The Exhibition and Experience Design Handbook

AMERICAN ALLIANCE OF MUSEUMS

The American Alliance of Museums has been bringing museums together since 1906, helping to develop standards and best practices, gathering and sharing knowledge, and providing advocacy on issues of concern to the entire museum community. Representing more than 35,000 individual museum professionals and volunteers, institutions, and corporate partners serving the museum field, the Alliance stands for the broad scope of the museum community.

The American Alliance of Museums' mission is to champion museums and nurture excellence in partnership with its members and allies.

Books published by AAM further the Alliance's mission to make standards and best practices for the broad museum community widely available.

The Exhibition and Experience Design Handbook

Timothy J. McNeil

ROWMAN & LITTLEFIELD
Lanham • Boulder • New York • London

Published by Rowman & Littlefield
An imprint of The Rowman & Littlefield Publishing Group, Inc.
4501 Forbes Boulevard, Suite 200, Lanham, Maryland 20706
www.rowman.com

86-90 Paul Street, London EC2A 4NE

Copyright © 2023 by American Alliance of Museums

British Library Cataloguing in Publication Information Available

Library of Congress Cataloging-in-Publication Data
Names: McNeil, Timothy J., 1965- author. | American Alliance of Museums.
Title: The exhibition and experience design handbook / Timothy J. McNeil.
Description: Lanham : Rowman & Littlefield, [2023] | Publication supported
  by the American Alliance of Museums. | Includes bibliographical
  references and index.
Identifiers: LCCN 2022056488 (print) | LCCN 2022056489 (ebook) | ISBN
  9781538157985 (cloth ; alk. paper) | ISBN 9781538157992 (electronic)
Subjects: LCSH: Museum exhibits--Handbooks, manuals, etc.
Classification: LCC AM151 .M43 2023 (print) | LCC AM151 (ebook) | DDC
  069/.5--dc23/eng/20221206
LC record available at https://lccn.loc.gov/2022056488
LC ebook record available at https://lccn.loc.gov/2022056489

♾️™ The paper used in this publication meets the minimum requirements of American National Standard for Information Sciences—Permanence of Paper for Printed Library Materials, ANSI/NISO Z39.48-1992.

Dedicated to my family near and far

Contents

Acknowledgments

This book was possible with the help, support, and expertise of many people. The list of contributors (both explicit and implicit) is immense and reflects my wonderful network of colleagues in the field who have generously supported this endeavor through their inspiration, sharing, and reviews. I am indebted to so many, and I dedicate this book to the comradery and passion inherent in the creative design industry.

Two people made this book a reality. My intellectual sparring partner Professor James Housefield in the UC Davis Department of Design: Thank you for your encouragement and wisdom. And my partner, Adrienne McGraw, who patiently, through thick and thin, provided advice, and researched and sourced 250 images.

The chapter visualizations for the Designer's Toolbox are drawn by different hands to exemplify the various styles of rendering (from hand to computer-drawn) used to capture a range of exhibition environments during the design development process. Each commission intentionally reflects today's multitude of styles, approaches, and voices from designers who are culturally and racially diverse and based in global design studios ranging from small to large. I would like to acknowledge the following designers for their exceptional contributions (in order of appearance): Kai Sase Ebens (who illustrated the informative diagrams), Zoey Ward, Claire Healy (special thanks for going first and helping to shape the overall visualization methodology), Asma Al-Dabal, Noor Al-Kathiri, Sarah Al-Maghlouth, Lydia Lee, Siddhartha Das, Roger Escalante Quintero, Evan Yang, Sayaka Koike, Jean-Pierre Dufresne, John Haden, Leidy Karina Gómez Montoya, and Magnús Elvar Jónsson.

This book benefited from the expertise and inspiration of many people during the research and review stages. I would like to particularly thank Tricia Austin, Cybelle Jones, Kathleen McLean, Liz McNeil, Susette Min, Merritt Price, Susan Spero, and Emma Thorne-Christy for taking the time to review and provide invaluable feedback on the book manuscript.

The following experts shaped the book's content directly or indirectly through conversations, reviews, insights, and guidance: Nick Bell, Craig Berger, Clare Brown, Jonathan Barnbrook, Barbara Fahs Charles, Tracy Corado, Frans Bevers, Nigel Briggs, Shirin Brueckner, Américo Castilla, Anne Chick, Abby Combs, Brenda Cowan, Mark de Jong, Tom Duncan, Nadja Fitchhorn, Stephanie Gibson, Peter Higgins, Elaine Heumann Gurian, Abigail Honor, Angela Iarocci, Lieke Ketelaars, Herman Kossmann, Christina Lyons, Sarah Maltby, Ann Marshall, Conal McCarthy, Noel McCauley, Suzanne MacLeod, Justin McGuirk, Ben Millstein, Bonnie Mitchell, Christopher Muniz, Britta Nagel, Lesley-Ann Noel, Victoria Noorthoorn, Eithne Owens, Judy Rand, Janette Ray, Tyler Rinehart, Rana Rmeily, Andrés Roldán, Paul Rosenthal, Steven Rosen, Pille Runnel, Jessica Sand, Marjorie Schwarzer, Avni Sethi, Bethany Shepherd, Katherine Skellon, Mahan Soltanzadeh, Tory Starling, Adam Taylor, Alin Tocmacov, James Volkert, Karina White, Paul Williams, Joe Zenas, and Tanja Zoeliner.

My gratitude to the Society for Experiential Graphic Design (SEGD) and the design studios at Atelier Brückner (Stuttgart), Event (London), Kossmanndejong (Amsterdam), Lorem Ipsum (New York), Ralph Appelbaum Associates (New York), and Thinkwell (Burbank), whose staff were generous and incredibly supportive as I launched this project.

I would like to recognize the three-thousand-plus University of California, Davis students I have taught so far and more importantly for what they have taught me. Particularly, Eleanor Bemis, Angela Cummings-Ingram, Julie Daseking, Olivia Easterly, Chloe Thepenier, Shaina Whaley, and Edward Whelan for their help researching this book. Acknowledgments go to my colleagues at the UC Davis Department of Design for their camaraderie and support; Marisa Kline, Leah Daugherty, and Kathleen Carroll for assistance with image acquisition; and the UC Davis College of Letters and Science for providing research and publication funding.

Thank you to the museums, attractions, studios, organizations, and people who generously gave their permissions and contributed photographs and images to this publication. Good-faith efforts were made to contact and obtain permission for all images used in this book. Should the rights owner come forth, we will obtain permission and include appropriate permissions wording in future printings of this book.

Finally, I would like to thank Kathy Borgogno for assisting with image research and rights; Joan Shapiro for indexing the book; at Rowman & Littlefield Publishers, Charles Harmon, and Erinn Slanina for their patient response to my endless queries; Jessica Thwaite and the designers of this book; and Dean Phelus and the American Alliance of Museums for enthusiastically supporting this project.

Designer's Toolbox: **Timeline**

Experiences permeate commercial, entertainment, cultural, and civic environments and reflect changes in society, taste, and technology, and the rise of the shared and participatory economy. Take a spin around the designer's toolbox to discover notable experiential events, and when design was consciously formalized, recognized, and commissioned to elevate standards of exhibition making.

Illustration: Eleanor Bemis, Julie Daseking, Kai Sase Ebens.
© Timothy J. McNeil

Practice
Behavior
Experience
Mode
Spiritual
– 150

Transdisciplinary
Virtual
Mixed Reality
Multimodal
Integrated Team
2021 – Present

Networked
Collective Team
2011 – 2020

New Media
Multidisciplinary
Participatory

Contract Team
991 – 2010

Social
Immersive
Inclusive
Interdisciplinary

2020 State of the art accessibility, U.S. Olympic & Paralympic Museum
2020 Digital Galleries, National Museum of Korea, Seoul
2019 Cutting-edge projection, Leonardo: Experience a Masterpiece, National Gallery London
2019 Design for all, Being Human, Wellcome Trust, London
2019 Graphic layers, Impact of the Bible in the World, Museum of the Bible, Washington, D.C.
2018 Contemporary versus historical context, National Museum of Qatar
2018 Humanoid robot "Pepper" answers visitor's questions at Smithsonian museums
2017 Selfie time, Museum of Ice Cream and Color Factory debuts in San Francisco
2016 Light projection fills in time, Temple of Mithras, Bloomberg Building London
2015 Dynamic object labels, Estonian National Museum
2015 Popup fashion museum, Het Nieuwe Instituut, Rotterdam
2014 Flexible space, National Exhibition and Convention Center, Shanghai
2014 Role play, Battle of Bannockburn diorama, Cooper Hewitt, Smithsonian Design Center, Stirling
2013 Immersive digital diorama, Confictura, Museo de Arte Moderno de Buenos Aires
2013 White cube 2.0, El círculo caminaba tranquilo, Museo de Arte Moderno de Buenos Aires
2013 "Pre" to "post-visit" moments, Making of Harry Potter, Warner Bros. Studio Tour, London
2012 "Wow" interactive wall of cats, Riverside Museum, Glasgow
2011 Salon-style wall of cats, Riverside Museum, Glasgow
2010 Mobile tablets, launch of the first generation iPad
2008 Artist collective Meow Wolf creates first installation
2007 Van Gogh immersive VR experiences begin international tour
2005 Nested information graphics, Sparking Reactions, Sellafield, Cumbria
2002 Interactive graphics gallery One, Cleveland Museum of Art
2002 Immersive and interactive film, secret Cinema
2000 Dynamic advances interaction design, Churchill Museum, London
2000 Paint manufacturers market lower-VOC coatings
2000 Engagement of senses, Guinness Storehouse, Dublin
2000 PlayZone interactive creative group team at founded, Millennium Dome, London
2000s Nested information graphics, Sparking Reactions
2000s Pine and Gilmore's book The Experience Economy
1998 Community building, Te Papa Tongarewa, New Zealand
1998 Pine and Gilmore's book, American Museum of Natural History
1998 Habitat Wall, American Museum of Natural History
1997 Universal Design Principles
1997 Guidelines for Accessible Exhibition Design
Mid-1990s LED light fixtures commercially available
1994 LED light fixtures commercially available
1993 Tower of Faces, U.S. Holocaust Memorial Museum
1993 Tower of Faces, U.S. Holocaust Memorial Museum
...to Gallery, National Gallery London

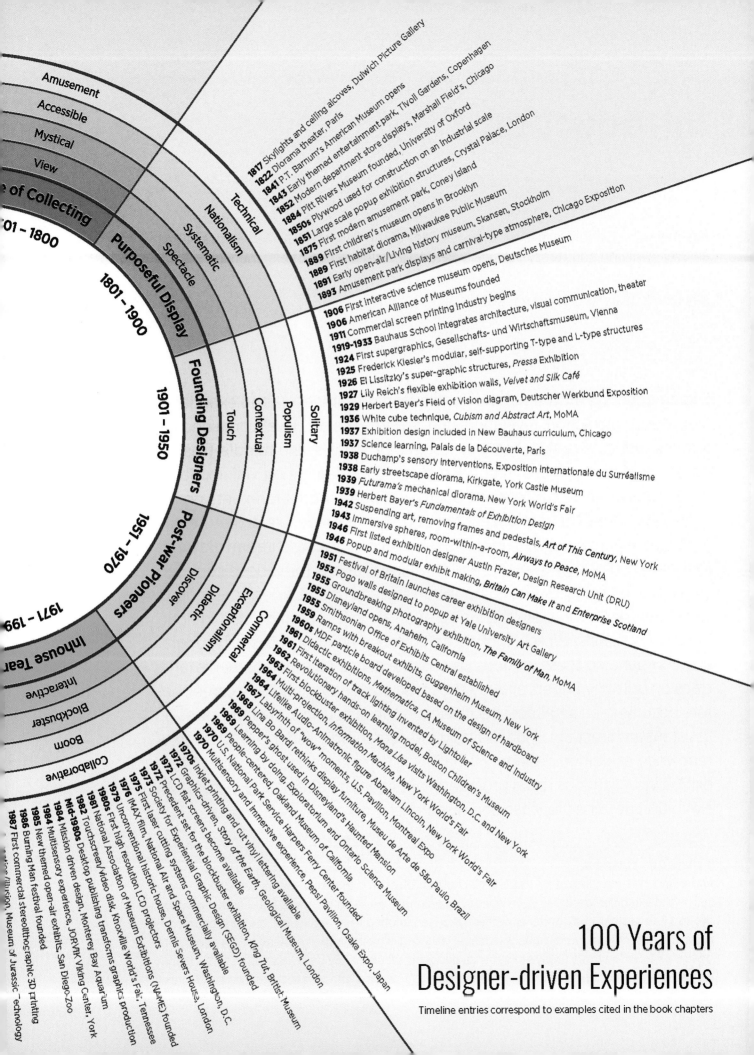

100 Years of Designer-driven Experiences

Timeline entries correspond to examples cited in the book chapters

Introduction

Key message: Exhibition design employs a set of rarely contextualized tropes within an ever-evolving and transdisciplinary field to inform a range of experiences.

Key words: history/theory/practice

Sliding open the drawers of the flat file storage cabinet was an experience tinged with attraction, revelation, and reward. The top level contained my father's meticulous sketches and watercolor studies; the middle files exposed his dog-eared architectural plans and renderings on vellum. Sandwiched between offcuts of matt board and scale-model remnants on the lower levels was the real prize. Stamped with his indelible signature and rendered in pencil, pen, and ink hid a series of design presentation drawings that depicted popup display stands and installations for various commercial exhibition projects. The compositions reeked of 1950s design—sinuous, structural frameworks like the inside of an aircraft's fuselage clad in floating display panels, clip-on lighting fixtures, and chunky slab-serif typography. As I handled these glorious visions, the dense 4B graphite marks left a trace on both my fingers and my subconscious. During his early career, before becoming an architect specializing in social housing, my father was an assistant architect at London's Design Research Unit under the tutelage of renowned exhibition designer Misha Black. Later in life, I realized that these exhibit visualizations had a profound impact on my decision to become an exhibition designer, teacher, and researcher.

T-shaped practitioners

Misha Black was conscious of the status of his chosen profession in those early years, self-deprecatingly calling the exhibition designers seen wandering amongst the excited crowds at the 1939 New York World's Fair "a small body of rather pathetic men" and noting that "architects" have instant recognition but not someone who happens to make designing exhibitions their profession.[1] This could not be further from the truth; today's experience designers would hardly be called pathetic, nor thankfully are they all men. Exhibition design and its skilled "T-shaped" practitioners are the precursors of

Design drawing for temporary exhibit pavilion by John McNeil, 1956.

Courtesy of McNeil Family

twenty-first-century multidisciplinary, collaborative, and human-centered design that permeates a workflow structure now commonly found in business, technology, and start-up environments. With this disclosure, the premise of this *book* is to prove that despite rapid advances in technology, the original methods used to shape the design of exhibition and experience environments laid the foundations for the dynamic devices of display we encounter today.

Design tropes

Having visited multiple exhibition environments in various parts of the world, I recognized a pattern of design practice—a series of recurring design tropes (you could also call them principles, or conventions), overlooked, and taken for granted in the exhibition design process. These design conventions go back to the formative years of exhibition and experience making and employ many of the same tools and techniques. Each illustrated chapter in this book investigates the origins, historical underpinnings, and implementation of one of these tropes using examples and three primary case studies scattered over a span of approximately one hundred years. Collectively, they chart a methodology for understanding exhibition design, plot the trajectory of exhibition development and making, and introduce design theory, techniques, and tools used to deliver successful exhibition-based experiences. I have validated this methodology successfully as a pedagogical framework in the classroom and during visits to exhibition spaces to witness the tropes in various degrees of application.

This methodology assesses, evaluates, and measures the impact of a multitude of experiences, and has the potential to enrich related disciplines such as interior architecture, graphic design, fashion design, product design, and more. This is particularly germane to the rapidly expanding metaverse and fields of User Interface (UI)/User Experience (UX) design, that create virtual exhibition and experience spaces in which elements are digitally rendered rather than physically built and allow for remote engagement. Indeed, the virtual worlds we find in gaming, Augmented Reality (AR), Virtual Reality (VR), and Mixed Reality (MR) applications employ—and thus can be enriched by—the same methods that help us to better understand the success of designed experiences in physical spaces.

Professional Exhibition Design Practice: A Brief History

"Novelty, charm, ingenuity, movement, people doing things, tricks and mystery, something really big and clever: These are the ingredients of successful display..."[2] James Gardner's and Caroline Heller's description from 1960 could have been written today. Exhibition makers tend to have a short memory span since the notion of exhibitions as places of entertainment and interaction is nothing new.[3] Large department stores of the late 1900s, World's Fairs, and eventually museums were developed to leverage commerce, entertainment, and culture resulting in the design of popular displays and interpretive experiences. Their merchandising principle called for attractive displays, careful selection and arrangement of objects, and the facilitation of visitor movement.[4]

The Paris World Exposition (1867) is considered the first to organize an exhibition space. Exhibits were arranged on an oval floor plan with corresponding galleries, and the overall pattern was expressed in the architecture of the building.[5] Encyclopedic national museums in nineteenth-century Europe and America commissioned architects to design purpose-built, uncompromising, monumental galleries filled with objects and displays by collectors, curators, and specialists. Exhibition techniques and standard practices were established by midlevel commissioners, and tradespeople, indispensable to exhibition making, fabricated the casework and corresponding elements. Without a formalized design intermediary to translate and interpret the curatorial vision, expressive and experimental installations by solitary artists and designers infiltrated the space, and eventually the role of the exhibition designer became increasingly commodified.

Exhibition design curricula

Professional exhibition design practice can be traced to the German Bauhaus School and its founding in the 1920s. Serving to unite art, craft, and industrial design, the Bauhaus was influenced by the preceding European Arts and Crafts Movements. The Bauhaus professors and their students designed experimental "set-like" environments that were purposefully interdisciplinary combining architecture, visual communication, and theater. Significantly, once the Bauhaus was shuttered by the Nazis in 1933 and its design talent dispersed across the globe, László Moholy-Nagy introduced "Display, Exhibition, and Stage" to the New Bauhaus curriculum in Chicago (1937). Around this time, formal exhibition design practice begins (see Designer's Toolbox: Timeline).

The Bauhaus model offers a successful but increasingly outdated base for contemporary design education. Scholars are grappling with the vexing task of teaching design amidst the escalation of various overlapping global crises associated with race, post-colonialism, economic disparity, health, and climate change. Pluriversal (where many worlds fit) rather than universal design (one world fits all) and ontological design thinking (design the world but allow the world to act back and reshape the design) are more in line with today's exhibition and experience making that champions inclusivity and participation.[6]

New Bauhaus curriculum diagram showing the course "Display, Exhibition, Stage."

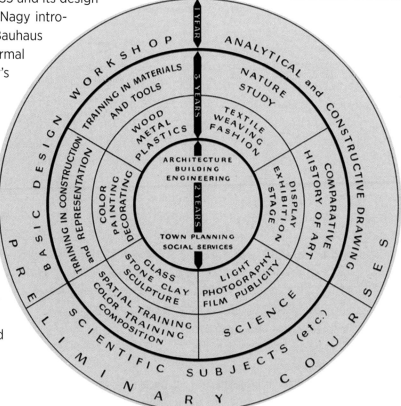

Contemporary practice

For such a young discipline, formal exhibition design practice has been through a remarkable transformation responding to societal changes, industry, commerce, entertainment trends, design thinking, tools, technology, and shifting economic models. Museums and attractions now compete with participatory and placemaking experiences, and likewise exhibition and experience makers come from a variety of disciplines and creative backgrounds.

Evolving from a solitary form in the first half of the twentieth century to become collaborative and interdisciplinary in the postwar years, exhibition and experience design practice in the mid to late twentieth century is defined by the formation of in-house and multidisciplinary teams that include people from a variety of backgrounds to shape content as well as form. Contemporary exhibition making is practiced through four distinct professional modes, each with a proclivity for a certain area of focus: architecture firm (emphasis on forms), design and media consultancy (emphasis on forms and narratives), museum or organization in-house teams (emphasis on objects), and art/design collectives or independent practitioners who behave like startups and tend to engage communities directly in their projects.

Prior to commercial consultancy firms, curators, educators, and designers were working together but often at odds (typically in the museum space). Once design consultancies emerged in the 1980s and grew in stature, these disciplines found a common home under one roof rather than as separate departments. Teams of exhibition researchers, developers, interpreters, and designers blurred disciplinary boundaries and

Critical and empowering design education curriculum incorporating ontological design thinking by Dr. Lesley-Ann Noel, 2020.

Courtesy of Dr. Lesley-Ann Noel

Design plays a central role in an exhibition team.

© Timothy J. McNeil

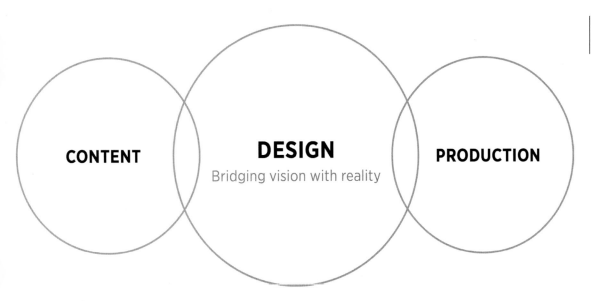

CONTENT — DESIGN
Bridging vision with reality — PRODUCTION

cross-pollinated. This flattened exhibit team structure was collaborative and coalesced as a group to deliver effective narrative, audience, and client-centric experiences. Design teams were no longer beholden to a singular museum type (art, history, etc.) and embraced interpretive excellence in the commercial, entertainment, and cultural sectors.

Future practice

Creativity, ideation (the process of refining multiple ideas), and imagination are the designer's greatest tools. The postwar generation of designers distilled complex subjects into large theatrical and sculptural forms that were dramatic rather than didactic and display case heavy. Scenographers like François Confino and exhibition designer Herb Rosenthal looked for comparative, everyday analogies to which audiences could relate.[7] Trained to build scale models and draw by hand, designers envisioned experiential spaces with the briefest of project information, rising above the challenge presented by four fixed walls to break down spaces rather than work within them.

Studios full of designers at drafting tables making drawings by hand over several weeks has been swapped for powerful software capable of rendering concepts in a fraction of the time. Poised to significantly alter the design process, Artificial Intelligence (AI) tools like Midjourney and DALL•E still require a point of origin, an idea, but with systems this powerful, where possible exhibition scenarios are quickly and accurately rendered, there is a shift in the role of designers. The time from idea to execution is cut exponentially, and the design control is now purely on concept and communication.[8] Access to design tools to visualize and participate in virtual environments are the hallmark of the twenty-first century. The lines between exhibition, interaction, experience, and the digital sphere are muddier than ever.

With expanding opportunities, greater diversity, and increased audience engagement and authorship, the conventional client-to-designer, concept-to-implementation design process is a model seeming less relevant. This book proposes an approach to exhibition making that learns from the success and failures of historical precedence, and argues for a revised methodology, one that can effectively guide the design of any type of exhibition, attraction, or experience environment regardless of its content, message, size, or budget.

Design at the helm

Today's multimodal, participatory exhibitions and attractions are bound by a desire to convey information, excite the viewer, and create social and narrative experiences. The earliest exhibitions were driven by spectacle, utilizing the visual impact of objects and artifacts. The twentieth century witnessed the professionalization of the exhibition field with a goal to educate, interpret, and explain as curators, administrators, and experts devalued spectacle in favor of content.

Advances in technology and new media, the shared gig, and attention-economy where breadth wins over depth, talented and persuasive design firms, generational change, and a desire for entertainment and instantaneous satisfaction/gratification has ushered in a renewed appreciation for visual experiences. Design is key to this transformation. Without design at the helm and employed effectively, experiential moments would fail to become lasting memories that inform and inspire an ever-increasingly sophisticated audience.

Scope: Whom Is This Book For?

Ultimately, use this book to become a better designer. The impetus for this project is embedded in my desire to identify the ideal resource for my teaching. The book structure follows the same pedagogical approach I use to introduce exhibition making in my courses, one that strives to seamlessly unite exhibition design history, theory, and practice. Comparable publications tend to start with an introduction and historical overview that is typically rooted in the evolution of museums (rarely the larger exhibition and experience design field), which then fails to return or link this context with the recurring methods used in contemporary practice. Armed with this deeper, richer depth of understanding enables exhibition development teams to formulate stronger concepts based on best precedence and pitch original ideas more effectively to clients and stakeholders. It is particularly relevant currently as exhibition design and scenography are central to the success of the experience and gig economy.

1	**CONTENT**	Develop compelling stories and objects
2	**AUDIENCE**	Know the audience
3	**SITE**	Understand the site
4	**MARKET**	Plan for pre/during/post experiences
5	**PRECEDENCE**	Learn from other examples
6	**SPACE**	Create dynamic spatial experiences
7	**STAGE**	Generate environments that engage the senses
8	**LAYER**	Vary the range of interpretive methods
9	**COMMUNICATE**	Establish a unified visual language
10	**DETAIL**	Specify clear, appropriate, and resolved designs

Ten Principles of Exhibition/ Experience Design

© Timothy J. McNeil

Audience

This book is aimed at a global audience with an emergent knowledge of the subject matter in places where exhibition/experience design are central to a growing experience economy and cultural tourism. This includes readers with a general interest in architecture, art, design, and cultural attractions, as well as professionals in the entertainment, museum, architecture, design, event planning, marketing, business, art, retail, urban planning, and landscape architecture industry. My hope is that students, instructors, and scholars in the educational fields of art, design, museum studies, communication, education, engineering, history, and business will expand and build on content between these pages. This book is broad rather than bottomless and will resonate with readers who make connections between museums, theme parks, retail, attractions, gaming, and interaction experiences.

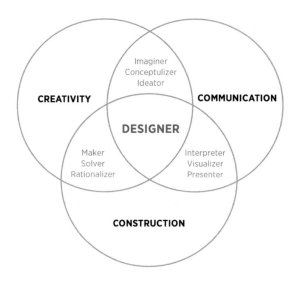

What Makes a Designer: Designers balance idealism with pragmatism.

© Timothy J. McNeil

People or participants

The ensuing chapters use the active and inclusive terms *people*, *participants*, or *audience* to describe the multitude of humanity who partake in exhibitions and experiences. Other current professional terminology aligns with each experience sector. *User* is favored by product and interaction designers but ignores experiences that are felt, witnessed, or multisensorial. *Visitor* is passive, with a shift to experience-based participatory environments. *Guest* appropriately describes those who attend hospitality-, entertainment-, and service-driven attractions. The term *actor* has entered the exhibition stage, and *participants* is apropos courtesy of Nina Simon.[9]

Design versus designing

Design is contentious and complex—ask scholars or practitioners to define the term and you will hear conflicting definitions. *Design* is both a noun and a verb spanning multiple disciplines and describes the rational creation of everything from skyscrapers to spreadsheets. *Designing* in the context of this book is synonymous with exhibition making, and *designer* is used to define a cohort of professionals—with and without formal design education/training—creating, communicating, and constructing the content that gives form to exhibitions and experiences. I acknowledge the designers who insert "context" into this relationship between form and content (thank you, Paul Rand) and leverage the exhibition medium as an instrument of agency, activism, and democratic co-creation (see co-design).

Exhibition versus experience

The terms *exhibition* and *experience* are used interchangeably to describe the book's featured projects. *Experience design* has evolved into an umbrella term that accommodates an expanding menu of subdisciplines. Interaction, virtual reality, and artificial intelligence infiltrate and vie to overshadow the design practice of placemaking, environmental, architectural, product, theater, and visual merchandising. I posit that all these subdisciplines constitute and combine into exhibition design—it is the mother of interdisciplinary, nay transdisciplinary, practice.

The difference between exhibitions and experiences is a matter of semantics and worthy of only a brief mention. Exhibitions consist of individual exhibits. Together they form a method of presentation that is designed to elicit an audience reaction and in turn create an experience. One can classify, but not necessarily comprehend, experiences as essence (what happens in the mind of

the audience) and offering (the product that is created and marketed).[10] Collectively, this creative process is referred to as exhibition design or scenography.

The design studio environment at ATELIER BRÜCKNER illustrates why creativity, ideating, and imagination are a designer's greatest tools.

Photo: ATELIER BRÜCKNER / Reiner Pfisterer

Top view of exhibition making

Exhibitions and designed experiences are everywhere and anywhere. The exhibition medium bridges the tabletop to the Big Top—and is a formidable facilitator for communication, creativity, expression, and advocacy. Designers talk about experience first, content second—the spectacle leads to engagement. This explains why museums sometimes struggle to be relevant and inclusive because their construct is firstly rooted in collecting objects and generating content, and why the edutainment industry often seems diametrically opposed. The best exhibition designers dip their toes in both worlds and let them cross-pollinate.

The following chapters intentionally rise above siloed or disciplinarity-based divisions to propose that design is design regardless of the content or venue. I see little distinction between museums, attractions, and branded exhibition environments. They share the same design methodologies and principles. What varies is content, intended audience, and concluding design expression. This top-view approach weaves together exhibition design practice, methods, and techniques with a historical framework for understanding how the discipline (both physical and virtual) contributes to cultural (museums, zoos, aquariums, and visitor centers), commercial (trade shows and retail), and entertainment (theme parks, attractions, festivals, and events) venues and the expansion of experiences for civic and community-based environments like parks, streets, and social-gathering spaces.

This book cites relevant professional case studies, design studio profiles, and historical and contemporary voices. It draws on my own creative practice and exhibition-making experience, as well as contributions from international museum, attraction, and design professionals. While primarily a title about the exhibition and experience design process, the book is positioned as a conduit between theory and practice and diverts the discourse about exhibition making from purely museology, commercial and professional practice, which has been the focus of comparable publications.

Author positionality

As with all research, it is helpful to understand and acknowledge my positionality. I am a white male who has practiced exhibition and experience design with bias and privilege—my family introduced me to design from an early age, I was fortunate to attend universities known for their design excellence, and my education and influences are predominately derived from a Eurocentric perspective. The established and accepted history and theory of the field is largely seen through a Western lens. Important work is just beginning to redress this imbalance. I have cited case studies and examples that are global and represent a diversity of cultures and voices. Some are lesser known; others are canonized; the majority are experiences I have witnessed and feel qualified to talk about.

Structure: Chapter-by-Chapter Overview

Our journey starts and ends with people and the intervening chapters follow the exhibition design process from story development, spatial planning and staging to communication and learning. Each of the twelve recurring design tropes form single chapters. Primary case studies—three to a chapter—are organized chronologically and are exemplary of an array of commercial, entertainment, cultural, and civic spaces. They represent milestones rather than the latest-and-greatest exhibition and experience projects. Other examples reinforce the trope's conventions over time, origins, context, and theoretical underpinnings. The case studies are intentionally brief and consistently structured to highlight three themes: design challenges, solutions, and impacts. Use the endnotes and bibliography to explore them further.

In the spirit of chapter 1, this book is organized with multiple entry points. The streaker (a reader who skims looking for the highlights) will appreciate the chapter headings and key themes, the stroller (a reader who craves more depth) the chapter visualizations and overviews, and the main text and bibliographical references will satiate the studier's (the reader who scrutinizes every detail) pursuit for depth.

Designer's Toolbox

The stunning visuals that convey exhibition/experience design concepts are often underappreciated or lost in the final melee of the iterative design process. Each chapter in this book begins with a double-page visualization that celebrates this significant and highly creative phase of a project. From Reykjavik to Riyad, each commission is by a different designer based in studios ranging from small to large and reflects the global diversity and future of the contemporary exhibition and experience design field. Spanning scale models, napkin sketches, and full renders, perspective and immersive viewpoints capture a variety of environments and drawing techniques. Collectively known as the Designer's Toolbox, these visualizations summarize each chapter, as well as the technical design methods and ingredients that constitute each trope. The reader is invited to open the toolbox and borrow what they need.

Timeline

The introductory timeline presents a cyclical synopsis of notable exhibition and experience design events that are captured within the pages of this book with a focus on the last one hundred years. Radiating out from the center, the role of the designer and their impact raises questions about when design was consciously commissioned to elevate the aesthetic quality, audience engagement, and standards of exhibition making. The timeline is a key reference point for understanding each chapter.

Chapters

While presented as twelve recurring design tropes, the chapters are structured to mimic the phased timeline for an exhibition/experience design project. Peel away the tropes, and chapters 1–3 focus on design planning; chapters 4–9 delve into spatial design; and chapters 10–12 explore interpretative design. Using the typical process-driven terminology, these align with the concept, development, and detail design phases. Ten Tips and Tricks are listed at the end of each chapter. These are a technical summary, intentionally pragmatic, serving to emphasize the publication's span from theory to practice.

Chapter 1 uses the trope "streaker, stroller, studier" to frame the designer's responsibility during the exhibition development process to understand audiences, plan welcoming and engaging environments, and interpret content in an informative and accessible manner.

Chapter 2 uses the trope "once upon a timeline" to illustrate how designers' structure, sequence, and bring to life an exhibition story, and how chronology is used repeatedly to organize and design experiential narratives.

Chapter 3 uses the trope "exit through the gift shop" to explore the comprehensive exhibition journey and the collaborative contribution the designer makes to market an entire experience and shape its visual message and identity.

Chapter 4 uses the trope "popup and modular" to assemble examples by designers who sculpt the exhibition experience from a variety of modular and memorable interventions made from a range of materials that take a multitude of forms.

Chapter 5 uses the trope "wow moment" to show how designers are responsible for people's emotive reactions and their behavioral responses to a variety of experiential triggers such as scale, color, lighting, and placement.

Chapter 6 uses the trope "beyond the white cube" to visualize how designers create cohesive flavors, atmospheres, and sensorial qualities for exhibition experiences, and react to the context and origins of the material to be presented.

Chapter 7 uses the trope "hanging salon style" to set the stage for how designers add visual variety, arrange elements, and draw on complex compositional design theory to engage people in exhibitions and experiences.

Chapter 8 uses the trope "trapped in glass boxes" as a metaphor for the variety of constraints designers work with to plan exhibitions and experiences, display objects, and create safe, people-centered environments.

Chapter 9 uses the trope "wraparound worlds" to reveal how designers create immersive experiences and are reinventing the tools to deliver on people's innate desire for escapism and alternative realities.

Chapter 10 uses the trope "smoke and mirrors" to dazzle the reader and demonstrate how designers deploy deception, illusion, and a little bit of magic to surprise and inspire people and transform experiential encounters.

Chapter 11 uses the trope "tombstones and text" to indicate the importance of clear but engaging communication, and how designers bring visual clarity, cohesion, accessibility, and consistency to exhibition graphics.

Chapter 12 uses the trope "hands-on, minds-on" to demonstrate that learning through doing requires a range of passive to interactive modalities that designers use to inform, engage, and educate a diverse and global community.

Finally, chew on this

As you streak or stroll through the upcoming chapters, remember that this book is about what is inside the exhibition container and not the building. You will not find a comprehensive list of exhibition design practitioners (although many are included) because I cannot quantify what qualifies as distinction, and I am bound to leave someone out. For brevity and where noted, I've chosen to include only the lead or primary designer/team for each project, knowing there is a much larger group of people and companies involved. This book does not tell you how to develop exhibition content—this exists elsewhere. It does not tell you how to design an exhibition from soup to nuts—this exists elsewhere. This book scratches the surface of exhibition design history, theory, and practice—and while not comprehensive, it is a start.

This book does provide a much-needed historical context for exhibition and experience design—a primer for practice. It offers a revisionist approach to understanding and reflecting on exhibition making by placing contemporary practice on a continuum with historical precedence to argue that nothing is new, just improved with more efficient and enhanced tools. The pages operate as a conversation starter, a preliminary survey of exhibition design practice, particularly at a time of rapid change and the profession's bleeding boundaries. Each chapter represents an updatable module—a framework to plug in content.

Lastly, like every other book, there is a mass of words, ideas, and research on the cutting-room floor. Each chapter in this book is a call to action. Any one of them has the makings of an entire book unto itself. I would love to see scholars and practitioners pick up the mantle and expand each trope further—a compendium of twelve volumes that will finally elevate the field of exhibition design to where it belongs—now that is what I call an experience!

Notes

1. Misha Black and Avril Blake, *The Black Papers on Design: Selected Writings of the Late Sir Misha Black*, 1st ed. (Oxford, New York: Published on behalf of the Faculty of Royal Designers for Industry by Pergamon Press, 1983), 119.
2. James Gardner and Caroline Heller, *Exhibition and Display* (London: B.T. Batsford Ltd., 1960).
3. Kathleen McLean, *Planning for People in Museum Exhibitions*, 5. repr. (Washington, D.C.: Association of Science-Technology Centers, 2009), x.
4. Michael Steven Shapiro and Louis Ward Kemp, eds., *The Museum: A Reference Guide* (New York: Greenwood Press, 1990), 202.
5. Shapiro and Kemp, 202.
6. "Ontological Design Has Become Influential in Design Academia—But What Is It?" *Eye on Design*, June 14, 2021, https://eyeondesign.aiga.org/ontological-design-is-popular-in-design-academia-but-what-is-it/.
7. Paul Rosenthal. Interview by Timothy McNeil about exhibition designer Herb Rosenthal. February 24, 2021.
8. Steven Heller, "The Daily Heller: There Is Nothing Artificial About AI Type Design," *PRINT*, September 26, 2022, https://www.printmag.com/daily-heller/the-daily-heller-there-is-nothing-artificial-about-ai-type/.
9. "Preface: Why Participate?—The Participatory Museum," accessed April 8, 2022, http://www.participatory museum.org/preface/.
10. Jan Packer and Roy Ballantyne, "Conceptualizing the Visitor Experience: A Review of Literature and Development of a Multifaceted Model," *Visitor Studies* 19, no. 2 (July 2, 2016): 131, https://doi.org/10.1080/10645578.2016.1144023.

Designer's Toolbox: **People**

Designers familiar with visitor studies and audience engagement methods advocate for inclusive and accessible design solutions that anticipate people's behaviors, expectations, and abilities. Dive into the designer's toolbox and welcome multiple audiences whether they stop or study for three minutes or three hours.

Illustration: Zoey Ward is an emerging exhibition designer based in Sacramento and the San Francisco Bay Area, U.S.A.
Scale model photography: Rachel McGraw is a San Francisco Bay Area photographer

STREAKER

STROLLER

STUDIER

CHAPTER 1

Streaker, Stroller, Studier

Experience-centered design is people-centered design.

Key message: Design facilitates the participation of everyone in the exhibition experience.

Key word: people

The most important thing about design is how it relates to people.[1] Exhibitions and experiences are inextricably linked to people. They are containers for human activity. French philosopher Henri Lefebvre argued that "(social) space is a (social) product"; rather than being something out there, disconnected from people, or an empty vessel to be filled, space is produced by people and their scalable actions over time.[2]

During the development process, designers work with other specialists to identify and understand their audiences before planning accessible, inclusive, welcoming environments that ideally interpret and present content in an informative, engaging, and appropriate manner for a broad range of people. Attention span, motivation, and time are other factors that impede or facilitate an experience, which is why exhibition makers equate the time spent experiencing with that spent engaging.

This chapter adopts the trope "streaker (seconds), stroller (minutes), studier (hours)," which exhibition professionals use to describe people's actions, attention span, and the pace in which they move. Streakers (people who crave a few highlights), strollers (those who diligently follow the intended narrative), and studiers (who scrutinize every detail), while relatable, is perhaps too simplistic a measure, and it may limit how designers think about audiences. Studies have found that many people exhibit all three behaviors in one visit, depending on the quality of the experience and other factors. However, if turned around, the trope helpfully defines how designers streak, stroll, and study in their own work when it comes to understanding people's preferences and interests. The "streaker, stroller, studier" model introduces the principles of universal and human-centered design, recurring tropes in the design industry that place people, the eventual end-users, first.

If you build it, *who* will come?
Awe, wonder, authenticity, vulnerability, dialogue, and contemplation are known to build empathy.[3] These are key experiential design ingredients. Designing inclusive exhibitions and experiences starts

with empathy—identifying and listening to the people who will visit, defining and advocating for their needs, and anticipating their preferences—the audience personae.

What motivates people to participate in exhibitions and experiences varies. Eilean Hooper-Greenhill defines *audiences* as those who might come, if the experience were judged (by them) to be worthwhile, in contrast to *visitors*, whom she defines as those who will actually come.[4] Howard Gardner's multiple intelligences summarizes people's proclivity for learning and thinking into visual-spatial, linguistic-verbal, interpersonal, intrapersonal, logical-mathematical, musical, bodily-kinesthetic, and naturalistic modalities.[5] John Falk classifies people as experience seekers, explorers, rechargers, hobbyists, facilitators, pilgrims, and affinity seekers.[6]

If you build it, *why* will they come?

Judy Rand's *Visitor's Bill of Rights* (1996) is a touchstone for the design of experiences. While originally intended for museums, it is applicable to every experience-making sector from the click of a mouse to one stomach-churning ride. Focusing on the whole person, it considers physical, intellectual, emotional, social, and cultural needs from an audience's perspective. Rand encouraged designers to use it as a standard, a set of visitor-centered goals that offers a why and what but does not dictate how—that is up to the designer's creativity.[7] Acknowledging the continued focus on diversity, equity, and inclusion, Rand's "call to action" remains remarkably present and relevant.

Welcoming People: Popularist Design

Exhibitions are not just collections of interesting things brought together at a certain place and time. They are human activities, human enterprises.[8] This was certainly true of London's Great Exhibition

Joseph Paxton's voluminous Victorian red Crystal Palace appealed to a broader populace.

Image from "Dickinson's Comprehensive Pictures of the Great Exhibition of 1851". Cooper Hewitt, Smithsonian Design Museum via Picryl.

(1851). The cornucopia of exhibits draped in Victorian red were drawn from art, natural history, and industry and placed in Joseph Paxton's voluminous Crystal Palace. The spectacle flung open its doors at a reduced price to a populace who had rarely crossed such a threshold before. Together with earlier Parisian fairs, this set the design tone for future World's Fairs, festivals, and trade shows with their crowds, impressive spaces, and stunning displays. The Chicago Exposition (1893) went a step further with a carnival-like atmosphere, themed villages, and exotic animals, where the attention of audiences was captured by displays that increasingly relied on entertainment value rather than educative content.

The customer is always right

The cyclical timeline preceding this chapter visualized the origins of people-centered experiences, from the spiritual spaces of churches and temples to the private cabinets of curiosity during the age of collecting. Access to these environments was restricted based on someone's faith or class. Even earlier, public markets, street fairs, and festivals welcomed all people. Driven by sales, these events turned into places of entertainment, where theater, music, and dance fueled commerce, and social interaction, and the competitive atmosphere encouraged traders to up their display tactics and exhibit their wares to outsell one another.

The fastest-paced exhibition design medium is the commercial trade-show industry, with sizeable teams, short turnarounds, and large rewards. Here people are classified as either B-to-B (business-to-business) or B-to-C (business-to-client) audiences. Trade shows and expos market rather than sell to a specific guest. It is about visibility and (mostly) friendly competition.

"Wear your guest shoes" means measuring and improving the visitor experience. This is embedded into Disney's DNA; it serves to guide every design decision.[9] Empathizing with exhibition audiences has not always been a determining factor for experience makers. Theme parks, festivals, and attractions were built on entertainment and amusing audiences, but museums grew out of collecting objects and scholarship before they primarily became places for people.

Popularist and egalitarian

Art, science, and exploration came together in the late nineteenth century, when, against a backdrop of colonial collecting and empire building in the Western Hemisphere, national and civically minded municipal museums were created that were free and taxpayer funded. These institutions rode the coattails and often inhabited former World's Fair and Exposition buildings. A focus on nationalism and the "people's collections" led to a systematic and didactic approach to exhibition organization

Public markets, street fairs, and festivals have always welcomed people with theater, music, dance, and exhibits.

Spring Festival on the River, Qing dynasty. The Metropolitan Museum of Art, New York. From the Collection of A. W. Bahr, Purchase, Fletcher Fund, 1947. Creative Commons CCO 1.0 Universal Public Domain Dedication

Event's design renovation continues to make Kelvingrove Museum and Art Gallery a place for the people of Glasgow.

Photo: Ian Dagnall Commercial Collection / Alamy Stock Photo

and a purposeful and intentional design to the displays. Glasgow's Kelvingrove Museum and Art Gallery (1901) was created as a museum of, and for, the people. It was a welcoming space where an egalitarian mix of classes, the educated, and the illiterate conjoined to set an inclusive tone contained within the wonderous Spanish Baroque Revival red sandstone architecture.[10] Kelvingrove remains one of the most visited cultural attractions, and gallery renovations (2006) responded faithfully to the wishes of Glaswegians to create a respectful (accessible) level of interpretation and exhibition design.

National collections, parks, and museums

The popularity of the vast Smithsonian Institution (est. 1846) in Washington, D.C., proves that free admission lessens the barriers to entry and the level of commitment for many people. Designing exhibitions and experiences for the world's largest collection, education, and research complex is undertaken by in-house teams or external consultancies following a robust set of design guidelines to actively engage audiences (see Smithsonian Guidelines for Accessible Exhibition Design). Crafting accessible exhibitions was not always a priority. Before 1948, in keeping with museological notions of the time, the Smithsonian had no centralized exhibition design planning or support beyond individual curators, preparators, taxidermists, and other museum staff who assembled exhibits on an *ad hoc* basis. As one of the first in-house museum design teams, the Office of Exhibits Central (1955) was created to consolidate these efforts and take responsibility for the design and production of permanent, special, and traveling exhibits in the United States National Museum and its successor museums.[11]

Freeman Tilden rationalized the process of understanding exhibit information, objects, and places. In *Interpreting our Heritage* (1967), he advocated for interpretation that relates to something within the personality or experience of the visitor.[12] This was counter to the overly explanatory texts that were common in most park museums at the time, and Tilden's work inspired exhibit makers at the Park Service to focus on the "trailside" outside the museum walls.

People, parks, and interpretative media

Visitor Centers, U.S. National Park Service (1916), Harpers Ferry Center (1970)
Designers: Various

Design challenge: **Mission 66**

The U.S. National Park Service (NPS) has an illustrious history, and the parks it oversees personify land conservation, interpretative excellence, and unparalleled outdoor experiences serving millions of visitors every year. To mark its fiftieth anniversary in 1966, the NPS rethought its museum/exhibition spaces with a program of change called *Mission 66*. Situated in most parks, often in historic buildings, interpretive exhibits suffered from a collective text-heavy malaise—technical information was presented in such a way that the park was regarded as an exhibit and the museum as an explanatory label.[13] Audiences of the 1960s were no longer paying attention.

New and renovated buildings were designed (often of architectural merit) to house a distinct breed of exhibits focused on improving visual communication and engagement in lieu of telling the comprehensive park story. Rather than tangential to the experience, these new visitor centers welcomed people, served as introductory hubs equipped with a variety of orientation services, and became integral to a park's interpretive program.

Design solution: **Different and suspect**

Visitor centers were the first piece in the interpretive puzzle. Second was the development and design of slick indoor exhibits using artifacts, models, artwork, and photographs and a series of interconnected outdoor wayside exhibits to interpret the landscape, flora, and fauna. The task of implementing this new "people's approach" fell to Bill Everhart, the founding director of the Division of Interpretation in Washington, D.C. (1962). To realize his vision, Everhart looked beyond in-house production staff and hired professional exhibition designers, filmmakers, artists, craftspeople, and

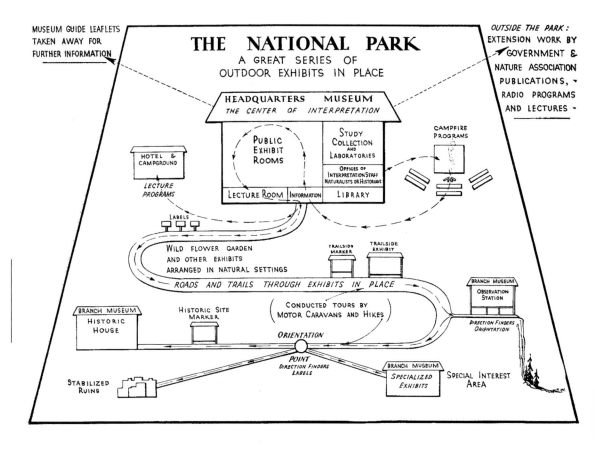

U.S. National Park's Service concept map illustrates an elaborate system of exhibits beginning at the visitor center.

Burns, NJ. Field Manual for Museums. Washington, D.C.

curators to modernize the exhibits, publications, and audiovisual productions.[14] Conservative ranks of the NPS viewed their ideas and products as different and suspect, and the "new look" was initially criticized for its eye appeal and superficiality, but there was a positive response to the interpretive design innovations from the public, and from contemporary design critics.[15]

Everhart's next step was to consolidate the creative/production team into one division at one location, which eventually became the Harpers Ferry Center (1970). The centralized team fostered interdisciplinary collaboration, and the exhibit designer worked alongside the curator from the very beginning of a project. This method was deemed a success, not just in increased efficiency, but also in increasing the quality of the exhibits.[16]

Design impact: Harpers Ferry today

The Harpers Ferry Center for Media Services and its work for NPS continues to inspire visitors through interpretive media. They offer a full range of services from exhibits and wayfinding to cartography, conservation, and digital solutions. Their design

standards, production guidelines, and creative process are used widely; are available on their website; are recognized by government agencies, nonprofits, and professional organizations; and have resulted in fulfilling experiences for the visiting public.[17]

The *Mission 66* Visitor Center remains the most complete and significant expression of the Park Service's modern style, and its influence is profound. New visitor centers (and the planning ideas and architectural style they implied) were used in the development or redevelopment of scores of state parks in the United States, as well as nascent national park systems in Europe, Africa, and all over the world.[18] Any criticism of the NPS process is that it instilled in a generation of designers an over-reliance on design standards that are too rigid and formulaic, overlooking a more nuanced approach to engaging a range of audiences with a variety of unscripted exhibit modalities.

Exhibits like this diorama in the visitor center at Riley Creek in Alaska are one of the first pieces in Denali National Park's interpretive puzzle.

Understanding People: Inclusive Design

Visitor studies and the fields of interpretation and education are full of excellent empirical research published in a plethora of books and journals (many are cited throughout this book). While much of these studies are focused on people and audiences, designers do not always see this type of research as critical to their work. Design has its own process for assessing audiences and the creative process called *design thinking*. Exhibition makers benefit from cross-pollination between both research areas.

Design thinking

Refining ideas based on a feedback loop of evaluation and testing before implementation has been used by designers for decades to foster creativity and solve complex issues. Branded as design thinking, this methodology is no longer driven by only the development of physical products, but it is also guided by the design of people's experiences, such as interaction and service design.

Design thinking is an overarching problem-solving framework grounded in iterative and collaborative processes with an emphasis on user research. The term *design thinking* originated from a Stanford University design program led by Jim Adams, which focused on creative thinking and conceptual blockbusting.[19] It has since been defined, taught, and embodied at the Stanford d.school, which developed a set of methods, toolkits, and strategies for interviewing and observing in the field, synthesizing insights, rapid prototyping, role playing, and testing with people, before being put into practice by multiple sectors and experience design agencies, notably IDEO.[20]

Human-centered design

Developed in the 1980s as ethnographic research to enable people to directly influence design decisions and build experiences around products or services, human-centered design starts with empathy attained through consultation throughout the process with the intended audience. As a form of co-production, it is deeply connected to understanding people and crafting experiences.

Designer Clare Brown aligns design thinking with exhibition making and the importance of "mindsets" that embrace ambiguity, empathy, and learning from failure as a routine part of the process. Brown suggests that exhibitions share goals with the tech industry and should adopt methods prevalent in this sector, such as incorporating values and principles at the outset of each project, shorter time scales, user and stakeholder testing, and divergent and convergent thinking throughout the iteration cycles.[21]

Equity, ethics, and empathy

Successful exhibition and experience design is empathetical and ethical. Historical and contemporary examples abound where design overpowers function, creates long-term problems (waste), or is ambivalent to audience access. The people who participate in experiences are the anarchistic element, and it is often easier to design around them rather than for them.[22]

Design research and evaluation directly focused on a person's specific identity may have to comply with human-subject IRB (Institutional Review Board) standards to prevent coercion and safeguard the sharing of sensitive personal data. Formative evaluation, prototyping, mockups, and most user-based design research falls outside of IRB regulations when they are anonymous and not focused on individual behaviors. Diversity, racial equity, and social justice should be part of any design thinking framework, and consider the appropriate conditions, actions, and intentions that will achieve inclusive, equitable outcomes.[23]

Emerging design scholarship and pedagogy seeks to upend the traditional canon, decolonize, and recognize the work of designers outside of Europe and North America who are often excluded from design research. *The Designer's Critical Alphabet* by Dr. Lesley-Ann Noel is an excellent tool for introducing audience empathy, critical theory, and awareness in the design studio.[24]

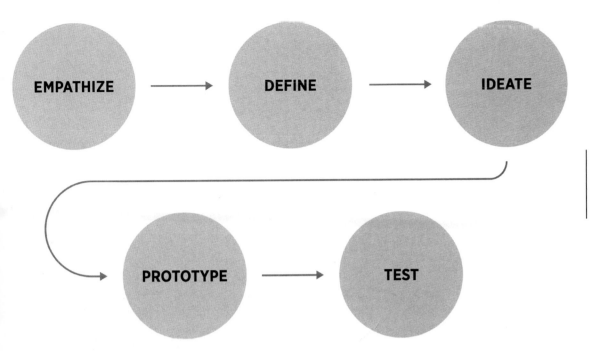

EMPATHIZE → DEFINE → IDEATE

PROTOTYPE → TEST

Empathy is the starting point for the IDEO design thinking process.

Adapted from http://longevity3
.stanford.edu/designchallenge/
design-thinking-process/.

Primary case study
People, politics, and prototyping

Oakland Museum of California (OMCA), 1969–present
Designers: Various

Design challenge: Community focused

From its inception, the Oakland Museum of California (OMCA) was envisioned as "the people's museum." Serving a traditionally diverse community with a celebrated history of social and political activism, the museum has consistently engaged methods of design thinking and human-centered design in the propagation of exhibits. The institution is a potent blend of contrasting collection areas, the result of merging three smaller institutions that collectively represented the many facets of California. This progressive and multidisciplinary premise makes the OMCA quite unique, and one level of the museum is dedicated to each of the disciplines of art, history, and natural science.[25]

Critical to the museum's success is its mid-century modern building. It was designed by Roche-Dinkeloo architects as a series of interlocking concrete tiers topped with a resplendent communal oasis—a terraced sculpture park integrating public indoor and outdoor spaces—considered the first green museum roof in the United States.[26]

In the 1970s and 1980s, OMCA was one of the first museums to collect contemporary culture—including artifacts from surfers, hippies, yuppies, and black power and gay rights activists' examples of the late-twentieth-century youth and political culture in California. Along with the objects, the museum took the radical step of collecting the owners' stories.[27] The museum's renovation in 2013 strengthened its role as a public forum, with new opportunities for people to participate in exhibits, gather, and share their own perspectives.

Design solution: Playground for designers

To balance the curatorial areas, a department of special exhibits and education was created in the early 1970s to advance collection interpretation and exhibition design. Ben Hazard oversaw this area and initiated new and exciting display concepts about objects and ideas that related to the community and made people feel it was their museum.[28] Consequently, OMCA exhibit staff came from a diversity of backgrounds, and it remains a playground for influential designers to this day.

Gordon Ashby (who had worked with the Eames Office and Kevin Roche on the 1964/1965 World's Fair) was appointed when the museum opened in 1969 to organize, populate, and transform the building's empty shell. Ashby's plan for the Natural Sciences Hall did not group objects into their sub-disciplinary fields (entomology, botany, etc.), but rather, it mixed them together as an imagined walk through a cross-section of California to illustrate the dynamic web of ecological relationships among living things in eight biotic zones. Essentially putting "nature back together again," this marked a radical improvement in the communication of the natural sciences for OMCA's audiences.[29]

Envisioned as a communal oasis, the terraced sculpture park at the Oakland Museum of California integrates public indoor and outdoor spaces.

Courtesy of the Hayward Area Historical Society, gift of the Oakland Tribune

Ted Cohen had a long design association with OMCA. He cleverly combined exuberant aesthetics, atmosphere, and object composition into a visual feast for visitors. Cohen was part of a generation of West Coast architects, artists, and designers whose work offered a counterpoint to East Coast modernism.[30]

Kathleen McLean's *Manifesto for the (r)Evolution of Museum Exhibitions* (2010) advocates for exhibit makers to consider their audience as partners.[31] McLean's recent work is an impassioned rethink of the exhibition development process to enable design and content to evolve together and iteratively using a humble design palette of object photocopies, handwritten words, and paper walls rather than slick "look and feel" image references, materials, and finishes, and outlines of narratives produced by most design studios. McLean is a prototyping

evangelist who creates exhibitions that challenge traditional design practice (based on architecture) with its steadfast phases that unwaveringly move through schematic, development, and construction documents and approvals. While this works for static/formulaic projects, OMCA's exhibition *Altered State: Marijuana in California* (2016) would have been denied its *high* following such a linear creative process. The success of the installation hinged on the ability to backtrack the process, iterate, and elaborate ideas, and the flexibility to evolve and change because of public engagement and visitor input.[32]

Design impact: Neither painter, nor babysitter

OMCA's legacy is one of civically minded museum incubator with a formidable lineage of exhibit makers who have shaped the exhibition design process over the last fifty years. Their educators studied and advanced museum learning and were not treated as schoolteachers or babysitters. Their designers employed human-centered design to promote professional legitimacy rather than painting the walls. OMCA's story is a microcosm of the San Francisco Bay Area in the later twentieth century (1980s), when educational theory fueled highly respected museum studies programs and design thinking methodologies ripened in Silicon Valley.

Oakland Museum of California's exhibition *Altered State: Marijuana in California* followed a non-linear design process.

Courtesy of Kathleen McLean

Including People: Participatory Design

Gordon Ashby's exhibition design marked a radical improvement in the communication of natural sciences for audiences at the Oakland Museum of California.

Courtesy of the Hayward Area Historical Society, gift of the Oakland Tribune

Gen Z and younger generations are increasingly concerned with the social impact and the credibility and authenticity of a product or service, referred to as ROE (Return on Engagement, Experience, or Emotion). Add a return on ethics and empathy, and if a designed experience is neither fun nor compelling, the consequential effects will show in decreased attendance and audience retention rate.[33]

Allowing people to design, alter, and control the outcome of an experience is prevalent across all exhibition sectors to varying degrees and has become a matter of survival to attract new and emerging audiences. With an emphasis on turning people and communities from passive spectator to an active participant, designing for diversity, equity, inclusion, accessibility, and belonging (DEIAB) is essential for today's experience-based outcomes.[34]

Participatory design

Understanding people and their desires means listening—really listening—and asking questions that define success as much as failure. The practice of "design interviewing" differs from regular audience interviewing in that there is both an explicit research agenda (what the interviewee hears) and an implicit research agenda (what the interviewer really wants to understand). It may sound deceptive, but as the Stanford d.school points out, it is a method to move beyond personal preferences and actions to needs and aspirations—design interviewing uncovers people's stories and their meaning.[35] These are techniques that can truly let people participate in the design process and affect the resulting outcomes.

Remember the Children: Daniel's Story (1992) at the United States Holocaust Memorial Museum was developed using interviews and feedback from children. People walk through an interactive room-to-room diorama that follows a Jewish boy's journey during Nazi occupation.

The environments are created with two- and three-dimensional painted backdrops and elements, like theater flats. The scene gradually shifts from his well-lit comfortable home to a dimly lit ghetto, and the hands-on elements go from colorful cookies and drawers full of playthings to scraps of fabric and colorless turnips cooking on a tiny stove.[36] Created by Darcie Fohrman Associates, the exhibition is designed so that children participate as observers without ever feeling in danger through an emotional, mental, and physical encounter.

While *Daniel's Story* is grounded in the dark reality of human injustice, the twenty-first-century emergence of social experiences that defy real life using performance-based exhibits, happenings, and festivals foster fantasy and escapism through active participation where people create the experience. London-based Artichoke stages public events that involve people in larger-than-life spectacles expanding the boundaries of what is possible. Improv Everywhere uses environmental satire to surprise, trick, and amuse. Secret Cinema hosts immersive showcases for film buffs who want a more interactive experience where they are expected to play a role. Meow Wolf creates dazzling, participatory artist installations that blend anything and everything from cosplay to steampunk.

At the opening of *Remember the Children: Daniel's Story* at the United States Holocaust Memorial Museum, two young visitors pause to read Daniel's diary.

Photo: United States Holocaust Memorial Museum. Photographer Bill Fitzpatrick. ©United States Holocaust Memorial Museum.

Co-design

It is one thing to be invited to participate at key moments to shape a design outcome; another to be treated as an equal, trusted collaborator, active partner, and co-creator during the whole design process. Co-design has its roots in the participatory design techniques developed in Scandinavia in

Artichoke's *Sultan's Elephant* is a public event that involves people in larger-than-life spectacles.

The Sultan's Elephant, Royal de Luxe, London, 2006. Produced by Artichoke. Photo by Sophie Laslett.

the 1970s and reflects a fundamental change in the traditional design-consultation relationship, where the intended audience or community become the experts of their own experience.[37]

A few radical organizations have adapted a community-centered approach that stresses cooperative development and co-design of exhibitions around collective research and action. The Santa Cruz Museum of Art & History (MAH) has developed a handbook/toolkit to help guide museums through the process of co-designing and building equity through low-risk events with their communities. This process was spearheaded by Nina Simon, the author of the *Participatory Museum*, which has been highly influential in inspiring exhibition makers to abandon the traditional curator-led exhibition model in favor of a more democratic approach. Simon's version is a form of anti-design, where aesthetic and polish are removed from the design equation in favor of content development and raw exhibit prototyping (see chapter 12).

Universal design

The world was not built with people with disabilities in mind, and because of that, the world we live in is inherently "ableist." More than one billion people globally have some form of disability, and Universal Design (see Tips and Tricks) is either mandated by law (through the Americans with Disabilities Act) or constitutes ethical design practice.[38] "Nothing about us without us" is the mantra of the disability rights movement,

which guided a series of creative workshops, led by designer Anne Chick, to explore co-design, and prioritize intellectual access for blind and partially sighted participants, their companions, and other volunteers.[39] The research resulted in an exhibition at the UK's National Centre for Craft & Design called *The Good, The Bad, and The Beautiful* (2017). The installation used 3D printing to create textured wayfinding pathways on the floor, contrasting colors, multisensory zones with tactile objects, Braille, audio descriptions, and legible graphics with open, large sans-serif fonts. All an outcome of a co-design process with the intended audience resulting in a design that worked for everyone.

Anti-ableist, inclusive, and intersectional design

Ableism is a set of beliefs or practices that devalue and discriminate against people with physical, intellectual, or psychiatric disabilities and often rests on the assumption that disabled people need to be "fixed" in one form or the other.[40] The goal of Universal Design is to include as many people as possible at the outset and use an iterative design process to arrive at a solution that increases that number further. It is the designer's responsibility to recognize that everyone is unique, to not conform to broad-brush labels, and to remember that variation in ability is a natural part of an audience's experience.[41]

Inclusive design is a newer term that, according to museum accessibility researcher Sina

Participants in Chaos at the Museum (2014) parade the streets of Buenos Aires with Museo Taller Ferrowhite to ceremoniously dispose of failed exhibition design ideas.

Museo Taller Ferrowhite and Fundación TyPA

***We're Still Here* (2019) at the Santa Cruz Museum of Art & History explored social isolation and was created by 186 seniors and advocates in the community.**

Courtesy of the Santa Cruz Museum of Art & History

Bahram, is more attainable for designers and developers. "Inclusive" constitutes a friendly invitation that aligns with most people's basic values. Inclusive and intersectional design move beyond physical disabilities and allow for differences in identity, age, gender, race, ability, fluency, and background, and reframes from making everyone the same.[42]

Accessible design

While universal and inclusive design address the larger view, accessible design addresses specifics like wide corridors, ramps, and automatic doors leading into exhibit buildings for those with mobility impairments. Once inside the exhibition, however, disabled visitors often find that the level of effort, resources, and consideration dedicated to providing equal access for all audiences is disappointingly low.[43] Examples that incorporate accessibility are increasing. *Sight Unseen* (2016) at the Canadian Museum for Human Rights featured work created by photographers who are blind for an audience who might also be blind or simply benefit from a multisensory experience. Several of the images were transformed into tactile 3D representations with audio descriptions, allowing people to see the images with their eyes, their ears, and/or their hands. Designer Corey Timpson was excited by the exhibition design's potential to push a passive exhibition (2D artwork) and make it both active and interactive as well.[44]

Beyond conventional exhibition object labels, image descriptions—textual translations describing what an image or object looks like—are helpful. They are designed as large-text and using Braille or digital Alt-text descriptions that are recognized and read aloud by screen readers. Lauded as one of the most accessible museums in the world, the United States Olympic &

The Good, The Bad, and The Beautiful used 3D printing to create textured wayfinding pathways that worked for everyone, the outcome of a co-design process.

Acoustic Nations

Sight Unseen at the Canadian Museum for Human Rights featured work by blind photographers and was designed as a multi-sensory experience.

Canadian Museum for Human Rights/Aaron Cohen

Paralympic Museum (2020) allocates every visitor an editable Radio-Frequency Identification (RFID) tag, which holds preprogrammed specific information to tailor the experience to their respective needs. As people go through the exhibits, the tag responds to a range of preferences from people's favorite sports to accommodations like audio descriptions or increased text size. RFID technology is a design tool that recognizes everyone is unique.

Design for neurodiversity

Most people's disabilities are invisible. These include people with seizure disorders, chronic pain, vision or hearing impairments, brain injuries, learning differences, and mental health disorders. The indiscernible nature of some illnesses and disabilities can lead to misunderstandings or judgment. The fastest-growing segment of the invisible disability population are people with sensory disorders, such as autism (including touch, taste, vision, sound, smell, and feeling pain or temperature).[45] Sensory-diverse people either crave (sensory seeking) or sidestep sensory experiences (sensory avoiding). Designing for neurodiversity means modifying spaces for areas of high- and low-sensory distraction and considering a range of hypersensitive factors, such as tolerance for bright lights, loud noises, ambient noises (whirring HVAC fan), stark contrast in colors (e.g., soft blue to electric pink), background odors (off-gassing materials or paint), textures (feeling of certain fabrics), and crowded spaces.

Design for well-being and healing

Health is defined as complete physical, mental, and social well-being and not only the absence of disease or infirmity. Engaging people in exhibition interaction, co-design, and co-curation is linked with positive psychology and well-being. The act of co-creating is the subject of intensive research that finds adding meaning and purpose to experiences results in bodily health and happiness.[46]

Objects are central to exhibition and experience design. They stir emotions, cause reflection, and serve as a call to action. Brenda Cowan's design research is founded upon the irrefutable knowledge that objects are both deeply meaningful and necessary in the lives of people.[47] Based on this relationship and understanding, *Psychotherapeutic Object Dynamics* uses the interrelated acts of releasing/unburdening, giving/receiving, composing, associating, making, synergizing, and touching to suggest that object-based exhibitions can be explicitly designed to enhance the psychological healing capacities of exhibitions and their participants.

Sustainable design

Reducing a project's ecological footprint is measured through the pillars of planet, profit, and *people*. Acting on these criteria is mandatory for many exhibiting institutions that represent science and natural history. Designers drive decisions that create healthy environments and influence practices that reduce waste and carbon emissions. These include energy-efficient lighting and climate controls, water conservation, building materials that conserve natural resources and are produced without using toxic chemicals, and systems of modular exhibition components that can be repurposed multiple times. Designers should work toward measurable outcomes that advance the understanding of environmental issues and sustainable design practices by contributing actively to a communal knowledge base with colleagues, vendors, stakeholders, and their audiences.

Psychotherapeutic Object Dynamics resulted in *Stories from Syria* (2019) at Stockholm's Medelhavet Museum which exhibited personal objects saved by Syrian refugees.

Brenda Cowan

Primary case study
People, participation, and healing

Conflictorium, Ahmedabad, India, 2013–present
Designers: Various

Design challenge: Discursive space

Part museum of conflict, center for social justice, and co-laboratory, the Conflictorium is designed around people, participation, and dialogue. A discursive space first, and exhibition space second, it lends a voice and listens to those who have none.[48]

The two-story refurbished historic house sits between a mosque and a Hindu temple and across from a church. By design, its location attracts a local population who might not find themselves seated together—confronting segregation, economic division, and long standing histories of communal tension in the city of Ahmedabad. From this vantage point, the Conflictorium seeks to directly reduce violent tension and find creative community-led solutions to conflict.[49]

The Conflictorium's *Memory Lab* encourages people to place notes about their personal conflicts into jars.

Conflictorium Archives

The building concept, creative spaces, and exhibits are based on Avni Sethi's (founder/artistic director) interdisciplinary design thesis project.[50] As a result, designers and artists are regularly employed as part of the museum's small staff.

Design solution: Participatory viewership

Intimate galleries for curating and creating new work contain six exhibit sections with themes that emphasize "participatory viewership" about the history and discourse of social conflict. The exhibition design employs simple aesthetic vocabularies that use everyday materials, fabrication techniques, and tools, and much of the content is community sourced. *Moral Compass* permits people to handle a replica of the Indian constitution; *Memory Lab* encourages people to place notes about a conflict in their lives into jars; and the *Sorry Tree* empowers people to tie their apologies to its branches outside the museum. Rotating, mixed media exhibitions are layered onto these already evocative installations to "activate dialogue."[51] Artist-in-residence programs, dance performances, moderated discussions, and open karaoke nights are open to all members of the community to capture a range of professional and amateur voices and perspectives.

Design impact: Relevance checking

The Conflictorium is continuously in the making, where participatory design means exhibitions and experiences are constantly transformed. The museum is an archive of the present challenging who writes history and who proposes the future. Rather than a collection of artifacts on display, it is a set of experiences attained by moving through the spaces, where technology is shunned in favor human interaction. A place for healing, well-being, and inclusivity, the Conflictorium continuously checks its relevance so as not to become an elephant in the larger public sphere.[52] Sethi considers the city as the archive of the conflict. Its memory, events, evidence, sometimes emotion, anger, hatred, or empathy—these are the things that come from the city and enter the museum.[53]

People open and close this book

This chapter and "Hands-on, Minds-on" (chapter 12) serve as bookends. They sandwich specifics about the history, theory, and practice of exhibition making and the experience design process. Understanding, accommodating, and including people is at the core of designing exhibitions and experiences. It is appropriate that people should get the first and last word.

The Conflictorium's *Sorry Tree* empowers people to tie their apologies to tree branches outside the museum.

Conflictorium Archives

The *Gallery of Disputes* at the Conflictorium uses everyday materials and community sourced content.

Conflictorium Archives

Tips and Tricks

Ronald Mace and design researchers at North Carolina State University (*The Center for Universal Design,* 1997) advocated for all people regardless of their age, size, ability, or disability. Their Universal Design Principles apply to people-centered exhibition and experience environments.[54]

1. **Equitable use:** Design is useful and marketable to people with diverse abilities.
2. **Flexibility in use:** Design accommodates a wide range of individual preferences and abilities.
3. **Simple and intuitive:** Design is easy to understand, regardless of the user's experience, knowledge, language skills, or current concentration level.
4. **Perceptible information:** Design communicates necessary information effectively to the user, regardless of ambient conditions or the user's sensory abilities.
5. **Tolerance for error:** Design minimizes hazards and the adverse consequences of accidental or unintended actions.
6. **Low physical effort:** Design can be used efficiently and comfortably and with a minimum of fatigue.
7. **Size and space:** Design provides approach, reach, manipulation, and use regardless of user's body size, posture, or mobility.

Finally, interpret Judy Rand's *Visitor's Bill of Rights* (1996) as a touchstone for the design of experiences.

Notes

1. Victor J. Papanek, *Design for the Real World: Human Ecology and Social Change*, 2nd ed., completely rev. (Chicago, Ill.: Academy Chicago, 1985).
2. Suzanne MacLeod, *Museums and Design for Creative Lives* (London ; New York: Routledge, Taylor & Francis Group, 2021), 17.
3. "Designing for Empathy—Elif Gokcigdem," accessed April 18, 2022, http://elifgokcigdem.com/designing-for-empathy/.
4. Eilean Hooper-Greenhill, ed., *The Educational Role of the Museum*, 2nd ed., Leicester Readers in Museum Studies (London; New York: Routledge, 1999), 255–68.
5. "Theory of Multiple Intelligences," in Wikipedia, March 29, 2022, https://en.wikipedia.org/w/index.php?title=Theory_of_multiple_intelligences&oldid=1079969403.
6. John H. Falk, "An Identity-Centered Approach to Understanding Museum Learning. Curator," *Curator: The Museum Journal* 49 (2006): 151–66.
7. Judy Rand, "The 227-Mile Museum, or Why We Need a Visitor's Bill of Rights," *Visitor Studies: Theory, Research and Practice* 9 (1997): 21.
8. Kenneth W. Luckhurst, *The Story of Exhibitions* (London, New York: The Studio Publications, 1951), 9.
9. Marty Sklar and Leslie Sklar, *One Little Spark! Mickey's Ten Commandments and The Road to Imagineering*, 1st ed. (Los Angeles; New York: Disney Editions, 2015).
10. Rosemary Spooner, "A Heritage Institution Exploring Its Own Ancestry: Glasgow's Kelvingrove Art Gallery and Museum," *International Journal of the Inclusive Museum* 6, no. 2 (April 2013): 60.
11. Smithsonian Institution Archives, "Record Unit 90 Exhibition Scripts, 1948–1978," text, Smithsonian Institution Archives (Smithsonian Institution, 1948–1978, 1948), https://siarchives.si.edu/collections/siris_arc_216697.
12. Freeman Tilden and R. Bruce Craig, *Interpreting Our Heritage*, 4th ed., expanded and updated (Chapel Hill: University of North Carolina Press, 2007).
13. "Field-Manual-Museums.pdf," accessed April 12, 2022, http://npshistory.com/publications/curation/field-manual-museums.pdf.
14. Barry Mackintosh, *Interpretation in the National Park Service: A Historical Perspective* (Washington, D.C.: History Division, National Park Service, Department of the Interior, 1986), 52.
15. Mackintosh, *Interpretation in the National Park Service*, 54.
16. David Harmon, ed., *People, Places, and Parks. Proceedings of the 2005 George Wright Society. Conference on Parks, Protected Areas, and Cultural Sites* (George Wright Society, 2006), 428.
17. "Harpers Ferry Center (U.S. National Park Service)," accessed April 12, 2022, https://www.nps.gov/subjects/hfc/index.htm.
18. "National Park Service: Mission 66 Visitor Centers (Introduction)," accessed April 12, 2022, https://www.nps.gov/parkhistory/online_books/allaback/vc0e.htm.
19. James L. Adams, *Conceptual Blockbusting: A Guide to Better Ideas*, 3rd ed. (Reading, Mass.: Addison-Wesley, 1994).
20. "Tools for Taking Action," Stanford d.school, accessed April 13, 2022, https://dschool.stanford.edu/resources.
21. Clare Brown, "Unboxing History Exhibitions: Experience design in museum practice," in MacLeod et al., *The Future of Museum and Gallery Design: Purpose, Process, Perception* (London; New York: Routledge, 2018), 213–24.
22. Atelier Brückner, Uwe Brückner, and Beverley Locke, eds., *Scenography. 2: Staging the Space = Szenografie 2: Der Inszenierte Raum* (Basel, Switzerland: Birkhäuser Verlag GmbH, part of Walter de Gruyter GmbH, 2019), 243.
23. In recent years, et al., "Five Emerging Trends in Design Thinking for 2020," *Design Thinking for Museums*, December 23, 2019, https://designthinkingformuseums.net/2019/12/23/five-trends-in-design-thinking-for-2020/.
24. "Critical Alphabet—By Lesley-Ann Noel, PhD," accessed April 18, 2022, https://criticalalphabet.com/.
25. "About OMCA | Oakland Museum of California," accessed April 18, 2022, https://museumca.org/about-omca.

26. Mark Dion et al., *The Marvelous Museum: Orphans, Curiosities & Treasures: A Mark Dion Project* (San Francisco; Oakland: Chronicle Books, Oakland Museum of California, 2010), 77.

27. Marjorie Schwarzer, *Riches, Rivals & Radicals: 100 Years of Museums in America* (Washington, D.C.: American Association of Museums, 2006), 133.

28. "Assignment Four—The Oakland Museum—Bay Area Television Archive," accessed April 18, 2022, https://diva.sfsu.edu/collections/sfbatv/bundles/208795.

29. Dion et al., *The Marvelous Museum*, 86.

30. Signe Mayfield and Ted Cohen, *The Object in Its Place: Ted Cohen & the Art of Exhibition Design* (San Diego; [Oakland]; San Francisco: Mingei International Museum; in association with the Oakland Museum of California and the Museum of Craft and Design, 2020).

31. Kathleen McLean, "Manifesto for the (r)Evolution of Museum Exhibitions," *Exhibition* 29, no. 1 (2010): 40–50.

32. Kathleen McLean, "Examining Process in Museum Exhibitions: A case for experimentation and prototyping," in MacLeod et al., *The Future of Museum and Gallery Design: Purpose, Process, Perception* (London; New York: Routledge, 2018), 121–31.

33. "ROE: The New Metric for Improving Customer Experience and Increasing Loyalty," *AMA New York*, July 1, 2021, https://www.amanewyork.org/resources/current-insights/roe-the-new-metric-for-improving -customer-experience-and-increasing-loyalty/.

34. Kathleen McLean, "Museum Exhibitions and the Dynamics of Dialogue," *Daedalus* 128, no. 3 (1999): 83–107.

35. *Introduction to Design Interviewing*, 2017, https://www.youtube.com/watch?v=gimBKfnrc7M.

36. Mary Jane Solomon, "A Boy's Life During the Holocaust," *Washington Post*, June 27, 2003, https://www .washingtonpost.com/archive/lifestyle/2003/06/27/a-boys-life-during-the-holocaust/2ba83cdc-7300 -48ae-9f83-03f0dc9fbb0c/.

37. Elizabeth B.-N. Sanders and Pieter Jan Stappers, "Co-Creation and the New Landscapes of Design," *CoDesign* 4, no. 1 (March 1, 2008): 5–18, https://doi.org/10.1080/15710880701875068.

38. "Welcoming the Widest Possible Audience," accessed April 19, 2022, https://www.tessituranetwork.com/ Items/Articles/Thought-Leadership/2019/Welcoming-the-Widest-Audience.

39. Anne E. Chick, "Co-Creating an Accessible, Multisensory Exhibition with the National Centre for Craft & Design and Blind and Partially Sighted Participants," *Conference paper*, 2017, https://www.semantic scholar.org/paper/Co-creating-an-accessible%2C-multisensory-exhibition-Chick/55831e9ce1f727cbcb c7dded7b4aed771c80a6dc.

40. "#Ableism—Center for Disability Rights," accessed August 31, 2022, https://cdrnys.org/blog/uncategorized/ ableism/.

41. Clare Brown and Janice Majewski, "What Makes an Exhibition Inclusive? A 20-Year Conversation about Universal Design," *Exhibitionist*, Fall 2015, 78–81.

42. Ellen Lupton and Andrea Lipps, eds., *The Senses: Design beyond Vision* (New York: Cooper Hewitt, Smithsonian Design Museum, Princeton Architectural Press, 2018), 25.

43. Lupton and Lipps, 24–25.

44. "Exhibitions—Corey Timpson Design," accessed April 19, 2022, https://coreytimpson.com/?page_id =366.

45. Heather Pressman and Danielle Schulz, *The Art of Access: A Practical Guide for Museum Accessibility* (Lanham, MD: Rowman & Littlefield, 2021), 77–91.

46. National Alliance for Museums, Health and Wellbeing, *Museums as Spaces for Wellbeing: A Second Report from the National Alliance for Museums, Health, and Wellbeing*, n.d., 5, https://museumsandwell beingalliance.files.wordpress.com/2018/04/museums-as-spaces-for-wellbeing-a-second-report.pdf.

47. Brenda Cowan, "Exhibitions and Objects of Wellness—Part 1" (October 21, 2019), accessed April 24, 2022, https://segd.org/exhibitions-and-objects-wellness%E2%80%94part-1.

48. *Panellist Avni Sethi, Dancer and Founder, Conflictorium at the IFA Conference*, 2018, https://www.you-tube.com/watch?v=jZHzoEpggxs.

49. "In Flux: The Making of Indian Museums and Their Audiences," Habiba Insaf, 42, accessed April 25, 2022, https://www.kulturmanagement.net/dlf/9d57bdbac3dc7514bd0af912978eefac,4.pdf#page=37.

50. "Conflictorium," Inquiry into the Civic Role of Arts Organisations, accessed April 25, 2022, https://civicroleartsinquiry.gulbenkian.org.uk/resources/conflictorium.

51. "Conflictorium."

52. "Conflictorium."

53. *Panellist Avni Sethi, Dancer and Founder, Conflictorium at the IFA Conference.*

54. "The 7 Principles | Centre for Excellence in Universal Design," accessed April 15, 2022, https://universaldesign.ie/what-is-universal-design/the-7-principles/.

Designer's Toolbox: **Narrative**

Designers respond to an exhibition's content with floorplans, diagrams, and visualization studies. This process creates the blueprint for the audience experience. Navigate the designer's toolbox to discover why spatial planning, narrative structures, and wayfinding principles are critical when it comes to moving people and telling a good story.

Visualization: Claire Healy designs and creates narrative environments and is an Associate Lecturer on MA Narrative Environments at Central Saint Martins in London. She is based between Dublin, Ireland and London, U.K.

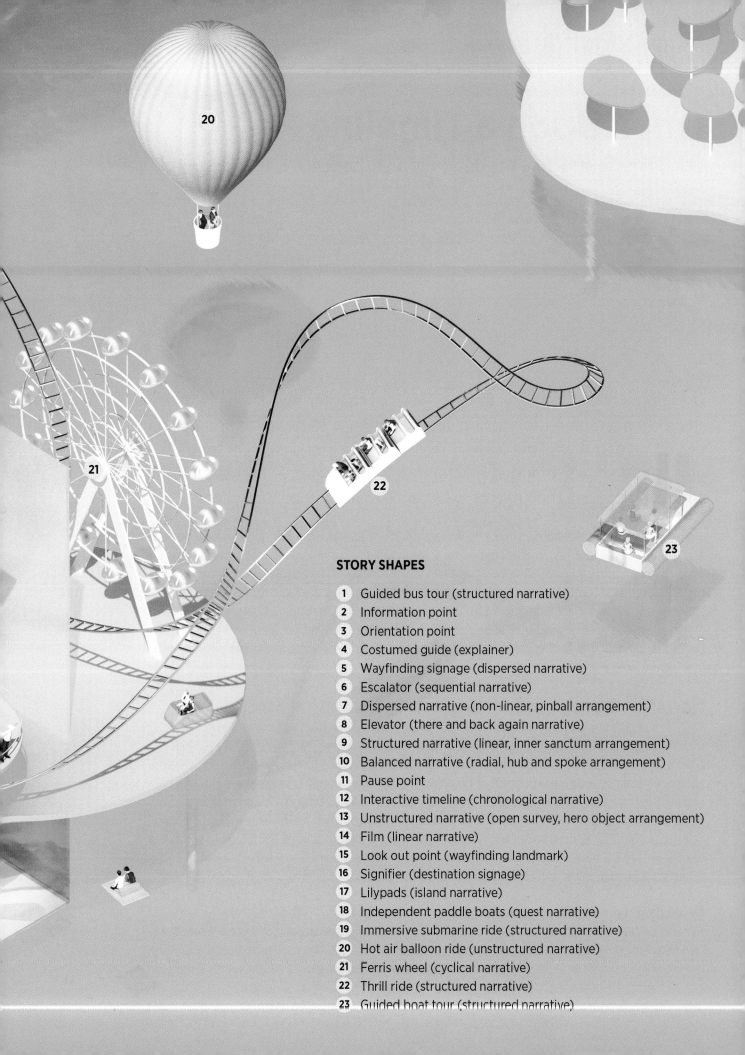

STORY SHAPES

1. Guided bus tour (structured narrative)
2. Information point
3. Orientation point
4. Costumed guide (explainer)
5. Wayfinding signage (dispersed narrative)
6. Escalator (sequential narrative)
7. Dispersed narrative (non-linear, pinball arrangement)
8. Elevator (there and back again narrative)
9. Structured narrative (linear, inner sanctum arrangement)
10. Balanced narrative (radial, hub and spoke arrangement)
11. Pause point
12. Interactive timeline (chronological narrative)
13. Unstructured narrative (open survey, hero object arrangement)
14. Film (linear narrative)
15. Look out point (wayfinding landmark)
16. Signifier (destination signage)
17. Lilypads (island narrative)
18. Independent paddle boats (quest narrative)
19. Immersive submarine ride (structured narrative)
20. Hot air balloon ride (unstructured narrative)
21. Ferris wheel (cyclical narrative)
22. Thrill ride (structured narrative)
23. Guided boat tour (structured narrative)

CHAPTER 2

Once Upon a Timeline

Using time to structure the design of an experience is timeless.

Key message: Design serves to structure, sequence, and bring to life an exhibition story.

Key word: narrative

Using time to tell a story is ubiquitous. This chapter reveals the relationships between time, storytelling, and experience to organize and design exhibition narratives. The trope is well-trodden, and designers for museums, trade shows, branded environments, interactions, and even retail spaces emphasize their role as experience makers *and* storytellers.

Experiences, like stories, have a beginning, middle, and end, where design dictates the pace and rhythm of the journey, from leisurely and self-guided, to controlled experiences that process large crowds in theme parks, attractions, and exhibition blockbusters. Leading people through experiences requires turning complex content into chronological or sequenced stories that unfold in space as a series of narratives, associated with objects, ideas, or information; visual metaphors summarize an idea or theme; or a timeline holds the exhibition themes together. Intuitive pathways, distinctive landmarks, wayfinding prompts, moving walkways, and people movers transition audiences from one space to another.

Narrative Structure: Communicating Exhibition Stories

Exhibitions are four-dimensional stories that unfold in space and time.[1] Whether history exhibitions, artist's retrospectives, or dinosaur installations, they all use timelines to hang themes and guide the audience's journey. While the concept of chronological time is globally understood, it does not acknowledge the entire worldview.[2] Native American cultures refer to time in the ethereal sense, with no beginning or end. In many African, Asian, and Indigenous societies, time is often seen as cyclical and related to ritual, reincarnation, and repetition. Where chronological time is spatialized according to change, cyclical time centers stability and is not conceived as external to lived experience.[3] Either approach has merit in the exhibition environment.

Developing chronological and thematic stories
Experience-based storylines are usually organized chronologically, thematically, or chrono-thematically (where themes divert from a chronological path). Chronological journeys use time-based narratives like history, evolution, or style, ending or sometimes starting with the most recent events. Thematic

Exhibits at the Estonian
National Museum feature
multi-language interpretation derived from people's
stories and oral histories.

Estonian National Museum

journeys break down content into sections and sub-themes, such as media, maker, or geography, and are less reliant on chronology.

Traditionally, museums organize their stories around their primary collections. For example: *European Art 1750–1900* (in a Gallery of Art), *Mass Extinction 252 Million Years Ago* (in a Natural History Museum), or *Car Pioneers 1886–1900* (in a Transport Museum). Alternatively, the J. Paul Getty Museum at the Getty Villa (2005) chose a thematic approach, where Greek, Etruscan, and Roman galleries were named *Gods and Goddesses* and *Mythical Creatures*, replacing the predictable geographical and chronological survey of the ancient world.

The International Spy Museum (2019) and the Museum of the Bible (2019) in Washington, D.C., are examples of thematic museums that leverage accessible topics. At the Museum of Broken Relationships (2010), everyday objects are given a different significance when they are placed in a display case and associated with compelling personal stories of unrequited love.

Everybody relates to a good story

Certain exhibitions and experiences grapple to identify or tease out obvious stories from complex content; others have an inherently clearer story to tell. H.C. Andersen's House (2021) in Odense, Denmark, is fortunate to be an attraction about the creation of world-famous fairy tales. Rather than present the life and work of Hans Christian Andersen in a predictable "once upon a time" manner, the museum is designed to provoke, and it turns things on their heads using sound, light, space, and scenery created in collaboration with twelve international artists. The "immersive theater" installation lets the indoor/outdoor space become the story, instead of an overbearing storyline dictating the space.

Telling stories—voice, emotion, and interpretation

An appropriate voice and language tone engages people in exhibition stories. Information written for a fifth-grade level has a greater chance of being understood than an academic treatise. Bilingual or multilingual storytelling increases access and facilitates inclusivity and global understanding.[4] Stories told in the third person dispel patriarchal "curator voices" and provide arm's-length commentaries. Exhibits at the Estonian National Museum (2016) in Tartu are multi-language and feature interpretive voices derived from people's stories and oral histories.

First-person narratives curtail misappropriation and offer emotional resonance and a human connection. A chilling example is the tapestry of audio and visual testimonies from 417 people describing their global whereabouts when the attacks took place on New York's World Trade Center in 2001. It is the visitor's first encounter upon entering the National September 11 Memorial & Museum (2014).

Designer Willhemina Wahlin advocates for critical distance between the designer and their practice, and she frames exhibitions with "difficult knowledge" as a performance of ideology, employing multimodal, semiotic resources as its actors.[5] *Curating Discomfort* acknowledges that discomfort—particularly to do with a legacy of racist ideology and centering whiteness—is necessary for genuine change. The Hunterian Museum in Glasgow is exploring ways outside of traditional museum authority to explore the interpretation of contested collections and to design and deliver a series of museum interventions that takes the museum out of the institutional comfort zone.[6] Social justice and human suffering, conflict, democracy, migration, slavery, decolonialization, and sites of consciousness present unique pedagogical challenges for both exhibition makers and audiences, in that first-person accounts are the only voices that matter.

Refer to Tricia Austin's book *Narrative Environments and Experience Design: Space as a Medium of Communication* (2019) for a comprehensive delve into the role of design, narrative, and storytelling in the exhibition and experience environment.[7]

Courting controversy

Exhibition storytelling was not always awake to societies' injustices. Paul Rudolph was establishing his architectural practice in 1954 when he received a call from the Department of Photography at the Museum of Modern Art in New York. Its director, Edward Steichen, went on to commission Rudolph for an installation that both would be celebrated as a milestone of design excellence and was an example of exhibition making that was tone-deaf to its controversial colonial connotations.[8]

Designers Local Projects use first-person narratives as a tapestry of audio testimonies for *We Remember* at the National September 11 Memorial & Museum.

Courtesy of Local Projects

Designer Willhemina Wahlin's *Ferguson Voices: Disrupting the Frame* (2017) at the University of Dayton framed difficult stories as a performance of ideology.

Photo: Chelsea Hall, Courtesy of the University of Dayton's Human Rights Center.

Event designed by H.C. Andersen's House to immerse audiences in the author's creative fairy tales through sensory-led stories.

H.C. Andersens Hus, photo by Laerke Beck Johansen

Human lives as human timeline

The Family of Man, Museum of Modern Art (MoMA), New York,
January 24–May 8, 1955
Designers: Edward Steichen; Paul Rudolph

Design challenge: Design facilitates

Featuring 503 images by 273 photographers originating in 69 countries, *The Family of Man* attained a significant role in the history of twentieth-century photography because of its international exposure. The U.S. Information Agency promoted the exhibition as an achievement of American culture by presenting ten different versions of the show in ninety-one cities in thirty-eight countries between 1955 and 1962, seen by an estimated nine million people.[9]

The exhibition displayed images from various magazine archives, including *Life* and *Vogue*, and photography agencies such as Magnum. Grouped in thirty-seven thematic sections that climbed around MoMA's temporary gallery space, the exhibition's chronology told the story of the human life cycle. A timeline of humanity from lovers and childbirth to family and death, ended with war and the H-bomb explosion. Significantly, a section on children at the exhibition's end provided a happy conclusion and atoned for this lack of optimism.

Criticism of the exhibition continues to this day because the choice of photographs painted a distorted portrait of an impoverished developing world through a Western perspective. Condemnation was also leveled at Steichen for imposing a populist thematic narrative structure on the exhibition—one that Rudolph's spatial plan accentuated—downplaying the historical context of the images, favoring journalism over art, and failing to amplify the photographers.[10]

Design solution: Chrono-thematic stories

Rudolph's floor plan responded to the chrono-thematic narrative. The work was spatially divided into a series of thematic groupings (open-ended and unstructured) connected by a contiguous (structured) path of travel to guide audiences from the entrance to exit. People were pulled through the space by the display of striking photography and glimpses of what lay ahead (see chapter 5).

Rudolph imbued the design with a sense of innovation and futurism. At the exhibition entrance,

photographs were attached to Lucite (a new transparent acrylic) panels, which made them appear to float.[11] Photos of pregnancy and birth were installed in a curved, white-curtained womb-like room evocative of a hospital operation theater. Exhibit wall colors corresponded to the chronology of life—white for birth, darkened red for the threat of continued war, and a naïve pink for the section on children. Unframed photographic enlargements were mounted to Masonite panels in a variety of contrasting heights, scales, adjacencies, and depths. The panels extended into the viewers' space to create a visual landscape that audiences were invited to explore.[12] Some attached to wall surfaces; others floated on poles, hung from wire from the ceiling, or they were arranged on platforms like an exploded three-dimensional magazine page.

Design impact: Responding to the narrative

Rudolph's design response to the exhibition's narrative structure received accolades for its engaging and dynamic display and for how it could be flat-packed and travel to multiple venues. *Photography and the City: The Evolution of an Art and a Science* (1968), designed by the Eames Office for the Arts and Industries Building of the Smithsonian Institution in Washington, D.C., was inspired to employ a similar approach.

The Family of Man's spatial compositions add a distinct architectural aspect to the narrative. Rudolph's subsequent architecture commissions for the Yale Art and Architecture Building (1958) and Miami residence (1961) incorporate floating window surrounds, setbacks, and articulations that soften brutalist concrete forms and reduce the heavy massing in the tradition of contemporary mid-century modern design.[13] This lighter stylistic touch to suspend forms in space is evident in the exhibition design for *The Family of Man*. The hovering rectilinear photographic forms served as a building block for Rudolph's later architectural compositions.

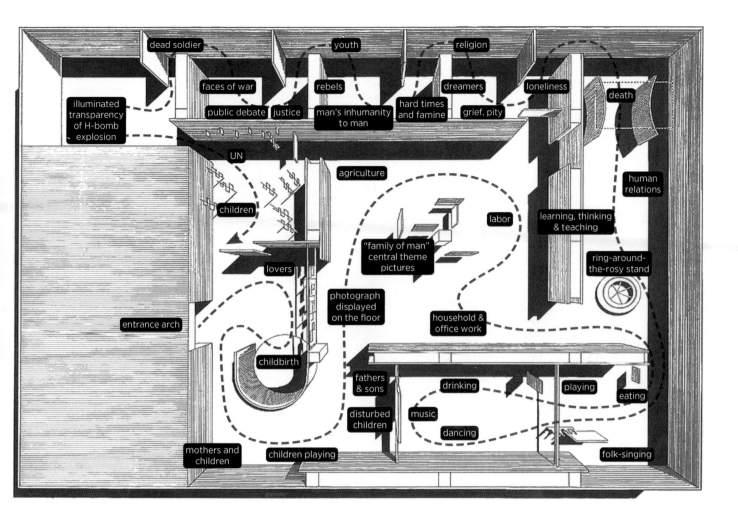

The following labels appear in the diagram: dead soldier, youth, religion, faces of war, rebels, dreamers, loneliness, death, illuminated transparency of H-bomb explosion, public debate, justice, man's inhumanity to man, hard times and famine, grief, pity, UN, agriculture, human relations, children, labor, learning, thinking & teaching, "family of man" central theme pictures, lovers, ring-around-the-rosy stand, photograph displayed on the floor, household & office work, entrance arch, childbirth, fathers & sons, drinking, playing, eating, disturbed children, music, dancing, mothers and children, children playing, folk-singing

Modes of Movement: Facilitating Exhibition Stories

Exhibitions blend the complexities of architectural space with the narrative concerns of book design.[14] However, the exhibition medium defies linearity and embraces what Falk and Dierking call free choice learning environments, which connect people socially and emotionally.[15] These connections are managed by carefully positioning structures, objects, atmosphere, and the presence of people to moderate pace, rhythm, and the flow of the story as it traverses any axis of the spatial environment. Exhibition designers employ multiple modes of physical movement to transport people and transform stories into fun, accessible, and comprehensible narratives.

Planning the journey and conveyance

People move through a story on walkways, stairs, escalators, elevators, and accessible ramps. Contiguous pathways or ramps at the Guggenheim Museum in New York (1959) or the Mercedes-Benz Museum in Stuttgart (2006) ensure there is no physical break in the story. This is particularly vital for experiences where interruptions en route challenge a person's suspended reality or feeling of total immersion—hence the elevator at Disneyland's Haunted Mansion seamlessly sets up the ghostly story as the walls appear to move while guests head to the Doom Buggies.

Other modes of movement utilize mechanical storytelling conveyances—people-movers, autonomous vehicles, boats, and monorails are omnipresent at global entertainment resorts. Roller coasters, thrill rides, and ribbon rides (autonomous cars that are guided by tracks on the ground, in water, or in the air) are a storytelling staple at attractions like York's JORVIK Viking

The Family of Man's chrono-thematic narrative grouped 37 thematic sections along a chronology of the human life cycle.

Based on *The Family of Man*, Museum of Modern Art, New York City, Plan / P. Rudolph, 1952. Library of Congress Prints and Photographs Division, LC-DIG-ppmsca-03530.

Centre (1984). Simulators that reenact a story, or theaters/rooms that revolve laterally or vertically to move people through a narrative, have a history of entertaining audiences. Early examples of this technique include Disney's Carousel of Progress and IBM's Information Machine, which debuted at the 1964/1965 New York World's Fair (chapter 10 expands on these projects).

Wayfinding—navigation, orientation, explanation

Judy Rand considers orientation a key comfort factor in the *Visitor's Bill of Rights*. Rui Olds calls for the freedom of movement and well-ordered and signposted spaces to arm people with competence in museums.[16] The strategies designers use to facilitate these actions is termed wayfinding—a problem-solving process by which people understand and make decisions about navigating architectural, natural, and urban spaces.[17]

Communication and wayfinding in the exhibition environment consist of three core explicit and implicit forms: (1) architecture—the physical clues in the environment (building attributes, lighting, and pathways); (2) people—the presence of someone to give verbal directions or advice (museum docents or park attendants); and (3) graphics—signs and maps that send a message or tell a story (directional signs at a trade show). Successful audience wayfinding and orientation is compromised if any of these key communication elements are removed.

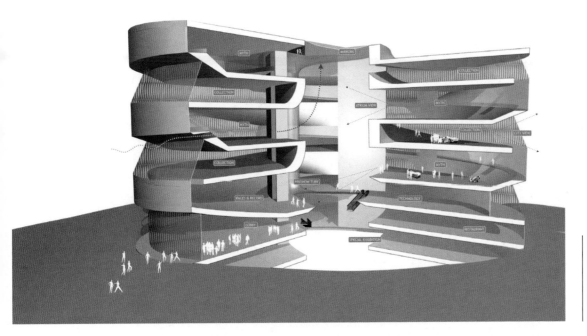

UNStudio and HG Merz's continuous circulation ramp seamlessly transitions people between stories at the Mercedes-Benz Museum in Stuttgart.

© UNStudio

Walt Disney's Carousel of Progress attraction at the Magic Kingdom Park in the Walt Disney World Resort brings the narrative experience to the audience using a revolving theater and Audio-Animatronic figures stage show.

© Disney

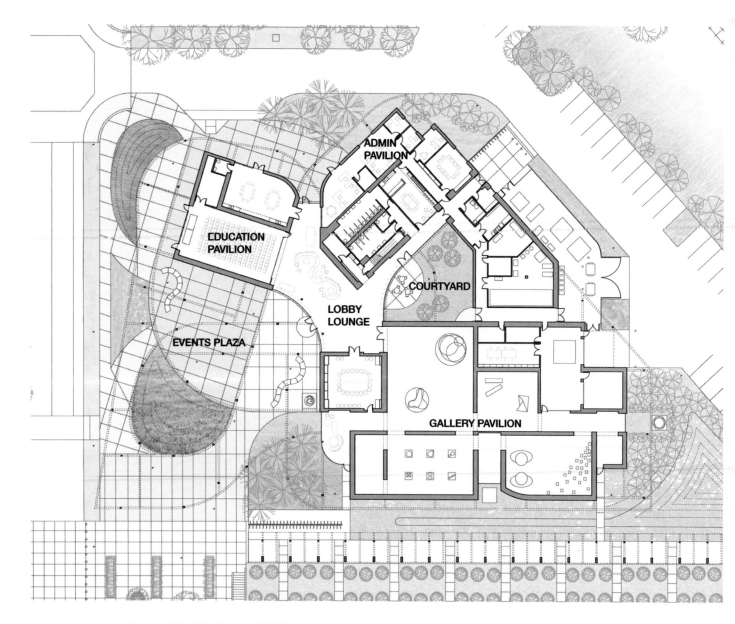

Plan view of the Jan Shrem and Maria Manetti Shrem Museum of Art (2016) where architecture, staff, and graphics tell a wayfinding story that orientates people to the site.

Courtesy of SO–IL, Bohlin Cywinski Jackson, Lutsko Associates

Primary case study

Navigating the site and story

Theme Parks and Attractions, 1543–Present
Designers: Various

Design challenge: Environmental storytelling

Bakken (1543) and Tivoli Gardens (1843) in Denmark were the first of countless pleasure gardens, theme parks, rides, and attractions around the world to use storytelling, characters, and fantasy themes to envelop audiences and lull them into a state of non-reality—whether contemporary adventure rides, journeys back in time, or treks into the future. Walt Disney Imagineering describes their process as "environmental storytelling" to distinguish it from film- and theater-based entertainment, which also

puts storytelling at the heart of their enterprise.[18] Parks and attractions typically occupy an expansive site segmented into a series of lands or zones, individually themed or re-themed to lure repeat audiences, and connected by a range of people-moving conveyances. It adds up to an experience that presents a unique and challenging wayfinding and story-sequencing model.

Design solution: Wayfinding strategies

Cities have evolved historic urban wayfinding models to serve as reference points for designers planning large-scale storytelling attractions.[19] These include: street models (gridded streets connected via compass points, numbers, or letter intersections, found in cities like New York or in Universal Studios' City-Walk); landmark models (focusing on major destinations that can be recognized from a distance, like the Colosseum in Rome or the roller-coaster rides at

SIX Flags Magic Mountain); connector models (utilizing a central location with surrounding developments, like found in the Forbidden City in Beijing or Disneyland's Magic Castle); and district models (the subdivision of a place into sections for ease of navigation, like those found in the Arrondissements of Paris or the in countries/lands at Disney's EPCOT).

Parks and attractions often rely on primary guest entry/exit points that connect to a central hub (plaza) with multiple spokes (pathways) that lead to the various zones. Common wayfinding strategies, such as aiming for recognizable landmarks; consulting maps, signage, and other navigational tools; following tracks/paths and markers; asking people for directions; or simply following the crowd, guide people from story point A to B.

Design impact: Multisensory navigation

Navigating the site and the story at parks and attractions is contingent on both physical (mechanical- and people-powered conveyances), and cognitive (intuition, deductive reasoning, and sensory perception) wayfinding. Former Walt Disney Imagineer Joe Rohde refers to stories that are multisensory, to include what guests smell, see, hear, feel, as well as the temperature and time of day—all factors that will impact how people personally choose to move through space and engage with the various attractions.[20]

Spatial Structure: Designing Exhibition Stories

Exhibition narratives and the storylines used to tell them span from the "big idea" to an object label's single idea. Stories adapt to the environment, the product, and the intended audience. A catchy retail summer sale message conveys a story of fun. A lengthier call to action activates a community popup exhibit. Researching and procuring the content for an exhibition (the assets) can take years depending on the complexity of the project—although shorter time frames are more common for temporary exhibition projects.

Establishing storylines falls to in-house development teams, external consultancies, or a combination of both. In-house teams, such as museums, have staff employed in various specific roles from different departments to develop content. External exhibition and experience design studios/consultancies work with either existing content or develop it from scratch. Larger design studios typically have three storytelling units: content, design, and new media developers. Exhibit

Parks and attractions often rely on entry/exit plazas to serve as central hubs connected to multiple spokes (pathways) leading to various storytelling zones.

Illustration: John Haden/Thinkwell Group

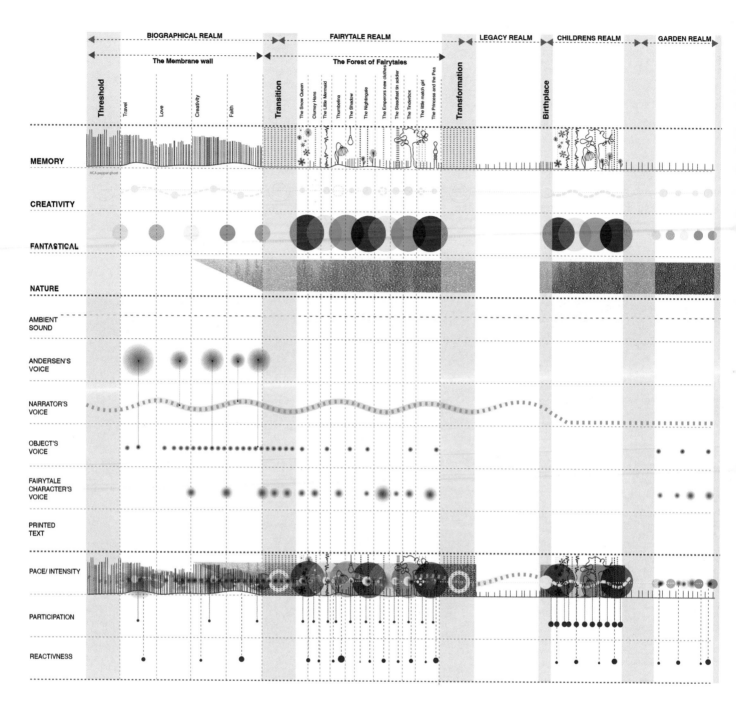

Event's experience storyboard for H.C. Andersen's House resembles the narrative structure found in film or a musical score.

Courtesy of Event

content teams include curators, experts, researchers, interpretive planners, writers, and producers. When the designer is invited to the collaborative table as the narrative is being developed, it will ensure the physical space can successfully tell the story, accommodate the amount of content, and satisfy specific object display requirements. Good designers are excellent visitor advocates. Early in the process, they can quickly visualize the experience, suggest methods to tailor the story, and recommend interpretive strategies.[21]

Transforming ingredients into experience

Essential elements guide the spatial narrative and inform the design process: (1) exhibition brief—written blueprint that summarizes the exhibition content and formulates the thematic structure around which the content is organized; (2) exhibition object list—visual blueprint for the content, which contains object images, dimensions, media, and other considerations; (3) exhibition parameters—goals, limitations, or practical constraints for the exhibition that influence design solutions; (4) exhibition script—storyboard (look book) that visualizes what the narrative might look like;

(5) massing diagrams—visualizations of the volumetric space required for the themes/sections; (6) the Big Idea—exhibition thesis: Everything should relate to a succinct statement that helps the team stay on track.[22]

Narratology

Exhibitions use sequence to build stories, emotion, and intellectual complexity. Sequencing, according to designer Katherine Skellon, is where objects and spaces gain impact and meaning for people through their juxtaposition with what precedes and follows them.[23] The six emotional arcs in cinematic stories proposed by Kurt Vonnegut—for example, boy meets girl, or rags to riches—track common narrative patterns found in exhibitions and experiences.[24]

The comparison to film does not end there. Exhibition stories follow spatial scripts that incorporate flashbacks to history or what was previously witnessed. Experiences employ methods that parallel film production/camera techniques, such as pan (panoramic rooms), long (object in the distance), close-up (looking closer at activities), aerial (overlooks from mezzanines), and establishing shots (sightlines through entrances to objects, colors, or images). Indeed, designer Tom Duncan compares the narrative structures of film with the physical architectural journey of the exhibition space in what have always been spatial, dynamic, and time based.[25]

The science and theory of storytelling is known as narratology and maps easily onto experience design. Gustav Freytag's narrative arc, or pyramid, illustrates how a story gradually builds in steps to a climax and then falls to a conclusion.[26] Another common circular pattern found in storytelling and applicable to exhibitions is called the Hero's Journey.[27] Let's imagine the hero heeds a call to adventure (decides to see the exhibition), crosses into the unknown with the help of a wise guide (the expert or curator), overcomes adversity to achieve a goal (contends with crowds or challenging content), and then returns to the place where he started (the exhibition entrance or, more often, the gift shop). The importance of pacing and the rhythm of an exhibition journey is explored in greater depth in chapter 5.

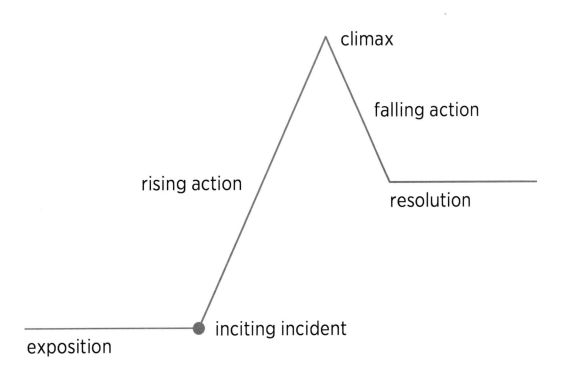

climax

falling action

rising action

resolution

inciting incident

exposition

Stories combine pace and rhythm with euphoria and adversity.

Gustav Freytag's Pyramid

Containers for human activity

Herbert Bayer's treatise *Fundamentals of Exhibition Design* (1939) rationalized spatial flow with story structure.[28] Consider the following spatial arrangements, which can be combined and interchanged (see Designer's Toolbox).

Structured (linear, directed, forced march): Few options to deviate from a prescribed route following the storyline in a deliberate sequence; keeps people moving; story builds in progression; frustrating for people who want to revisit previous exhibit areas.

Unstructured (nonlinear, undirected, open survey): Free to roam with few obstructions and dip into any exhibits/stories; open-ended discovery; personal connections; people may feel overwhelmed by choice.

Balanced (hub and spoke, radial, central core): Experience starts at a central hub and radiates out in multiple directions; good for orientation; focus on a central theme; people gain from a balance of structured and unstructured.

Dispersed (multidirectional, random, pinball): Variety of objects or exhibits free standing in a larger space; open-ended; ability to stagger route and backtrack; people may find the experience exhausting without a clear navigational guide.

Mapping stories—development/structure/concept

Exhibitions and experiences originate from either tailoring the story to an existing environment (changing the museum gallery) or allowing the story to shape the construction of a brand-new space (World Expo pavilion) where the architecture follows the narrative. Once the story, content, and exhibition elements are decided, the design team explores the chronology, themes, and concepts using a series of architectural massing studies and diagrams where the content is mapped onto the site or space to establish the basic spatial organization—a kind of "journey blueprint" for the exhibition. This process reveals any overarching problems conveying the narrative or accommodating the number of objects and/or stories in the given space. It may necessitate a major change in planning or how the architecture of a building must adapt to tell the exhibition story.

Primary case study
Layering stories

National Museum of African American History and Culture, Washington, D.C., 2017–present
Principal Designer: Ralph Appelbaum Associates

directly from the African American community—a major museum first.

Ralph Applebaum Associates (RAA) relied on their successful record of connecting stories, objects, and people; sequencing experiences; and designing the interstitial spaces between the exhibits to carry an emotive narrative. With offices all over the world and a cadre of designers, they have left their footprint on contemporary exhibition design practice.

Design challenge: Storytelling museum

One of the most dramatic and long-awaited examples of the storytelling museum to emerge in the last decade is the National Museum of African American History and Culture (NMAAHC).[29] The museum was visited by over 1.2 million people in the first six months after its opening, and it remains one of the most popular museums on the Mall in Washington, D.C. The interpretive story of the African American struggle took over ten years to develop. The museum team juggled a complex historical story told through 160 media presentations, 3,500 photographs and images, and 3,000 artifacts. Many of these objects were crowd-sourced

Design solution: Spatial narratives

Questions about structuring the NMAAHC story focused on whether a linear storyline would imply a triumphal march toward inevitable racial change and progress, and in doing so, obscure existing racial injustices.[30] Should the exhibition start in Africa, how would slavery be remembered and interpreted, and would racial and sexual violence be presented? Just how hopeful should the telling of the African American experience be?[31] Ultimately, the team decided clarity, accessibility, and audience comprehension would be best served by a chronological account. A slave stone auction block marks the beginning of the story—the tragedy of over one thousand bare feet—where men and women were torn from each other and their children, shackled, bound, bought, and sold.[32]

The celebrated museum, designed by the architectural team of Freelon Group/Adjaye Associates/Davis Brody Bond/Smith Group, was initially conceived with four floors aboveground for orientation, events, and temporary exhibitions about contemporary African American experiences, and one below ground level for the history galleries—the ground plane marks the period before and after emancipation. RAA was hired to develop the exhibits well into the construction planning and intervened at a late stage in the design process to advocate for a major change to the architecture's volumetric relationships. The exhibit designers recommended the history galleries increase from one to three subterranean levels to encapsulate a comprehensive overview of the African American diasporic experience and accommodate a more expansive storyline.[33] A series of mezzanines and overlooks were added to punctuate the levels, connected by a contiguous ramp between the floors. Lead designer Aki Carpenter cites the use of "dark, deep" colors in the underground galleries, which then embrace rich, bright hues like goldenrod as the galleries build toward the present day, and the typography (created by African American designer Joshua Darden) gets bolder and more contemporary as people ascend through the story.[34] This radical alteration to the original scheme served to strengthen the emotional and conceptual links across time, throughout the story, and between the exhibits. The resulting change is one of the most distinctive features of the museum journey.

Design impact: Narrative immersion

Museums are at their best when the collaboration among designers, curators, and educators sharpens the interpretive and visual edges of the exhibitions, making the past accessible in a way that provides both emotional and intellectual sustenance, says founding director Lonnie G. Bunch III.[35] The National Museum of African American History and Culture demonstrates the value in placing storytelling, difficult knowledge, and the exhibition experience ahead of architectural form and the short-term constraints of cost and change orders.

Metaphorically, the building embodies an untold story: change rising from the past, embracing the present, and continuing upward into the future. In remarks at the museum's opening, President Barack Obama said, "This building reaches down seventy feet, its roots spreading far wider and deeper than any tree on this mall, and on its lowest level, after you walk pass remnants of a slave ship, after you reflect on the immortal declaration that all men are created equal, you can see a block of stone . . ."[36]

The National Museum of African American History and Culture is a dramatic example of a building reinforcing a narrative.

Image courtesy of the Smithsonian Institution National Museum of African American History and Culture, Photograph by Alan Karchmer.

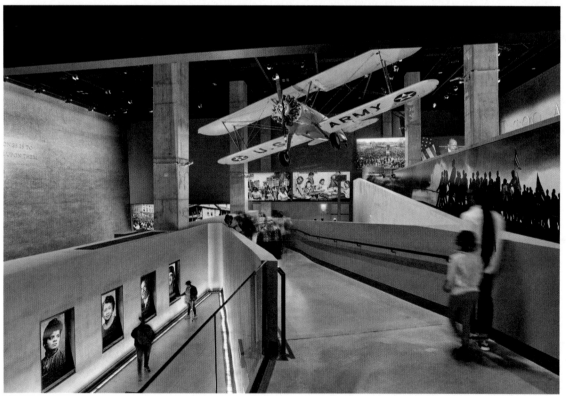

Exhibition designers for the National Museum of African American History and Culture advocated that the history galleries increase to three subterranean levels to accommodate a more expansive storyline.

Image courtesy of the Smithsonian Institution National Museum of African American History and Culture, Photograph by Alan Karchmer.

Mezzanines and overlooks at the National Museum of African American History and Culture punctuate levels connected by ramps that strengthen the emotional and conceptual story links between exhibits.

Image courtesy of the Smithsonian Institution National Museum of African American History and Culture, Photograph by Alan Karchmer.

On the Block

A strong iron collar was closely fitted
by means of a padlock round each
of our necks. A chain of iron about
a hundred feet long was passed
through the hasp of each padlock...
we were handcuffed in pairs.

CHARLES BALL 1837

The auction block was a site of fear, humiliation,
and uncertainty where loved ones were separated
for life. Auction blocks could be found from
colonial times well into the antebellum period.
They were often seen in the public square, slave-
trading offices, hotels, at the docks, in jail yards,
and at courthouses. African Americans endured
being sold on the block and being devalued to
mere laboring hands, feet, backs, and wombs.

A slave stone auction block marks the beginning to the exhibition journey at the National Museum of African American History and Culture.

Image courtesy of the Smithsonian Institution National Museum of African American History and Culture, Photograph by Alex Jamison.

This chapter presented options for organizing content based on linear time, cyclical time, and thematic groupings. While it considered people's method of movement, form of conveyance, and how they navigate stories successfully while at a venue, the next chapter will expand storytelling beyond the present to discuss the before and after—the pre- and post-experience.

Tips and Tricks

Develop spatial flows, people-centered experiences, and narrative structures that respond to the story using the following design techniques:

1. Integrate spatial interludes (liminal or intersectional) to punctuate the story and make the exhibition/experience less overwhelming.
2. Measure the volume of the space against how people respond to themselves as a fixed unit of measurement—cathedrals versus homes.
3. Utilize distributional and transitional space: entrances or exits (lobbies, atria), connecting one place to another (doorways, corridors); key vistas (pacing and orientation).
4. Incorporate collecting spaces: to meet or gather (classrooms, auditoriums, exhibit halls).
5. Allow for people's exhibit fatigue, sensory overload, and overstimulation/exertion (seating, quiet spaces).
6. Keep transitions smooth, make the journey contiguous, and accommodate everyone (ramps, elevators, and accessible pathways).
7. People tend to turn right upon entry, following the right wall, and stopping at the first exhibit on the right side.
8. All things being equal, people prefer intuitive wayfinding, visible exits, and the shortest route.
9. Let the narrative drive the spatial experience and content arrangement—structured or unstructured, balanced or dispersed.
10. Use linear and nonlinear "storyshapes" to design pathways around objects, exhibits, attractions, or buildings.[37]

Notes

1. Herman Kossmann and Mark W. de Jong, *Engaging Spaces: Exhibition Design Explored* (Amsterdam: Frame, 2010), Introduction.
2. Richard Lewis, "How Different Cultures Understand Time," *Business Insider*, accessed August 22, 2021, https://www.businessinsider.com/how-different-cultures-understand-time-2014-5.
3. "Can We Teach Graphic Design History Without Chronology?" *Eye on Design*, October 29, 2020, https://eyeondesign.aiga.org/can-we-teach-graphic-design-history-without-chronology/.
4. "Gateway Project," accessed June 24, 2021, https://gatewayproject.blog/.
5. Willhemina Wahlin, "The Ligatures of Life: Communication Design and Difficult Exhibitions" (Australia, Charles Sturt University, 2018).
6. "Curating Discomfort," *The Hunterian Blog* (blog), February 11, 2021, http://hunterian.academicblogs.co.uk/curating-discomfort/.
7. Tricia Austin, *Narrative Environments and Experience Design: Space as a Medium of Communication*, Routledge Research in Design Studies (New York: Routledge, Taylor & Francis Group, 2020
8. "Paul Rudolph (Architect)," in *Wikipedia*, June 15, 2021, https://en.wikipedia.org/w/index.php?title=Paul_Rudolph_(architect)&oldid=1028664580.
9. Alise Tīfentāle, "*The Family of Man*: The Photography Exhibition That Everybody Loves to Hate—FK," July 2018, https://fkmagazine.lv/2018/07/02/the-family-of-man-the-photography-exhibition-that-everybody-loves-to-hate/.
10. Louis Menand, "'The Family of Man' Revisited," Substack newsletter, *Backbencher* (blog), May 20, 2021, https://timothynoah.substack.com/p/the-family-of-man-revisited.
11. Marjorie Schwarzer, *Riches, Rivals & Radicals: 100 Years of Museums in America* (Washington, D.C.: American Association of Museums, 2006), 137.
12. Alise Tīfentāle, "*The Family of Man*: The Photography Exhibition That Everybody Loves to Hate—FK."
13. "Paul Rudolph (Architect)."
14. "*Eye* Magazine | Feature | From Object to Observer," accessed June 28, 2021, http://www.eyemagazine.com/feature/article/from-object-to-observer.
15. John H. Falk and Lynn D. Dierking, *Learning from Museums: Visitor Experiences and the Making of Meaning*, American Association for State and Local History Book Series (Walnut Creek, CA: AltaMira Press, 2000).
16. Anita Rui Olds, "Sending Them Home Alive," *Journal of Museum Education* 15, no. 1 (December 1, 1990): 10–12, https://doi.org/10.1080/10598650.1990.11510128.

17. Paul Arthur and Romedi Passini, *Wayfinding: People, Signs, and Architecture* (New York: McGraw-Hill Book Co, 1992).

18. "Imagineering in a Box | Storytelling | Arts and Humanities | Khan Academy," accessed June 28, 2021, https://www.khanacademy.org/humanities/hass-storytelling/imagineering-in-a-box.

19. David Gibson, *The Wayfinding Handbook: Information Design for Public Places*, Design Briefs (New York: Princeton Architectural Press, 2009), 45.

20. "Imagineering in a Box | Storytelling | Arts and Humanities | Khan Academy."

21. Polly McKenna-Cress and Janet Kamien's book *Creating Exhibitions: Collaboration in the Planning, Development, and Design of Innovative Experiences* is a great resource for collaborative working methods, exhibition teams, and their roles in the process. Hoboken, NJ: John Wiley & Sons, 2013.

22. Beverly Serrell, *Exhibit Labels: An Interpretive Approach*, 2nd ed. (Lanham, MD: Rowman & Littlefield, 2015), 1–8.

23. "Re-XD: Chaos at the Museum," accessed May 5, 2021, http://re-xd.org/.

24. "The 6 Emotional Arcs of Storytelling, Why You Should Use Them, and Which One Is Best," No Film School, November 29, 2016, https://nofilmschool.com/2016/11/emotional-arcs-6-storytelling-kurt-vonnegut.

25. "Beyond the Museum: A comparative study of narrative structures in films and museum design," in Suzanne MacLeod et al., eds., *The Future of Museum and Gallery Design: Purpose, Process, Perception,* Museum Meanings (London; New York: Routledge, Taylor & Francis Group, 2018), 239–53.

26. "Dramatic Structure," in *Wikipedia*, May 31, 2021, https://en.wikipedia.org/w/index.php?title=Dramatic_structure&oldid=1026141991.

27. Ellen Lupton, *Design Is Storytelling* (New York: Cooper Hewitt, Smithsonian Design Museum, 2017), 26–33.

28. "Fundamentals of Exhibition Design," Rare Book Division, *The New York Public Library Digital Collections*, 1940-01 1939, https://digitalcollections.nypl.org/items/90f27111-9714-4fc1-e040-e00a18064ba4.

29. Philip Hughes, *Storytelling Exhibitions* (London; New York: Bloomsbury Visual Arts, 2021).

30. Lonnie G. Bunch III, "How Lonnie Bunch Built a Museum Dream Team," *Smithsonian,* accessed June 23, 2021, https://www.smithsonianmag.com/smithsonian-institution/how-lonnie-bunch-built-museum-dream-team-1-180973132/.

31. "How Lonnie Bunch Built a Museum Dream Team."

32. NMAAHC, *President Obama at the NMAAHC Grand Opening Dedication*, accessed June 23, 2021, https://www.youtube.com/watch?v=0chICwsnRZw.

33. "How Lonnie Bunch Built a Museum Dream Team."

34. Ainsley Harris, "How the Exhibit Designer behind the Obama Presidential Center Captures the Attention of Children and Adults Alike," *Fast Company*, December 11, 2019, https://www.fastcompany.com/90430034/how-the-exhibit-designer-behind-the-obama-presidential-center-captures-the-attention-of-children-and-adults-alike.

35. "How Lonnie Bunch Built a Museum Dream Team."

36. NMAAHC, *President Obama at the NMAAHC Grand Opening Dedication*.

37. UAL, "MA Narrative Environments," May 24, 2021, https://www.arts.ac.uk/subjects/architecture-spatial-and-interior-design/postgraduate/ma-narrative-environments-csm.

Designer's Toolbox: **Journey**

Experience makers create exhibition identities with a cohesive visual language that extends from the pre-visit to the post-visit and everything in-between. From teaser trailers and transactional merch to ticket booths and trash cans, travel through the designer's toolbox to see the array of promotional elements that augment the audience's journey.

Visualization: Asma AlDabal leads a team of emerging designers including Noor AlKathiri, and Sarah AlMaghlouth at National Talents in Riyadh, Saudi Arabia

EXIT THROUGH THE GIFT SHOP

STREET BANNERS

BUS WRAP

SOCIAL MEDIA

WINDOW POSTER

DYNAMIC BILLBOARD

FLOOR GRAPHIC

Pre-visit

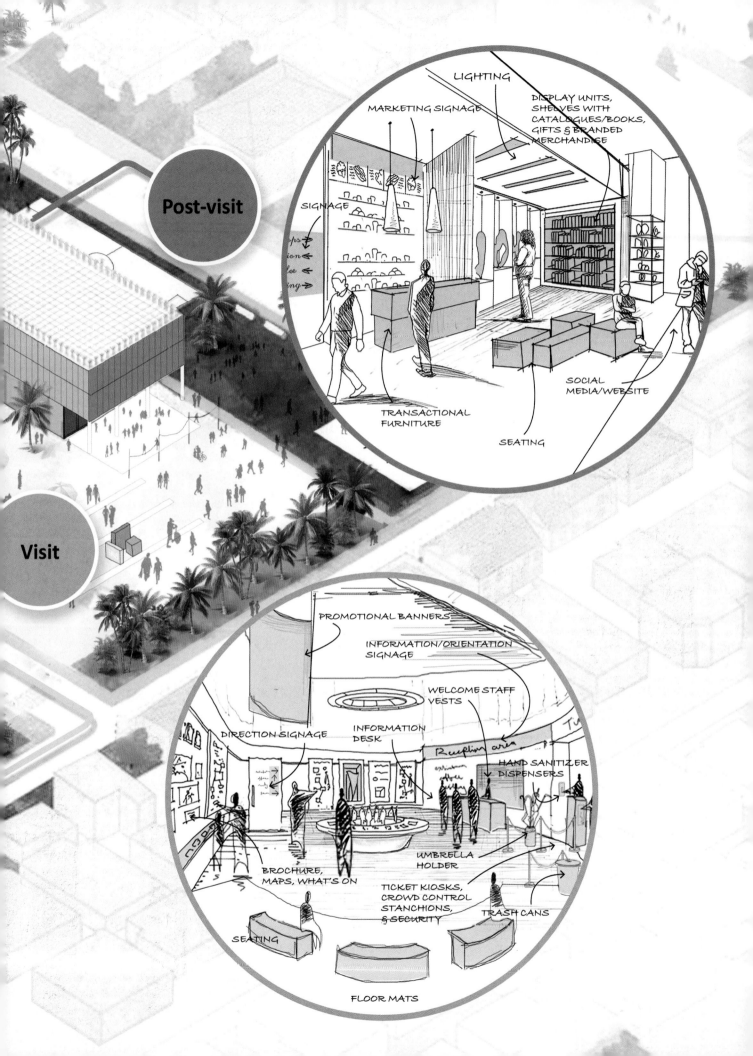

Post-visit

Visit

LIGHTING

MARKETING SIGNAGE

DISPLAY UNITS, SHELVES WITH CATALOGUES/BOOKS, GIFTS & BRANDED MERCHANDISE

SIGNAGE

SOCIAL MEDIA/WEBSITE

TRANSACTIONAL FURNITURE

SEATING

PROMOTIONAL BANNERS

INFORMATION/ORIENTATION SIGNAGE

WELCOME STAFF VESTS

DIRECTION SIGNAGE

INFORMATION DESK

HAND SANITIZER DISPENSERS

Reception area

UMBRELLA HOLDER

BROCHURE, MAPS, WHAT'S ON

TICKET KIOSKS, CROWD CONTROL STANCHIONS, & SECURITY

TRASH CANS

SEATING

FLOOR MATS

CHAPTER 3

Exit Through the Gift Shop

Exhibition design is about the pre-, present, and post-experience.

Key message: Design considers and tackles the comprehensive exhibition journey.

Key word: journey

Compared to commercials (thirty seconds long) and social media (three minutes long), brand-based experiences can captivate audiences and take them on a fee-paying and social journey for up to three hours—this is gold for exhibition marketers *and* makers. Designing exhibitions and experiences is primarily a commercial enterprise. Today's economic climate is not only about cultural, entertainment, and educational outcomes; every project must justify its Return on Investment (ROI), Return on Equity (ROE), and Customer Experience (CX), whether that is financial through ticket sales, part of a wider endeavor to attract sponsorship and philanthropic support, or to increase, include, and diversify audiences. A recognizable or *catchy* exhibition brand and experience counts for so much regardless of the topic or venue. Promotion begins online, occurs on-site, and ends with both through future visits, sales, and word-of-mouth recommendations. The added exposure and fiscal value of extending the exhibition design identity to a website, merchandise, and social media is imperative to any marketing strategy to bolster name recognition, extend the experience and take it home, lead to repeat visitation, and complete the comprehensive exhibition journey. For institutions and for brands, satisfaction and return visits can bring the benefits of long-term loyalty.

This chapter exits through the gift shop (immortalized by the film of the same name celebrating artist Banksy), a trope commonly used in the museum field to refer to the commercialization of the exhibition experience that occurs when people are forced to leave via the retail store in the hope that they will be tempted by a range of visual merchandise and branded goodies. The trope is used here metaphorically to examine the collaborative contribution the exhibition designer makes to market the entire pre-, present, and post-visit experience and shape its visual message and identity.[1]

Marketing, the Media, and *Mona Lisa*'s Smile

Crowds of people waiting to enter an exposition pavilion, concert venue, or museum are bound to put a smile on the face of organizers who commit the up-front capital investment. Another smile wound its way up the Hudson River in 1962 as one of the world's most famous women left Paris and sailed across the Atlantic for her debut at the National Gallery of Art in Washington, D.C., and the Metropolitan Museum of Art in New York (1963). *Mona Lisa*'s romantic journey from France captured the imagination of the world. After twenty-seven days, over half a million people had waited in line to spend a few precious moments in front Leonardo da Vinci's painting and its world-renowned smile.[2]

  Mona Lisa's success demonstrated to museum directors that "celebrity" loan exhibitions could significantly increase attendance and ticket revenue. The event also highlighted deficiencies in crowd management and audience orientation during the arrival experience, and the financial promise of promotion and merchandise sales during the exit experience. Scott A. Lukas breaks down people's experiences at events into *pre associations* (anticipation and the desire to escape), *internal monologue* (thoughts and reactions), and *post associations* (takeaway reflections).[3] He applies these associations to audience behavior across a range of experiential environments from cruise ships to casinos. Theme parks, department stores, and attractions were designed to accommodate crowds; charge for tickets, towels, and tote bags; and appeal to diverse audiences; eventually museums were influenced by these experience-based venues.

Crowds viewing the *Mona Lisa* at the Metropolitan Museum of Art proved blockbuster loan exhibitions increased revenue and highlighted design deficiencies in the audience experience.

Image copyright © The Metropolitan Museum of Art. Image source: Art Resource, NY

Pre-exhibition Experience: *King Tut* Awakens the In-house Museum Design Department

The discomfort of queuing outside for hours to visit an exhibition or attraction has largely become outdated with timed-tickets, pre-web sales, and the likes of Disney's MagicBand. The 1.7 million people who lined up in 1972 to see the exhibition *Treasures of Tutankhamun* recall it was worth the wait.[4] The British Museum was the first venue to exhibit the jaw-dropping collection of fourteenth-century-BCE Egyptian artifacts, including the infamous gold death mask, the iconic image for the show's catalogue. The exhibition traveled to seventeen international venues, garnered unprecedented media attention, and was seen by over ten million people in ten years. Referred to as the world's first "blockbuster" exhibition because audience numbers mirrored those of the commercial film industry, *Tut* influenced how museums contracted exhibition design. The blockbuster cemented two formidable in-house museum design teams led by Margaret Hall at the British Museum in London (who wrote one of most influential books on exhibition design, *On-Display: A Design Grammar for Museum Exhibitions*) and Gaillard "Gil" Ravenel at the National Gallery of Art in Washington, D.C., where the exhibition opened in 1976. Both were responsible for large teams of design and technical staff—up to thirty-five people in the department at the British Museum at its height of operation—and crafted the philosophical design aesthetic for the entire museum.[5] Larry Klein, head of an equally expansive design empire at the Field Museum of Natural History in Chicago, where *Tut* opened in 1977, credits them with advancing the professionalism of centralized museum design departments.[6] This shift in the internal museum power structure placed them on equal footing with curatorial departments who had enjoyed control of the exhibition spaces. As design leaders, they gained the respect of their colleagues through the quality of their work, and permission to actively advance display standards and position design at the center of exhibition making.[7]

Primary case study
Designing for crowds and souvenirs

Treasures of Tutankhamun
British Museum, London, March 29–
December 31, 1972. Designer: Margaret
Hall and team; National Gallery of Art,
Washington, D.C., November 17, 1976–
March 15, 1977. Designer: Gil Ravenel and
team; Field Museum of Natural History,
Chicago, April 15–August 15, 1977.
Designer: Larry Klein and team; and fourteen other venues

***Design challenge:* New exhibition design standards**
Tut captured the public's imagination, commodified the exhibition medium, and launched the blockbuster design template. The mysteries of the pharaoh's tomb and its riches excavated by Howard Carter in 1922 are well documented in multiple resources.[8] Less documented is how the design of *Treasures of Tutankhamun* defined a new genre of museum display and elements to enhance the entire exhibition journey. New ticket systems—until then, the purview of sporting events and concerts—addressed the visitor volume at each venue and rescued museum staff tasked with orientating lines of people standing, sitting, and reclining outside without the capacity to handle them on the inside. Requirements stipulated by loan agreements for the irreplaceable objects advanced shipping standards, and adaptable exhibition design and display furniture templates were conceived by Margaret Hall and her team to travel between multiple venues.

***Design solution:* Flags, death masks, and jewelry**
While each museum design team learned from each other, not every venue matched Hall's initial design. The Field Museum accommodated up to twelve thousand people a day and stayed open until 9 p.m.[9] Kiosks did eventually allow people to purchase tickets in advance and wander the museum before their time slot. A flag emblazoned with their exhibition identity flew on the north side of the building to signal if tickets were available. When lowered, the tickets were gone for the day.[10]

Sophisticated exhibition graphics and promotional signage set new standards and evolved at each venue. The Field Museum's team was particularly effective at communication. Large banners flanked the exterior entrance to the building and hung above the ticket desk in the lobby. Interior and exterior wayfinding signage informed people where to stand and directed them to the galleries. The emblematic exhibition identity employed a stylized version of the iconic death mask in orange on top of a striking yellow-gold field. This improved on the less-recognizable hieroglyphics used by the British Museum and the National Gallery of Art.

Hall's design for the exhibition sequence replicated archaeologist Howard Carter's path of discovery through the tomb and ended with the pharaoh's coffin. Temporary walls defined a series of connected tomb-like spaces set within the perimeter architecture. Accessible display cases made the objects easy to view despite the jostling crowds. Dramatic lighting transformed the gold artifacts into shimmering jewels. Large photographic backdrops and interpretive text panels provided context for the objects. Some venues installed silk-screened Plexiglas signs above the display cases so people could identify the objects from a distance.

Each venue bookended the journey with an information desk at the entry and a gift shop at the exit. The merchandise included three hundred *Tut*-themed items, which ranged from postcards to posters and clothing to catalogues.[11] *Tut*-inspired jewelry collections brought new display, inventory, and storage challenges. Designers were tasked with shaping the shop and the retail furniture. The space required clear sightlines to monitor security and had to be large enough to accommodate studiers and the streakers who breezed through without making a purchase—it was the main exhibition exit, after all.

Design impact: Raising the bar for exhibition design

Tut provided a range of takeaways, from experiencing rare artifacts and participating in an international sensation, to purchasing a set of keepsake earrings. While the *Tut* gift shop was not a museum first, the volume of sales, expanded range and quality, and success of the exhibition merchandise set a new international standard. Rather than stifle design flourish and expression, the exhibition's copious footfall, commercialism, and constraints bred innovation. *Tut* influenced the design of future large-scale exhibitions with crowd-control contingencies, improved wayfinding and circulation, state-of-the-art display cases, and new promotional platforms with a cohesive visual identity. Significantly, museum directors were keen to replicate the success and raise the profile of in-house museum design teams.

Sophisticated promotional exhibition graphics greeted people as they queued in all weathers to see *Treasures of Tutankhamun* at the Field Museum.

AP Photo/Charles Knoblock

Treasures of Tutankhamun
**established exhibition
design templates and
marketing standards that
evolved at each venue like
the Field Museum.**

Courtesy Field Museum. GN58_8T

Treasures of Tutankhamun
**sales at venues like the Field
Museum set new international
standards for exhibition
merchandise and giftshop
design.**

Courtesy Field Museum. GN61T

Margaret Hall's model for the British Museum's *Treasures of Tutankhamun* replicated the journey through the tomb bookended by the information desk and giftshop.

Courtesy of British Museum Central Archive, Photo: The Sunday Times / News Licensing

During-exhibition Experience: Engaging the Five Senses at the Guinness Storehouse

Close your eyes and imagine the sound of spring water, the aromas of hops and malt, and the texture of barley and yeast—these visceral elements are the first dramatic acts that ignite people's senses and pull them into the brand story when they tour Dublin's Guinness Storehouse. Attractions that house brand experiences, or brand homes, are one of the only forms of product marketing that engage all five senses and connect with audiences on many levels.[12] Corporate museums, attractions, and movie-studio tours sell brand stories packaged as destination tourism. They immerse audiences in Pine & Gilmore's premise that while commodities are fungible, goods tangible, and services intangible, experiences are memorable.[13] Brand homes have a clear narrative arc from start to finish. Audiences travel on carefully choreographed journeys that leave an impression, often with a sampling of the product at the conclusion.

Primary case study
Designing the brand story

Guinness Storehouse, Dublin, Ireland, 2000–Present
Principal Designers: Imagination (2000); Event (2008)

Design challenge: Recognizable global brand
Located in a converted 1902 fermentation plant for the St. James's Gate Brewery, the Guinness Storehouse was the first multilevel steel-framed building in Ireland. At the heart of the attraction is a partially glazed atrium that tapers downward to resemble the shape of a Guinness pint glass. This connects all seven levels, each with a different story to tell, to the top-floor observation lounge, which includes the Gravity Bar.[14] The design firm Imagination created the exhibit spaces for the original scheme and event for a refresh in 2008. Their scope was to tell the story of Arthur Guinness, who founded the brewery, the distinctive dark stout brewing process, and the history behind this recognizable global brand. The building presented some challenges because orientation, access, and wayfinding are crucial for a positive audience experience in which the story unravels through multiple levels. In 2015 the Storehouse was named Europe's leading tourist attraction, and it welcomes 1.7 million international visitors yearly.[15]

Design solution: Performative experiences
People begin the Storehouse journey on the first floor, where they are ticketed, oriented by staff, and introduced to the Guinness story. Guests are guided through the stages of the brewing process. A multisensory, immersive journey connects visitors with the drink's history and main ingredients on a massive, performative scale. The sound of a cascading waterfall dominates the environment, humidity emphasizes the importance of fresh Irish water, and hops and barley cover the floor and are contained in glass walls, their smell alluding to the distinctive Guinness aroma. Film projection, dramatic lighting, soundscapes, and supersized sans-serif typography applied directly to the industrial surfaces, brewing equipment, and fermentation chambers explain the process. The journey continues via escalators through levels of staged environments and exhibits on storage, shipping, and Guinness' renowned advertising campaigns using a continuation of visual media, hands-on activities, and a range of historical and contemporary objects associated with the Irish stout. And then the reward—a view of Dublin and a pint of the dark nectar in the top-floor observation lounge for those who want to finally taste what they have been experiencing. People return via elevators and spill out into the well-stocked gift shop to browse and purchase from an array of branded merchandise before they exit.

Design impact: Lack of the hard sell
The Guinness Storehouse tells the story of the history, heart, and soul of Ireland's most iconic beer.[16] People journey through a scripted experience to learn about the brand legacy, ingredients, and brewing process. Everything leads to the communal "pub-like" moment when the tour concludes, people socialize, and visitors learn to enjoy a Guinness stout correctly in the Gravity Bar. The pint that awaits offers a multisensory experience that is distinctly gustatory but incorporates all the senses. Looking out over Dublin, audiences reflect on the Guinness brand and the journey they have taken from water to the pint, to the tap. The journey echoes the distinctive Guinness pour, with its slow-then-rapid ascent to a distinctive head.

The final peak experience defies gravity. During various updates, the Storehouse has seen attendance, retail sales, and net profits increase, with over 80 percent of people saying they felt greater closeness to the Guinness brand after their visit.[17]

The experience captivates the streaker and is deep and discoverable for the studier. A successful triangular story arc anchors the experience with exhibits along each axis and distinct emotions at each of the three points—the dramatic brewery pre-experience, the reflective Gravity Bar experience, and the gift shop post-experience. The Guinness Storehouse avoids a hard sell. The best brand homes do not need to upsell their wares to a captive audience who has already paid for brand immersion. If the experience is exceptional, their audience will do the heavy lifting, take a piece of the magic home, and share the experience with their social networks.[18]

The Guinness Storehouse has seven levels; each tells a different part of the brand story ending with the top floor observation lounge that includes the Gravity Bar.

Photo: Werner Dieterich / Alamy Stock Photo

The journey at the Guinness Storehouse begins and ends at the giftshop and a plethora of merchandise celebrating the dark nectar.

Photo: Kay Roxby / Alamy Stock Photo

Aromas, film projection, dramatic lighting, soundscapes, and super-sized typography applied to industrial surfaces engage the five senses at the Guinness Storehouse.

Photo: Smith Ranger / Alamy Stock Photo

Looking over Dublin, audiences reflect on the Guinness brand and the Storehouse journey they have taken from water to the pint, to the tap.

Photo: Martin Thomas Photography / Alamy Stock Photo

Post-exhibition Experience: *David Bowie Is* and Continues to Be a Marketing Sensation

Social media platforms coupled with endless merchandising opportunities make the post-event experience profitable and everlasting. Behind it all is a team of content developers, marketers, future forecasters, and, yes, designers. The presence of a gift shop is now an indispensable part of any experience, be it themed attraction, festival, or museum. A mind-blowing assortment of expensive to affordable trinkets translate visual identities through a design exercise to infuse image, color, and typeface onto multiple products and surfaces.

David Bowie Is was no exception. Disciples all over the world lapped up the related exhibition swag. Striking tote bags slung over the shoulders of post-visitation punters promoted the exhibit tour on the streets of London, São Paulo, and New York. After its run, thousands of people installed the app version of the exhibition onto their mobile devices.[19] Together, these elements constitute a virtual encore that ensures the exhibition experience and visual identity extend beyond the somatic encounter.

Primary case study

Designing a comprehensive exhibition graphic identity

David Bowie Is, Victoria and Albert Museum (V&A), London, March 23–August 11, 2013 (plus eleven other global venues ending at the Brooklyn Museum, New York on July 15, 2018) Principal Designer: Jonathan Barnbrook Studio

Design challenge: Philosophical and creative direction

The celebrated *David Bowie Is* exhibition displayed about five hundred objects, including costumes, photographs, films, and music ephemera. The performer's private archive and collection was a key source—Bowie famously kept everything, keenly aware of its stylistic significance for future generations. Rather than read lengthy gallery text, audiences accessed audible stories and Bowie's music using high-quality headphones and AMBEO 3D sound by Sennheiser.[20] This kept the crowds flowing in time with their ticketed entry, since the "Bowie Crush" made it the most complex exhibit to mount in some venues' history.[21] The exhibition team at the V&A developed installation and identity guidelines to ensure a level of design consistency when the exhibition components were adapted by each venue to fit their space and marketing requirements.

London-based designer/typographer Jonathan Barnbrook and his studio were the artistic advisors to the V&A curators. They defined the exhibition's philosophical and creative direction and set the all-important tone to guide exhibition staff at other museums.[22] Barnbrook was selected because he had a long association with Bowie, having designed multiple album covers for the pop icon.

Design solution: Myriad of shifting applications

Barnbrook Studio established the design template for exhibition promotion, merchandise, print collateral, catalogue marketing, and the "Berlin" or *Black & White Years* section of the exhibition with the design team at 59 Productions. The exhibition's simple and infinitely adaptable visual language maintained the Bowie brand across a voracious and varied tour schedule. A clever element was the endlessly extendable phrase *David Bowie Is*, created by Paul Morley, which was used to explain the many facets of Bowie. The present tense affirmed his continued influence today.[23] Each phrase is set in the distinctive font Albertus, chosen in part because of its association with street signs in the London borough of Lambeth, where Bowie was born.[24]

Instantly recognizable is the identity's striking field of Pantone Orange 021, which permeates a plethora of graphic applications and is paired with the iconic album cover photograph of *Aladdin Sane*, which is in the V&A's collection. Judging by his stage outfits and hair, orange was arguably Bowie's favorite color, and it complements the famous facial lightning bolt.

Design impact: The show must go on

Visual identities for pre- and post-visit experiences boil down to design recipes. *David Bowie Is* had them all in right measure. The carefully crafted identity was designed to deploy easily across a myriad of shifting platforms and environments and deliver when one of the key ingredients was changed. If a venue chose another image, the identity's font and color held it together. If they defaulted to their house-typeface, the image and color carried the message.

David Bowie Is: The AR Exhibition app sustains the show's spectacle in perpetuity, as does a documentary film about the exhibition.[25] Experiences now outlive their run dates. Websites, as well as AR applications for handheld or VR for gaming consoles, blend exhibition and UI/UX design to create virtual formats and adapt them to an ever-increasing range of post-, present, and pre-experiences.

An adaptable visual language maintained the Bowie exhibition brand across a varied tour schedule with the endlessly extendable phrase *David Bowie Is.*

Photo: Thom Moore / Alamy Stock Photo

Instantly recognizable, the *David Bowie Is* identity's striking field of orange permeates promotional banners and signs at the Victoria and Albert Museum.

Photo: travelpix / Alamy Stock Photo

DAVID BOWIE
IS
SAYING YOU'RE
WONDERFUL
GIVE ME YOUR
HANDS

Each of the identity's phrases was originally set in the distinctive font Albertus and continued into *David Bowie Is* exhibition graphics.

Photo: Matthew Chattle / Alamy Stock Photo

At each exhibition venue, disciples all over the world responded to the simple design and lapped-up the *David Bowie Is* merchandise.

Photo: Matthew Chattle / Alamy Stock Photo

David Bowie Is: The AR Exhibition app sustains the show's spectacle in perpetuity and adds to an increasing range of exhibition post, present, and pre-experiences.

Photo: dpa picture alliance / Alamy Stock Photo

Non-exhibition Experience: Color Factory to Candytopia and the Virtual Exhibition

Tut catalogues are still treasured as a memento of a cultural phenomenon.[26] Personalized pint glasses transport people to the Gravity Bar overlooking Dublin. Virtual Bowie pulsates from mobile devices. The experience maker's mark continues well beyond the initial exhibition and audience encounter. These emotional souvenirs are a product of the experience economy.[27] Pine and Gilmore's book had a profound effect on the value of services combined with goods to enhance consumer interaction and experiences. The four realms of experience (entertainment, education, escapist, and esthetic) were put forward as compatible areas that actively comingle to create personal rich, compelling, and engaging encounters. Their advice was to choose not one realm, but to explore how aspects of each realm add value across a range of services. Design is at the heart of these services: It shapes, colors, and guides the consumer journey and enables the experience to be profitable. Blockbuster exhibitions like *Tut* and *David Bowie Is* represent culture as commodity, and the Guinness Store-house exemplifies all four realms of experience using a variety of transmedia.

Revisiting the Experience Economy

The tangible services Pine and Gilmore envisioned in 1998 came before hybrid and remote experiences or the delivery-based gig-economy. Non-visit experiences are now commonplace, and the designer deploys quite different development tools with less control over the audience journey.

Explore how aspects of each realm from the four realms of experience add value across a range of designed experiences and services.

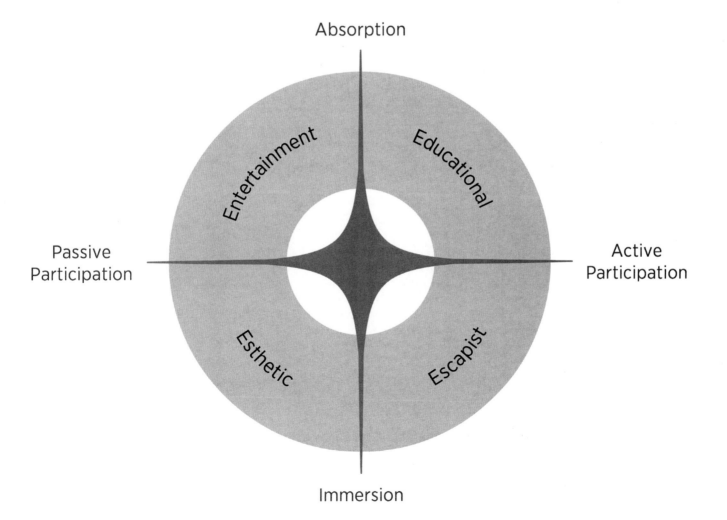

The ease of video production means that pre-exhibition trailers, teaser interviews, and behind-the-scenes technical insights exist on sophisticated web platforms. Social media outlets extend this material further where it is amplified by blogs, vlogs, and channels before, during, and after an event. Whereas designers of an earlier generation might have sought total control to maintain a coherent journey for their audiences, designers today increasingly relinquish control in favor of inclusivity and co-design and share their tools with talented social media influencers.

Social media–ready experiences

Attention now focuses on adding value to experiences and how post-impression and post-visit reflections contribute to people's health and well-being.[28] Younger generations shun spending their resources on material objects in favor of experiences that are active; create a sense of purpose; provide digital artifacts, souvenirs, and memories; and offer rapid escapism. Museum of Ice Cream founder Maryellis Bunn says her generation "does not want to spend six hours doing anything."[29] Her design philosophy is "socially squared" to encourage interaction between strangers. Events by Secret Cinema, installations by Meow Wolf, Immersive Van Gogh, and selfie fests like Color Factory and Candytopia have proven popular adult playdates, particularly with generations who self-market these vibrant attractions using visual-ladened social media. Critics easily dismiss these popup experiences for using museology as a crass design tactic, but they occupy a vital liminal design zone, as part attraction, museum, and brand home, where a non-visit is entirely plausible when friends share their virtual experiences.[30]

Social media–ready experiences create a sense of purpose, provide digital artifacts, memories, and offer rapid escapism.

Photo: Larry Brownstein / Alamy Stock Photo

Post-pandemic experiences

During the COVID-19 non-economy, attractions temporarily closed, museums shuttered, exhibitions postponed or transitioned online or outdoors. The pandemic reset what was normal. The experience economy went screen based and design UI/UX driven. It forced exhibition venues to extend additional value to audiences who could no longer visit in person and those who were geographically distant. Once organizations moved past simply adapting their physical content to online content, a rich array of well-designed virtual tours and novel exhibitions blossomed, with new ways to charge admission and have people exit through the online gift shop. The Louvre in Paris has made its entire art collection available online for free.[31] Accessible twenty-four hours a day and without standing in line, *Mona Lisa*'s smile is now just a click away for a global audience.

Tips and Tricks

Develop a unified experience, message, and exhibition promotional journey using the following design techniques:

1. Keep visual identities to basic design recipes: (1) message ingredients: title, key image, dates, venue (name or logo), sponsor (if applicable), and (2) graphic ingredients: color, typeface, layout, image treatment, spacing, and format (size).
2. Work with simple, connected, and interchangeable graphic elements. If one is substituted, the others step in to maintain the brand identity.
3. Use an iconic image or illustration that is legible—do not try to capture the exhibition with many small, illegible images.
4. Choose the most-recognizable images for the broadest audience.
5. Treat the pre-journey like a breadcrumb trail (directed and on-message) and the post-journey like a roundabout (undirected and reflective).
6. Make the gift shop spacious and optional, and accommodate a variety of merchandise tastes and price points for families/student groups.
7. Make the wayfinding journey as intuitive as possible—do not make people frustrated or feel like they have missed something.
8. Begin the journey with a "wow" moment to pull people in and end with a "wow" moment to instill a memory.
9. Innovate UX design—see the virtual space as a new frontier, not one to house content better suited to traditional platforms.
10. Provide a reason to return and remain connected to an audience post-visit; these are critical to ROI and ROE.

Notes

1. John H. Falk and Lynn D. Dierking, *The Museum Experience* (Washington, D.C.: Whalesback Books, 1992). Establishes "Before, During, and After the Visit."
2. Christie's, "Smile On: How the Ultimate Pop Icon Conquered the US," Auction Preview, Christie's, April 24, 2015, https://www.christies.com/features/Warhol-Mona-Lisa-5898-1.aspx?PID=newsviews_landing_morefeatures1.
3. Scott A. Lukas, *The Immersive Worlds Handbook: Designing Theme Parks and Consumer Spaces* (New York: Focal Press, 2013), 139.
4. Meredith Hindley, "*King Tut*: A Classic Blockbuster Museum Exhibition That Began as a Diplomatic Gesture," *Humanities: The Magazine of the National Endowment for the Humanities*, October 2015, https://www.neh.gov/humanities/2015/septemberoctober/feature/king-tut-classic-blockbuster-museum-exhibition-began-diplom.
5. Simon Muirhead, "The designer's role in the display of ethnographic costume and textiles," *Newsletter (Museum Ethnographers Group)*, no. 20 (1987): 55.
6. Larry Klein, *Exhibits: Planning and Design* (New York: Madison Square Press: Distributors in North America, Robert Silver Associates, 1986), 64.
7. Note the corresponding elevation of Stuart Silver at the Metropolitan Museum of Art. Alex Traub, "Stuart Silver, Designer of Museum Blockbusters, Dies at 84," *New York Times*, June 9, 2021, sec. Arts, https://www.nytimes.com/2021/06/09/arts/stuart-silver-dead.html.
8. Hindley, "*King Tut*: A Classic Blockbuster Museum Exhibition That Began as a Diplomatic Gesture."
9. William Mullen, "City to Get Another Taste of Tut," chicagotribune.com, accessed April 2, 2021, https://www.chicagotribune.com/news/chi-0412020230dec02-story.html.
10. Hindley, "*King Tut*: A Classic Blockbuster Museum Exhibition That Began as a Diplomatic Gesture."
11. Hindley, "*King Tut*: A Classic Blockbuster Museum Exhibition That Began as a Diplomatic Gesture."
12. Christian Lachel, "The Brand Benefits of Places Like the Guinness Storehouse," *Harvard Business Review*, October 20, 2015, https://hbr.org/2015/10/the-brand-benefits-of-places-like-the-guinness-storehouse.
13. B. Joseph Pine II and James H. Gilmore, "Welcome to the Experience Economy," *Harvard Business Review*, July 1, 1998, https://hbr.org/1998/07/welcome-to-the-experience-economy.
14. Guinness Storehouse, *The Guinness Storehouse—Experience More*, 2017, https://www.youtube.com/watch?v=tVfb5Y qskHE.
15. "Guinness Storehouse Named Europe's Best Tourist Attraction," *Irish Times*, accessed March 24, 2021, https://www.irishtimes.com/business/transport-and-tourism/guinness-storehouse-named-europe-s-best-tourist-attraction-1.2341826.
16. "Welcome to the Home of Guinness," Guinness Storehouse.
17. Lachel, "The Brand Benefits of Places Like the Guinness Storehouse."
18. Amber Brown, "Correspondence with Marketing Manager, Guinness Storehouse," January 21, 2022.
19. "*David Bowie Is*—The AR Exhibition," accessed March 26, 2021, https://davidbowieisreal.com.
20. David Weiss, "Audio is Art: David Bowie 'is' at the Brooklyn Museum," *SonicScoop* (blog), March 7, 2018, https://sonicscoop.com/david-bowie-brooklyn-museum-art-audio-art/.
21. N. Parsi, "'David Bowie Is…' a Project: To Mount the Most Complex Exhibit in Its History, a Museum Team Flexed Its Creativity without Losing Its Focus," *PM Network* 29, no. 4 (2015): 40–47.
22. "*David Bowie Is* Exhibition Graphics," Barnbrook, accessed March 26, 2021, https://barnbrook.net/work/va-david-bowie-is/.
23. "*David Bowie Is* Exhibition Graphics."

24. Indra Kupferschmid, "David Bowie Is the Subject," Fonts in Use, March 5, 2013, https://fontsinuse.com/uses/3336/david-bowie-is-the-subject.

25. *David Bowie Is* Exhibition Graphics."

26. "Luxor's Valley of the Kings: Magnificent Tombs and a Reunion with King Tut," *Modern Postcard Travel Blog* (blog), January 23, 2020, https://www.themodernpostcard.com/luxors-valley-of-the-kings-magnific-ent-tombs-a-reunion-with-king-tut/.

27. Lachel, "The Brand Benefits of Places Like the Guinness Storehouse."

28. "Are Museums Good for Your Mental Health?" MuseumNext, May 16, 2020, https://www.museumnext.com/article/are-museums-good-for-your-mental-health/.

29. Anna Wiener, "The Millennial Walt Disney Wants to Turn Empty Stores into Instagram Playgrounds," *Intelligencer*, October 4, 2017, https://nymag.com/intelligencer/2017/10/museum-of-ice-cream-maryel-lis-bunn.html.

30. "The Existential Void of the Pop-Up 'Experience,'" *New York Times*, accessed March 26, 2021, https://www.nytimes.com/2018/09/26/arts/color-factory-museum-of-ice-cream-rose-mansion-29rooms-candytopia.html.

31. "The Louvre Just Made Its Entire Art Collection Available Online for Free," designboom | architecture & design magazine, March 29, 2021, https://www.designboom.com/art/the-louvre-art-collection-available-online-free-03-29-2021/.

Designer's Toolbox: **Form**

Experience makers manipulate movement through an exhibition using a series of spatial dividers and interventions to guide the story, contextualize the content, and control people's behavior. Enter the designer's toolbox and select from a range of popup walls, rooms, and objects, that can be fixed, movable, modular, and reconfigurable.

Visualization: Lydia Lee is an emerging experience designer based in San Francisco, U.S.A.

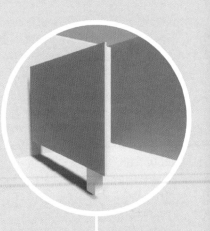

End detail: step-back with float

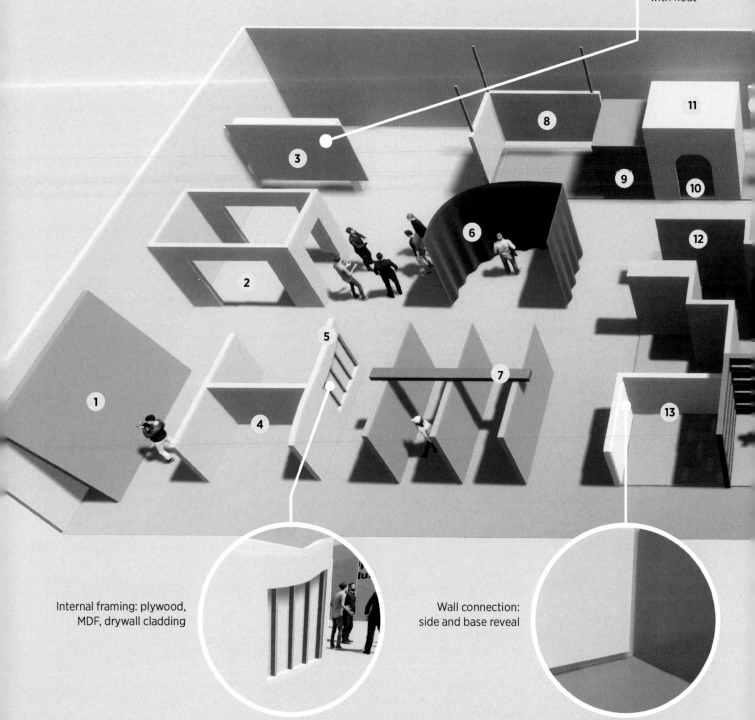

Internal framing: plywood, MDF, drywall cladding

Wall connection: side and base reveal

SCULPTING SPACE

1 Slant wall	13 U-shape wall
2 Open room	14 L-shape wall
3 Cantilever wall	15 Free-standing wall
4 H-shape wall	16 Floating wall
5 Asymmetrical wall	17 Circular wall
6 Fabric wall	18 Full-height wall
7 Top beam	19 Fin-style wall
8 Hanging wall	20 Partial-height wall
9 Transition vestibule	21 Semi-open ceiling
10 Arched opening	22 Dome
11 Room within a room	23 Fabric over frame
12 Accordion wall	24 Fabric ceiling
	25 Curved wall
	26 Articulated wall
	27 T-shape wall
	28 Modular wall

Wall connection:
lap join

End detail:
recessed reveal

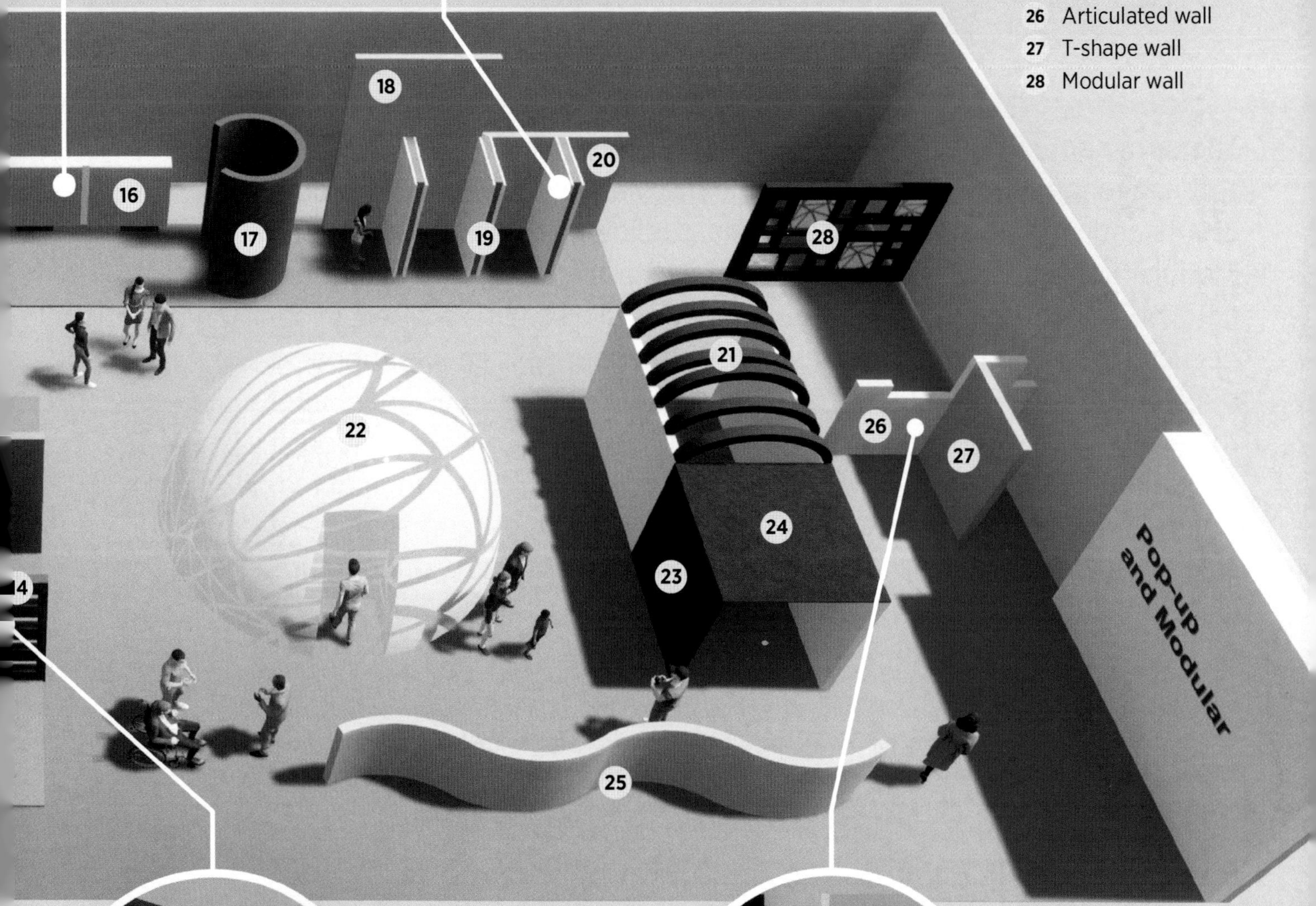

Wall connection:
open with slats

Wall connection:
butt join

Pop-up
and Modular

CHAPTER 4

Popup and Modular

Sculpting dynamic and memorable spatial experiences is at the core of exhibition design.

Key message: Design creates a permanent or temporary architectural form that reacts to the exhibition content.

Key word: form

The term *popup* has become ubiquitous. Popup exhibitions span solid to soft and range from roll-up to inflatable. They are well-suited for outdoor events and when communities invest in public placemaking. Popup and modular applies to all exhibitions at some level since depending on budgets, object loans, audience preferences, and sliding time frames, experiences are inherently transient and ever-changing. This chapter unpacks the trope "popup" and uses it as a lens to look at how designers alter the exhibition experience using a variety of partitions, dividers, modular structures, and memorable interventions. Fashioned from a range of materials, these insertions take on multiple scales, shapes, and forms that are the mainstay of temporary commercial, entertainment, and cultural exhibition industries.

Design pioneers in the early to mid-twentieth century challenged the constraints of existing sites and sculpted exhibition spaces in innovative ways, carving them out with an experimental palette of materials and architectural forms. The design of the exhibition environment deviated from the surrounding architecture, responded to the exhibition content, and embraced a stripped-down aesthetic influenced by the theme or narrative being told.

Back to the Wall: Evolution of Exhibition Interventions, Partitions, and Dividers

The first purpose-built exhibition venues stifled any changes to the architectural flow because of their fixed environmental imprint. Structural constraints and a fashion for decorative embellishment resulted in spaces with obstructive columns or a series of smaller connecting rooms with solid walls punctured by on-axis doorways. The Crystal Palace for London's Great Exhibition in 1851 is considered one of the first popup exhibition structures because of the speed and method of construction. The building's airy and open steel frame and glass surfaces ushered in a flexible container but continued to follow a rigid internal formula—the overwhelming number of objects, exhibition furniture, and decorative display components were at odds with the simple architecture. Exhibits were arranged in a traditional manner with orderly rows to create designated pathways. Popup buildings at subsequent World's Fairs favored function and adaptation, placing equal design emphasis on the interior organization and the exterior architecture. Museums and other exhibition spaces were inspired to do the same.

In 1920s Vienna and Berlin, theater and art-exhibition designer Frederick Kiesler experimented with modular, self-supporting T-type and L-type structures that could be dropped into galleries and reconfigured to make dividing walls, drop ceilings, and display surfaces. Kiesler's interventions were associated with the De Stijl movement, and his work was carried out against a backdrop of avant-garde art theory and practice.[1] His free form stands remain refreshingly contemporary. The system of grid-like components predate off-the-shelf, click-and-build assembly products used in today's retail and trade-show environments.

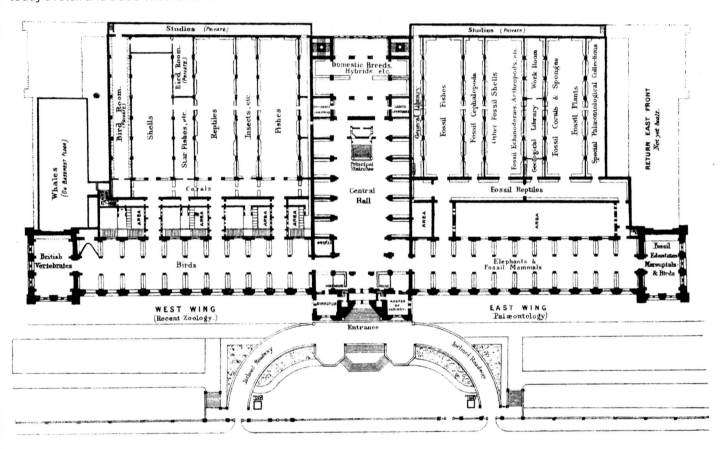

Fabricating Divisions: Softer Partitions, Fabrics, Drapes, and Wrapped Surfaces

Curtains, scrims, and backdrops have long been used to alter theatrical scenes and film sets because they can quickly cover large expanses. Exhibition designers gravitated to the merits of these flexible substrates to shape, sculpt, and contain their spatial experiences. Rigid plaster or wood surfaces are easier to hang things on, but stretching fabric, vinyl, or paper composites over a wood or metal frame reduces cost, build time, and the weight associated with similar solid-framed structures. Fabric-covered dividers or surfaces are excellent sound absorbers. They can be loosely draped or stretched taut. Coverings with synthetic fibers, like Lycra, are more forgiving and coalesce around extreme forms, and come in a range of textures, colors, and opacities that can be dramatically lit with light sources from behind or in front of the material.

Designer George Nelson pushed the potential of temporary popup structures for the 1959 American National Exhibition in Moscow.

© Vitra Design Museum, estate George Nelson, photographer unknown

Lilly Reich was one of the first designers to challenge the rigidity of the exhibition space. Born in 1885 and into a male-dominated design field in Berlin, Reich designed furniture, clothing, and shop-window displays early in her career.[2] From 1924 to 1926, she worked as a designer for the Trade Fair Office in Frankfurt and met architect and designer Ludwig Mies van der Rohe (forming a romantic relationship). They were both members of the Deutscher Werkbund (Mies was vice president; the organization was established to promote German companies in the global market). Together, Lilly Reich and Mies van der Rohe collaborated on furniture and interior design projects with groundbreaking results.[3]

Frederick Kiesler experimented with modular, self-supporting T-type and L-type structures that predate today's retail and trade show environments in *City in Space*, the Austrian pavilion at the Exposition Internationale des Arts Décoratifs, Paris, 1925.

© 2022 Austrian Frederick and Lillian Kiesler Private Foundation, Vienna

Primary case study
Dividing space using interventions

Café Samt & Seide (*Velvet and Silk Café*), Berlin Fashion Exhibition, 1927 Designers: Lilly Reich and Ludwig Mies van der Rohe

Design challenge: Fabricating divisions

Lilly Reich's best-known project is the *Velvet and Silk Café*, which she designed with Mies van der Rohe in 1927 for the Association of German Silk Weavers (Verein Deutscher Seidenwebereien) as its contribution to the trade exhibition Die Mode der Dame. Housed in the trade fair halls near Kaiserdamm in Berlin, the exhibition of women's fashion was organized by the Imperial Association of the German Fashion Industry and traveled afterward to the Netherlands.[4] The café served coffee and respite to weary fashionistas.[5] The challenge was to design a café that could adapt to the available space at each venue, as well as provide a level of privacy and separation for the fashion models to change and hang out between runway performances.

Design solution: Visual feast

Reich and Mies designed a space that even by today's standards feels highly original—the sensorial sweep of the curved fabric walls created a series of rooms within a room—the perfect antidote to the voluminous trade fair interior. Panels of silk and velvet were suspended like curtains from steel pipes at different heights to form zones sprinkled with the now-eponymous Mies tubular-steel chairs, which audiences found strikingly modern at that time. Subdividing the space with textiles rather than solid walls gave a tantalizing impression of fluidity and a nod to the open-plan spaces of modernist architecture.[6] It also made it faster, easier, and cheaper to ship, install, and dismantle. Lost in the black-and-white photographs of the café is the lushness of the black, orange, and red velvets, and the shimmering silks in gold, silver, and yellow—it would have been a visual feast.

Design impact: Fashioning fabric forms

Fabric divisions and interventions are a mainstay of the temporary event industry due to their ease of assembly, light weight, and small packing footprint. Reich drew on her previous retail design experience. The *Velvet and Silk Café* is one of the first examples where the exhibition form follows the narrative or content—why wouldn't an exhibition about fabrics use the very same materials to define the design of the environment? Reich's fashioning of the fabric form anticipates the parabolic

The fabric forms in the *Velvet and Silk Café* define the exhibition environment and respond to its fashion narrative.

Artist: Mies van der Rohe, Ludwig (1886-1969) © 2022 Artists Rights Society (ARS), New York / VG Bild-Kunst, Bonn. Photo Credit: Digital Image © The Museum of Modern Art/Licensed by SCALA / Art Resource, NY.

algorithms employed in the work of architect Zaha Hadid—another female designer in a man's world—whose studio designed *Mathematics: The Winton Gallery* at the Science Museum London in 2012. Inspired by the Handley Page aircraft hanging in the middle of the exhibition space, the design was conceived through observing equations of airflow used in the aviation industry. The layout and lines of the gallery represent the movement of air that would have flowed around this historic aircraft in flight, a metaphor that extends from the positioning of the display cases and benches to the billowing fabric–covered surfaces of the suspended hollow structures.[7] Bathed in a wash of iridescent purple light, Hadid's billowing overhead forms owe much to Reich's exploration of spatial division—placing a wall between the audience and the atmosphere rather than the café and the catwalk.

Zaha Hadid's design studio were inspired by aviation equations of airflow for the billowing forms at *Mathematics: The Winton Gallery* at the Science Museum London.

Mathematics: The Winton Gallery by Zaha Hadid Architects. Photograph by Luke Hayes.

Lighter, Quicker, Modular: Materials and Structures Become Nimble and Reconfigurable

The global post-WWII rebuilding boom encouraged a wave of commercial displays—referred to as "propaganda exhibitions"—sponsored by private industry, commerce, and government agencies.[8] These trade shows, precursors to brand homes, opened the door to temporary exhibit structures fashioned from lighter, cheaper, and more flexible materials that emerged during wartime production. Semipermanent exhibitions were shipped in; built on-site using fabrics, fiberglass, aluminum, plywood, and framing; and then packed up for travel. This popup and modular approach allowed designers to break free from time-consuming bespoke interventions and the architectural constraints of a site.

Exhibition design codified

One of the most influential postwar design consultancies was the Design Research Unit (DRU), founded in 1943 in London by Marcus Brumwell, Milner Grey, and Misha Black. A one-stop shop for multidisciplinary design, DRU employed architects, industrial, and graphic designers. DRU's 1946 design team listed Austin Frazer as exhibition designer, one of the first codified citations of professional practice in the field.[9] DRU fashioned themselves beyond the formalities of architecture to leverage design as a form of mass communication. Many famous British brands owe their identity to their philosophy.[10] Director Misha Black edited the book *Exhibition Design*, published

James Gardner and Basil Spence's design for *Enterprise Scotland* consisted of modular frame-like structures and drapes of fabric to pull the eye upwards.

Photo: Design Council Slide Collection at Manchester Metropolitan University Special Collections.

by the Architectural Press: London in 1950. Prior to this publication, little had been written about the field except Herbert Bayer's treatise *Fundamentals of Exhibition Design* in 1939.[11] Black's book cites various case studies to explain the commercial exhibition design process, and the examples look startlingly contemporary even by today's standards. It is a wonderful read for the exhibition design enthusiast.

The Design Research Unit embraced the lightweight modularity provided by post-war materials for this Short Bros. and Harland exhibition stand in 1948.

Courtesy of Scott Brownrigg

Modular frame-like structures for *California: Designing Freedom* (2017) at the Design Museum London.

Luke Hayes Photography

Pre-fabricated components and composite materials resulted in rapid construction and new experimental exhibit forms after WWII. Illustration from *Exhibition Design*, Misha Black, 1950.

Courtesy of Scott Brownrigg

Design lifting the spirits

DRU were instrumental in the design of the Festival of Britain (1951), a celebration of British manufacturing, industry, and ingenuity that deployed a range of progressive temporary structures, exhibits, and environments with a World's Fair feeling on London's South Bank.[12] Billed as a "tonic for the nation," it succeeded in lifting the spirits of a country struggling to emerge from the austerity imposed by WWII and launched the career of a cadre of postwar design pioneers who went on to shape exhibitions and experiences throughout the world.[13]

The Victoria and Albert Museum hosted a prelude to the Festival of Britain called *Britain Can Make It* (1946). The chief designer for the exhibition was James Gardner, who was responsible for the overall creative team, which included Misha Black. A year later, Gardner worked with Scottish architect Basil Spence on the exhibition *Enterprise Scotland* (1947).[14] Each exhibition featured exciting new products and manufacturing techniques, matched by an equally innovative shift to popup and modular exhibition making. *Enterprise Scotland* consisted of open, modular kiosks (display stands) tethered to the floor and ceiling and not the walls. Gardner's design employs a light touch—round, tubular, frame-like structures encircle the product displays—and the response has buoyancy in stark contrast to the existing perimeter architecture. Tall drapes of fabric fan out from the ceiling and pull the eye upward to highlight the vertical nature of the space. Lighting, inside and outside, cleverly accentuates the fabric's contours and pleats and illuminates each of the product displays below, thus creating a division of space that is soft and permeable rather than hard edged and fixed, and allowing people to glance through the exhibits to what is beyond—in this case, the future.

The buildout of these exhibitions rejected plaster and lath in favor of concrete, fiberglass, and faux finishes. This new experiential vernacular influenced the design of countless scenes and fantasy environments in the retail and entertainment sector, and it inspired the design of flexible, modular museum display systems.

Primary case study
Reusable and reconfigurable temporary wall systems

Yale University Art Gallery, 1953
Designers: Louis Kahn; renovation of
wall system, Staples & Charles, 2006

Design challenge: Innovative gallery spaces

The American architect Louis Kahn was a young man in 1951 when he took on his first significant commission to design the Yale University Art Gallery in New Haven, Connecticut. Hailed as his first masterpiece, the building occupies the site of what was the oldest university art museum in the Western Hemisphere, the Trumbull Gallery, founded in 1832.[15] This project set Kahn on a path to design future innovative gallery spaces, such as the Kimbell Art Museum in Houston, known for its interior travertine wall finishes, and beautiful use of diffused natural light from the coffered skylights—the best type of light for viewing the artworks below.

Yale University Art Gallery employs architectural features that define a new generation of exhibition spaces. Masonry, concrete, glass, and steel fuse together to create five open-plan levels, connected by a central cylindrical main staircase. The galleries are celebrated for their beauty, geometry, and light, but also for the structural and engineering innovations.[16] The muscular tetrahedral ceilings of reinforced concrete, whose indentations cleverly conceal the ductwork and gallery lighting, are the first example of recessed lighting in an American museum.[17] The strength of the tetrahedral ceiling span allows the galleries to be completely modular. Kahn designed a system of corresponding floating "pogo" panel walls that can be temporarily fixed at 90- or 45-degree points along the ceiling grid to create a flexible environment to curate different displays.

Design solution: Pogo walls

The walls consist of a wooden frame covered with 3/8-inch plywood painted to match the gallery finishes. The side profile is an elegant three inches. The panel dimensions adhere to the architectural ceiling grid and measure 10 x 5 feet. They can be placed next to each other to increase the wall width. At the top of the wall are two metal poles (aluminum polecats)—hence the "pogo" reference—these serve to float the wall on metal feet (with neoprene pads), allowing it to be anchored and positioned. The plain design of the outer wall belies the inner structure, and the stability required to support heavy and fragile art objects on such minimal forms. In 2004, the design firm Staples & Charles (formally of the Eames office) were commissioned to refurbish the wall system and update its functionality.[18] Kahn adopted this same signature wall intervention when he was invited back to Yale between 1969–1974 to design the Yale Center for British Art. This time the walls were covered in Belgian linen to match the gallery finishes and hide any installation holes.[19]

Design impact: Temporary wall systems

Kahn's pogo-wall design addressed the ongoing needs of gallery and exhibition makers to rearrange artworks, sculpt space, and provide new vistas and sightlines for audiences. We can deduce that Kahn was influenced by the design of popup wall systems favored at World's Fairs—he cut his teeth working on the Sesqui-Centennial International Exposition in Philadelphia during his first job after graduation in 1926.[20] Kahn's design for the galleries represents

a break from the rigid, solid, and restrictive architecture common in permanent collection galleries at art museums in the mid-twentieth century. Even today's vast, high-ceiling contemporary art spaces struggle to accommodate temporary wall systems to divide space, stay up, and feel like a natural extension of the exhibit architecture. If there are no built-in floor anchor/support systems, exhibition designers resort to weighted bases, ceiling anchors, and multiple wall-to-wall attachments. Safety infrastructure in the ceiling, such as fire sprinkler clearances, complicate the installation further. There are many commercial off-the-shelf temporary exhibit wall systems, but Kahn's bespoke version is articulate and one of the first. The design feels appropriately elegant, integrated, purposeful, and the "pogo" remarkably clever.

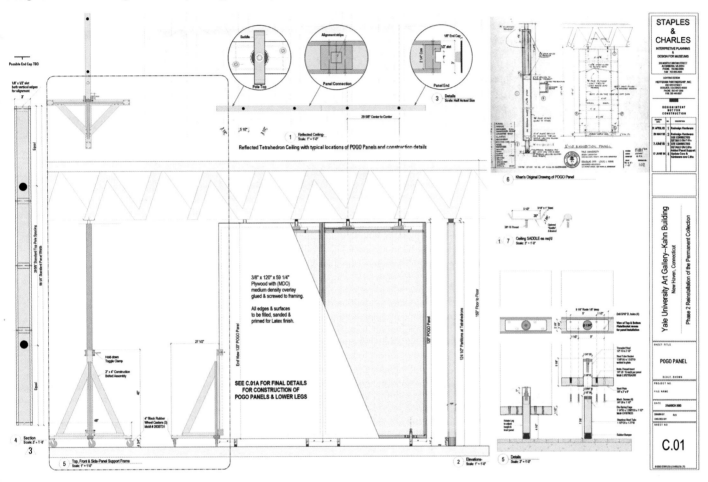

Based on Louis Kahn's original concept, designers Staples & Charles re-engineered how the walls at the Yale University Art Gallery were constructed including the signature metal "pogo" legs.

Courtesy Staples & Charles, Yale University Art Gallery.

Popup to Placemaking: Display Systems, Islands, and Themed Interventions

Consider popup experiences as rapid response, something designed and assembled quickly to serve an immediate need, such as the COVID-19 vaccination centers. Popup displays originated at medieval fairs and markets, where goods were brought to a temporary stall to be displayed, bartered, and sold. The retail sector uses the term POP (Point of Purchase) to describe small temporary displays (often made from cardboard) promoting featured products. Branded exhibit stands at trade shows and expositions with elaborate canopies, built-in lighting, product placement, VIP rooms, retractable graphics, and people facilitating the experience are the ultimate popups. Quick assembly and rapid deployment personify these exhibit types (see NECC case study in chapter 6). World's Fairs, the Olympics, and music festivals ramp popup to the next level, where temporal cities are created for events with varying degrees of lasting permanence. The Burning Man festival is the extreme popup on this scale. Overnight a barren desert becomes a fantasy playground for eighty thousand people with the purpose of leaving no trace nine days later.[21]

Tactical urbanism and a surge in public placemaking in neighborhoods, parks, and streets has expanded the definition of popup exhibition. "Popup to Permanent" is a movement that expounds the use of interim interventions to avoid slow, expensive, and sometimes exclusionary preplanned approaches to quickly prototype and test what works in community spaces. It advocates meaningful public engagement to allow people to experience what is possible, rather than looking at speculative design renderings.[22] Placemaking initiatives increase and celebrate what Oldenburg terms *third places*.[23] Contemporary and more nimble design collectives like The Decorators in London tailor their furniture interventions to these free, non-home, non-work public environments with an emphasis on social well-being and choreographing community interaction.[24]

Emma Thorne-Christy's pop-up exhibit *Filed Away* (2015) salvages filing cabinets that contain objects connected to undocumented persons and their experiences.

Emma Thorne-Christy

The Santa Cruz Museum of Art & History developed a popup museum where their content comes from participants rather than museum staff. An uncomplicated design approach sets out folding tents, tables, signs, and frames so that when people pass by, they can write a label for their object and leave it on display.[25] Popup events have moved exhibition making from the indoors to the outdoors, from the sanctioned to the unsanctioned, and directly into communities where people live and work—an analogy is the food truck revolution where the dining service goes to the consumer rather than the consumer to the restaurant.

The Exploratorium's *Middle Ground* (2018) is designed to encourage participants to engage in popup activities that help them better understand each other.

Photo by Amy Snyder, © Exploratorium, www.exploratorium.edu

Popup Museum—transforming the entire space

Temporary Fashion Museum, Het Nieuwe Instituut, Rotterdam, Netherlands. September 13, 2015–May 8, 2016 Principal Designers: EventArchitectuur; Studio Makkink & Bey

Design challenge: Ready to change

While museums have toyed with popup experiences—the Santa Cruz Museum of Art & History on a small scale, or the larger architect commissions for the annual pavilion at the Serpentine Galleries in London's Kensington Gardens—these are additions beyond permanent exhibition areas. Het Nieuwe Instituut (The New Institute) in Rotterdam is purposefully programmed to be entirely responsive. This museum of architecture, design, and digital culture engages thinkers, designers, makers, and diverse audiences to critically reflect on the "now" and ways to enact the future.[26] Known for its experimental approach to exhibition making and curatorial rigor, the museum challenges design teams to transform galleries with a toolbox of temporary divisions, display furniture, activity stations, and participatory popup components; nothing remains static, not even the gift shop or the café.

For a one-year period, the institute morphed into the Temporary Fashion Museum. There is no dedicated home for fashion collecting in the Netherlands, and the initiative was intended to advance exploration of a future national museum. Several design firms were commissioned to turn the galleries on each level of the institute into a series of fashion exhibitions. They set out to create an accessible, popup, and multimodal environment where audiences select how they experience the exhibits and collections. The museum's motto was intelligently named *prêt à toucher* (ready to touch).

Design solution: Open storage and display

The Temporary Fashion Museum's largest gallery was devoted to a series of unique collections, from Eva Maria Hatschek's private haute couture to public archives in the form of a vintage store, with iconic pieces from the history of Dutch and international fashion. Stacked modular shelves (3 feet wide x 10 feet high)

that resemble open storage in a warehouse displayed the garments, some on body forms, others in archival boxes. People requested objects using a catalogue that corresponded to a graphic letter and numbered sign system on the display units. Exhibition staff located the appropriate box in the open-shelved archive and laid the garments out on tissue paper for gloved viewers to unfold and inspect.[27]

The New Haberdashery exhibit contained open shelves to display a variety of fabric bolts, where people cut patterns and made their own garments on large tables that resemble a fashion-making studio. An exhibit titled *Hacked* focused on the ethics and waste associated with fast fashion. Other exhibit areas presented the speculative history of Dutch fashion, featuring the work of contemporary designers with the option to wear some of their items, test various perfumes, and of course, purchase products.

Design impact: Museum in motion

Het Nieuwe Instituut exhibits ooze temporality and are quickly assembled as if constructed as prototypes in an architecture or design atelier. There is a raw, experimental quality to the exhibition elements, materials, and visual communication methods. Less preoccupied with finish, they are nimble, immediate, and assertive—part trade show, part science center. Fashion theorist Marco Pecorari called the Temporary Fashion Museum a "museum in motion," which gains an agility when freed from being a canonical museum with economic and collecting restrictions.[28] The provocative exhibition design engaged audiences in what museums can do to facilitate how people understand fashion. Popup and modular retail-like displays responded to the museum narrative, highlighted the ephemeral quality of fashion, and questioned the role of audience as either visitor or consumer.

Rotterdam's Het Nieuwe Instituut is designed to be purposefully responsive and for a one-year it became the Temporary Fashion Museum.

Het Nieuwe Instituut, Rotterdam. Photo by JW Kaldenbach.

Warehouse-like shelving at the Temporary Fashion Museum displayed collections that included archived and iconic Dutch and international pieces.

Het Nieuwe Instituut, Rotterdam. Photo by Johannes Schwartz.

Popup surfaces allowed archived garments to be retrieved for gloved viewers to unfold and inspect at the Temporary Fashion Museum.

Het Nieuwe Instituut, Rotterdam.
Photo by Johannes Schwartz.

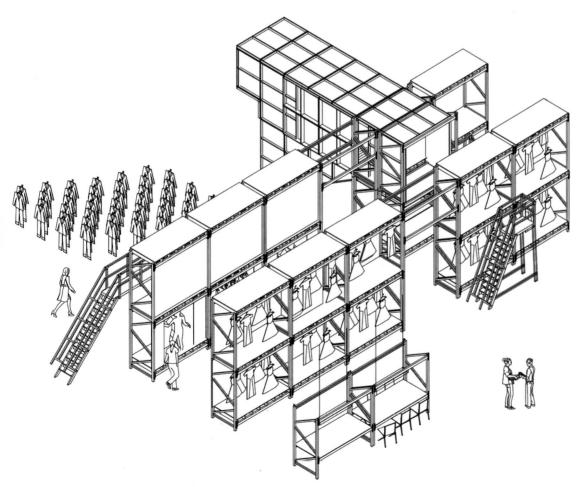

Modular retail-like concepts responded to the Temporary Fashion Museum's narrative and questioned the role of audience as either visitor or consumer.

Courtesty of Studio Makkink & Bey

Ultimate object of design is form

In the book *Pattern Language,* architect and design theorist Christopher Alexander says the ultimate object of design is form.[29] This is at the heart of systems thinking and modularity—the shape or pattern designers give materials when brought under an organizing idea, shaped in response to context and within constraints. Designers create their exhibit forms in response to the physical site and cognitive themes and content. Spatial manipulation and the design of spatial forms are key experiential design tools in this process.

Tips and Tricks

Create a strategy and purpose for spatial divisions, structures, and interventions using the following design techniques:

1. Activate the space visually using diagonal and curved walls/surfaces.
2. Provide respite by using transitional and interstitial zones to break up space.
3. Vary physical space using wall height, ceiling height, and aisle width.
4. Utilize free-standing display cases or embed them in thicker temporary walls.
5. Consult experts about the stability of dividers/walls and fire-safety systems.
6. Use a rough-scale model to quickly plan spatial relationships.
7. Keep physical access in mind—pathway widths, ramps, floor textures, visual exits.
8. Reuse exhibition dividers and wall systems when possible.
9. Work to a modular grid to save time and improve the design aesthetic.
10. Employ a full range of wall surface materials and vary their levels of opacity.

Notes

1. Mary Anne Staniszewski, *The Power of Display: A History of Exhibition Installations at the Museum of Modern Art* (Cambridge, MA: The MIT Press, 2001), 4.
2. "Lilly Reich Biography—Infos for Sellers and Buyers," accessed April 7, 2021, http://www.lilly-reich.com/.
3. "Alice Rawsthorn on Instagram: 'Lilly Reich | 4. One of Lilly Reich's Most Seductive and Ingenious Projects Was the Velvet and Silk Café, Which She Designed in 1927 In...,'" Instagram, accessed April 7, 2021, https://www.instagram.com/p/CBkaqmdBOcS/.
4. "Café Samt & Seide, 1927—Projekt MIK," accessed April 7, 2021, https://projektmik.com/en/moderne-in-krefeld/mies-in-krefeld/cafe-samt-seide-1927/.
5. Staniszewski, *The Power of Display*, 43.
6. "Alice Rawsthorn on Instagram."
7. "Inside Zaha Hadid Architects' Mathematics Gallery for the London Science Museum," *ArchDaily*, December 7, 2016, https://www.archdaily.com/801015/inside-zaha-hadid-architects-new-mathematics-gallery-for-the-london-science-museum.
8. Misha Black, ed., *Exhibition Design* (London: Architectural Press, 1950), 11.
9. Michelle Cotton, *Design Research Unit, 1942–72* (Cubitt Gallery London touring exhibition, Koenig Books, 2010), 114.
10. Cotton, *Design Research Unit, 1942-72*, 8.
11. "Fundamentals of Exhibition Design," accessed May 31, 2021, https://digitalcollections.nypl.org/items/90f27111-9714-4fc1-e040-e00a18064ba4/book#page/1/mode/2up.
12. Harriet Atkinson, "'Lines of Becoming': Misha Black and Entanglements through Exhibition Design," *Journal of Design History* 34, no. 1 (March 1, 2021): 37–53, https://doi.org/10.1093/jdh/epaa046.
13. "V&A · The Festival of Britain," Victoria and Albert Museum, accessed April 14, 2021, https://www.vam.ac.uk/articles/the-festival-of-britain.
14. "Enterprise Scotland" (1947), 2014, https://www.youtube.com/watch?v=p_AbpHYLF48.
15. "Yale University Art Gallery," in *Wikipedia*, March 5, 2021, https://en.wikipedia.org/w/index.php?title=Yale_University_Art_Gallery&oldid=1010525633.

16. "Architecture | Yale University Art Gallery," accessed March 6, 2022, https://artgallery.yale.edu/about/architecture.
17. "Yale University Art Gallery Renovation and Expansion," accessed October 29, 2021, https://www.architecturalrecord.com/articles/7411-yale-university-art-gallery-renovation-and-expansion.
18. Barbara Fahs Charles. Interview by Timothy McNeil about pogo walls at the Yale University Art Gallery, October 29, 2021.
19. Wendy Lesser, "Whispers of Louis Kahn's Vision at the Yale Center for British Art," *New York Times*, April 28, 2016, sec. Arts, https://www.nytimes.com/2016/05/01/arts/design/whispers-of-louis-kahns-vision-at-the-yale-center-for-british-art.html.
20. "Kahn, Louis Isadore (1901–1974)—Philadelphia Architects and Buildings," accessed April 14, 2021, https://www.philadelphiabuildings.org/pab/app/ar_display.cfm/21829.
21. "Burning Man 2021," Burning Man, accessed April 19, 2021, https://burningman.org/event/brc/.
22. "From Pop-Up to Permanent: Five Lessons in Tactical Urbanism," Global Designing Cities Initiative, April 18, 2018, https://globaldesigningcities.org/2018/04/18/from-pop-up-to-permanent-five-lessons-in-tactical-urbanism/.
23. Ray Oldenburg, ed., *Celebrating the Third Place: Inspiring Stories About the "Great Good Places" at the Heart of Our Communities*, 1st ed. (New York: Da Capo Press, 2002).
24. "About the Decorators," accessed June 20, 2022, http://the-decorators.net/About.
25. Nora Grant, "Pop-Up Museums: Participant-Created Ephemeral Exhibitions," *NAME Exhibitionist* 1, no. 34 (Spring 2015): 14–18.
26. "Home," Het Nieuwe Instituut, accessed April 7, 2021, https://hetnieuweinstituut.nl/en/home.
27. "'Prêt-a-Toucher'—Inside a Very Special Fashion Archive," HuffPost UK, March 16, 2016, https://www.huffingtonpost.co.uk/brooke-robertsislam/pretatoucher-inside-a-ver_b_9459396.html.
28. "Re-Fashioning the Institution: Reflections on the Temporary Fashion Museum," Temporary Fashion Museum, April 26, 2016, https://tijdelijkmodemuseum.hetnieuweinstituut.nl/en/refashioning-institution-reflections-temporary-fashion-museum.
29. "PatternLanguage.Com," accessed May 31, 2021, https://www.patternlanguage.com/.

Designer's Toolbox: **Spectacle**

Design dictates behavior. A space that is bright and intimate rather than dark and cavernous will determine if people's emotional responses are active or passive, social or solitary. Exhibitions and experiences employ a range of methods to attract and provoke reactions from audiences. Dip into the designer's toolbox and anticipate what techniques elicit a wow!

Visualization: Siddhartha Das is an exhibition designer and educator whose multidisciplinary studio is based in New Delhi, India

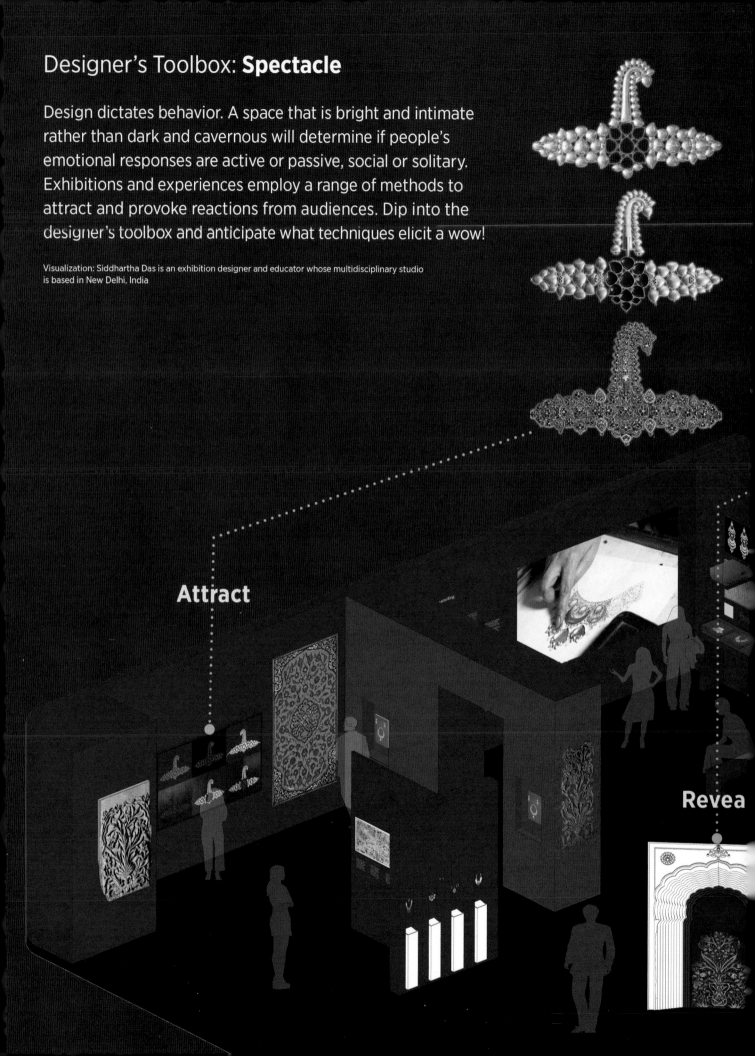

Attract

Revea

Reward

CHAPTER 5

"Wow" Moment

Experiences that surprise, reveal, and attract are central to the designer's playbook.

Key message: Design is responsible for the emotional and behavioral reactions of the exhibition audience.

Key word: spectacle

"We need a 'wow' moment" is a common exclamation in the entertainment industry and this trope is cast to conjure up captivating exhibitions and experiences. Also referred to as the "wow" factor, "aha" moment, or visual magnet, these spectacular incursions prey on people's emotive reactions and their subsequent behavioral responses to a variety of design triggers, such as architectural form, scale, color, image, light, and the composition and placement of objects.

To create an "experience" is to cause a reaction. Designers of exhibition environments want their work to elicit a reaction—joyful or moving, chaotic or contemplative, participatory or passive, a response from people signals a level of engagement that translates into learning or plain old fun. The element of surprise is a well-worn trope. The art of attraction, building anticipation, and providing a reward are other ploys. Placing key objects on sightlines, providing a glimpse of what lies ahead, making things larger than life, and starting, punctuating, and ending the exhibition journey with "wow" moments is what Walt Disney called "creating a wienie."[1] Designers have crafted a multitude of manipulative techniques to lure and guide people, stop them in their tracks, as well as keep them, often subconsciously, moving purposefully through an exhibition environment.

"Wow" Factor: Emotional and Behavioral Responses to the Exhibition Journey

Memorable experiences contain magical moments that make audiences pause, stop in their tracks, open their eyes wide, and gasp audibly. A healthy dose of wonder, spectacle, and awe brings people together to create meaningful social interactions. "Wow" moments can be intimate—peering through a magnifying glass to marvel at the microminiature eye-of-a-needle scenes by Hagop Sandaldjian at the Museum of Jurassic Technology; or expansive—the awesome approach along rim road to capture the natural wonder of the Grand Canyon from the visitor center.[2] Regardless of scale, micro to macro experiences rely on anticipation, surprise, and reward to build indelible experiences and memories. Remove "wow" moments and exhibitions are flat, and the level of active participation low.

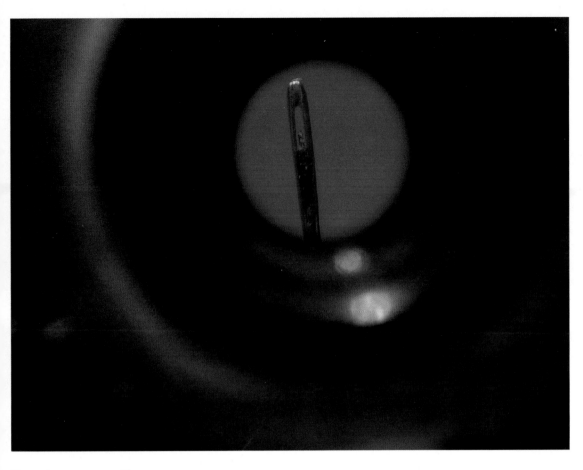

Experience as emotion

Falk and Dierking identified that people's perception and interpretation of an exhibition experience is shaped by their personal context and values.[3] These include past experiences and emotional biases/preferences based on socioeconomic background, race, or gender. Exhibition design firm Duncan McCauley explores this further to challenge people's sensory and emotive perceptions.[4] Using joy, laughter, empathy, fear, surprise, and sadness, their work engages audiences in a series of emotional sequences that respond to the exhibition themes and translate into spatial narratives and compositions that facilitate the communication of knowledge. Their work respectfully plays with peoples' emotions and accepts the responsibility of the design team to harness the multimodal power of the exhibition medium, respond to audiences' preferences, and craft positive emotional experiences, be they physical, cognitive, or visceral.

Exhibition design like the fields of UX and service design use principles of cognitive science and psychology to break down how people process an experience. Each level builds on the other to foster emotional connections: (1) visceral—how it appears and looks, (2) behavioral—how it works, its ease of use and feel, and (3) reflective—how it appeals, relates to past experiences, memory, and self-image. Don Norman's studies on emotional design suggest the first two levels of processing are about the "now" whereas reflective is about the "future," and how people will interpret an experience after the fact.[5] User experience design maps closely with exhibition design. More is known about people's habits through online experiences. Data tracks the actual, rather than the anecdotal behavior common in exhibition evaluation, where people tend to say what they think the institution wants to hear. With "big data" at their fingertips, experience makers can better serve their audiences.

Experience as memory

Entertainment and commercial industries such as attractions and retail have tracked people's emotional responses tied to behavioral economics for some time using the pleasure, arousal, and dominance model.[6] Increasingly, the rapid rise in user-experience studies and the ease of data collection in the digital sphere informs audience experience in the physical realm. Each sector grapples with designing for experience versus memory, which are related but systematically different. UX designer Curt Arledge advocates for memory designers who understand that each of us has two selves—the experiencing self and the remembering self—but the remembering self does the learning, judging, and deciding.[7]

Exhibition experiences benefit from both narrative and emotional arcs punctuated by peaks and troughs ranging from frenzy and excitement to reflection and calm. Designer Katherine Skellon compares this journey to a musical score where the tempo changes from decrescendo to crescendo with a series of interludes.[8] It is important to balance and vary the intensity of "wow" moments. A content-heavy exhibition with a harried design creates audience fatigue and overload. By contrast, one that is too empty, neutral, and sedate fails to excite and hold people's attention.[9] Theme parks offer moments of respite between rides, and art museums introduce interactive spaces to break up the potential monotony of the experience.

UX designers strive for peak moments and endings because online experiences are vulnerable to unexpected snags and glitches. Peak moments create a buffer against unforeseen problems in the user experience, and one single emotional high point can override a series of otherwise disastrous low points. For instance, a pulsating peak-end to an experience offsets a nonfunctioning interactive touch-table, or long lines for a theme park ride. The significance of ending well cannot be overemphasized as it retroactively frames people's memories. "Wow" moments foster positive overall experiences that build resilient memories, which can be shared, and count for much more overall.

Tracking experience and memory

Cookies, user data, and analytics make it easy (too easy) to track a person's experience in the digital environment. Retail environments use emotional journey maps to measure a consumer's energy—their curiosity, pleasure, and satisfaction, or alternatively their doubt, frustration, and anger. Exhibitions and attractions employ a variety of evaluation, survey, and observational tools to gauge footfall and success. Emotional impact is measured by mapping dwell time in a particular area.[10] Tracking people's eye movements reveals the popular parts of certain exhibits.[11] Careful staging of space, sightlines, and atmosphere creates multisensory clues that lure and lead people to the most memorable "wow" moments.

Visual Magnets: Wondrous Objects and Features Control the Exhibition Journey

Sneak peeks through portals, sightlines to prominent features, objects that reveal themselves around corners: These are techniques that place the audience in front of the narrative—a fundamental exhibition design principle to build anticipation and deliver awesome rewards. Former Walt Disney Imagineer Marty Sklar called these prompts "visual magnets" that pull guests from the Matterhorn to Mickey Mouse (attraction A to B).[12] These methods of attraction originated with the spectacle found in *Wunderkammer* ("rooms of wonder" or Cabinets of Curiosities) and other early object-based collections and exhibition environments. The cascading taxonomy of flora and fauna tumbling down the walls of Levinus Vincent's 1715 palatial Dutch home with his guests scrutinizing the specimen trays, must have been breathtaking for audiences unaccustomed to such wonders.[13]

The earliest depiction of a natural history cabinet of curiosities is the fold-out engraving from Ferrante Imperato's *Dell'Historia Naturale* (1599). Commonly associated with the origins of the modern museum, it demonstrates the overwhelming attraction of immersive object display.

Mapa de experiencia del visitante

- ● El sabio
- ● La sensible
- ● El grupo
- ● El intelectual
- ● El inquieto
- ● La entusiasta
- ● La moderna
- ● El ocupado

1 Se amplía la **zona de transición** entre el espacio público y la biblioteca

2 La colección se establece como **corazón de la biblioteca**

3 **Sala infantil** ubicada estratégicamente para mejor control de su público específico.

4 Nuevo acceso desde el **barrio Carlos E. Restrepo**

5 Integración de la biblioteca con la **Torre de la Memoria**

Nivel 1
...

Mapping experiences and exhibition dwell time with people's personalities at Parque Explora, Medellín, Colombia.

Courtesy of Parque Explora

A myriad of creatures suspended from the center of the ceiling create a tense alliance with the people underneath. The upside-down crocodile serves as a clever foil—a disarming compositional focal point and visceral takeaway image from the experience—it would have made for an excellent "wow" moment selfie.

Objects as magnets

Every designed experience, whether cultural, entertainment, or commercial, takes people on a consecutive journey that attracts, reveals, and rewards—something catches their eye, pulls them closer and reveals itself, and assuming it is worthy, rewards them with beauty, scale, human endeavor, humor, or fun. Audiences go out of their way to bask in the celebrity presence of Leonardo da Vinci's *Mona Lisa*. The Louvre team cleverly installed the painting at the heart of the museum to build anticipation and make people work for the experience. The towering *Self-Conscious Gene* by sculptor Marc Quinn anchors the entrance to the Medicine Galleries at London's Science Museum. This monumental bronze sculpture of Rick Genest draws in people from a distance into the space, and a closer look reveals his full-body tattoos.[14] The immersive tanks of teeming ocean life at the Monterey Bay Aquarium reel people in with staging and lighting. Like the crocodile in the *Wunderkammer*, the inches-thick glass between shark and viewer elicits an uneasy but rewarding emotion.

Wunderkammer (Cabinets of Curiosities) are associated with the origins of the modern museum and immersive object display.

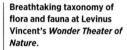

Ferrante Imperato, Dell'Historia Naturale, Naples 1599. Collection of Biblioteca di agraria UNINA provided by Wikimedia Commons. CC-PD

Breathtaking taxonomy of flora and fauna at Levinus Vincent's *Wonder Theater of Nature*.

Illustration from *Wondertooneel der Nature a Cabinet of Curiosities*, between 1706 and 1715. Collection of the Universities of Strasbourg, provided by Wikimedia Commons. CC-PD

Art of Attraction: Sightlines and Look-Throughs

Visual targets lead people clearly and logically through an exhibition. Teaser sightlines from one space to another use a vocabulary of architectural vistas, corridors, windows, and portals. Sightlines feature signature objects, super-graphics, bright color fields, lighting, and sound effects to pull people through or anchor a space. Studies show people move to larger, well-lit openings, are attracted to brightness with an aversion to darkness, and consistently gravitate to the biggest object and space.[15] As a social species, humans are attracted to crowds of other humans, but when their personal space is violated, they retreat, seeking greater isolation. Theme parks, attractions, and expositions are adept at the art of attraction, and designers deliberately create environments that manipulate audience tendencies and instincts.

Primary case study
The Attract

U.S. Pavilion at the Montreal Expo, Canada, 1967
Principal Designers: Cambridge Seven Associates; R. Buckminster Fuller

Design challenge: Radical designers that shaped a generation

Buckminster Fuller's 62-meter (203-foot) design for the Montreal biosphere used the art of attraction to dominate the skyline and entice people to a vision of the future. Expo 67 is considered one of the most successful World's Fairs of the twentieth century, with a single-day attendance record of 569,500 and participation from sixty-two nations.[16] The U.S. Information Agency's Jack Masey was responsible for the Pavilion and commissioned Fuller's biosphere and the emerging firm of Cambridge Seven Associates to design the exhibits inside.[17] Designers Ivan and Peter Chermayeff, Alden B. Christie, Paul E. Dietrich, Tom Geismar, and Terry Rankine pulled off a radical design concept against a backdrop of the Cold War when the United States and the Soviet Union were jostling for global power and the race to space. American architecture and design consultancies like Cambridge Seven, the Eames office, and Herb Rosenthal enjoyed a period of expanding exhibition opportunities, and their firms influenced current professional practice—Cambridge Seven's Chermayeff and Geismar are now today's C&G partners.

Design solution: Labyrinth of anticipation and attraction

Buckminster Fuller's geodesic dome is synonymous with the liberated lifestyles of the late 1960s. The geometric forces of physics engineered it to be strong, easy to construct, modular, and lightweight. Cambridge Seven requested that the monorail be routed through the sphere at the equator, adding another kinetic experience to the space. Heatherwick Studio's UK pavilion at the Shanghai Expo (2010) is the direct descendent of Fuller's ambitious and omnipresent spherical exposition form. The biosphere contained a series of interconnected terraced exhibit environments, like a tower of landing pads that floated free of the thin, outer acrylic membrane.[18] People moved rhythmically in all directions and traversed the labyrinth via a series of overlapping moving walkways, which Masey described as Piranesian in feeling.[19]

NASA's moon landing exploration, Hollywood movies, and abstract expressionism were some exhibit themes that expressed the diverse creative spirit and a softer side of America—controversially not the military hardware or heavy industry associated with former expositions. The design team leveraged the vantage points that the multiple platforms afforded. Strategically placed artworks, banners, suspended objects, and film projection animated the various planes and surfaces to attract people's gazes and pull them through the cascading space. Audiences described the pavilion as having a dreamlike quality. People were mesmerized by the vertical ascent/descent through the tiers of exhibits against the backdrop of Fuller's geodesic dome with its diaphanous skin affording spectacular views over the entire exposition site.[20]

Design impact: Psychology of attraction

The U.S. Pavilion was designed to maximize sightlines and toy with the psychology of attraction. Vistas to objects, other people, and external views tease and tempt. Level changes and overlooks trick and tantalize. The spatial shift from open to intimate keeps people engaged. The visible crowds on the higher levels instinctively draw people upward. Using David Dean's terminology to describe these behaviors, *megaphilic* (attraction to size) tendencies lure people to the large moon-landing capsule and parachutes; *chromaphilic* (attraction to color), to the bright fields of color and graphics; and *photophilic* (attraction to light), to the ever-changing light-play in the dome.[21] Such behavioral characteristics are deeply ingrained. The designers manipulated these predispositions to deliberately slow, stop, and pace people through the exhibition environment.

Buckminster Fuller's Montreal Expo 67 biosphere used the art of attraction to entice people to a vision of the future.

Photo: Archives de la Ville de Montréal, VM94-EX136-779

Element of Surprise: Revealing Content and Not Giving the Game Away

Curiosity is instinctive. What is behind the curtain, through the peephole, under the microscope, beneath the flap? Should one push the button, gesture in front of the screen, interact with the smiling costumed guide? The act of anticipation before something reveals itself verges on a "wow" moment. The aftermath may surprise when objects move, jump out, or make a sound. While opening a drawer is small scale, designers also use larger spatial interventions, such as baffle walls, switchbacks, and overlooks, to hide and reveal a myriad of content to keep audiences on their toes. Historic houses, science centers, and themed attractions combine magical settings with an element of surprise, without completely giving the game away.

Level changes and overlooks trick and tantalize at the Montreal Expo 67 U.S. Pavilion.

Image courtesy of Chermayeff & Geismar & Haviv

Strategically placed artworks, banners, and film projection create a labyrinth of anticipation, attraction, and reward at the Montreal Expo 67 U.S. Pavilion.

Artists: Ellsworth Kelly © Ellsworth Kelly Foundation, Courtesy Matthew Marks Gallery. Tom Wesselman © 2022 Estate of Tom Wesselmann / Artists Rights Society (ARS), NY. Image courtesy of Chermayeff & Geismar & Haviv.

The Reveal

Dennis Severs House, London, 1979–present
Designer: Dennis Severs

Design challenge: Driven to design outside the box

Tucked away behind London's Liverpool Street station is a five-story Georgian terraced house on Folgate Street that belies the remarkable "wow" moments that await inside. Historically, this borough welcomed generations of immigrants seeking work and religious freedom. The gentrification of this East End district has since swapped these escapees for business-seeking office workers in high-rise architecture and traded the once thriving food market of Spitalfields for trendy restaurants and shopping zones.

Local community members bought houses on Folgate Street in the 1970s to save them from the wrecking ball. One of those was Californian transplant Dennis Severs, who was compelled to return his house to its Georgian roots. He removed modern conveniences, favored candles over electricity, and eschewed flushing toilets for chamber pots. Severs continued to transform his home and domestic surroundings until his death in 1999. The house now operates as a private foundation and is open to the public by appointment.

Severs maintained that the house was occupied by the Jervises, a Huguenot silk merchant and his family who escaped France because of religious persecution in the seventeenth century and settled into the silk industry in the East End. Each level of the Dennis Severs House tells their rags-to-riches Hogarthian story—from well-furnished lower-level rooms to attic spaces in a state of neglect and disrepair. The unfurling story is based loosely on historic facts, and the fantasy Severs formulated to serve as narrative for the design and thematic interpretation of each level of the house. Not only does each floor tell part of the story, but so does each room, and not necessarily in chronological order.

Design solution: Still-life drama

Rooms in the house evoke a cabinet of curiosities. Historical furniture, domestic objects, and knick-knacks are not necessarily period accurate. Even the commemorative plate for the 1981 Royal Wedding of Charles and Diana looks at home on the living room mantelpiece. Critics cite this "jumble of history" as misleading, and unlike comparable historic sites, the presentation of objects, and the renovation of the interior, take great liberties with authenticity and accuracy.[22]

Accuracy was never Severs's intention; he was fascinated by "still-life drama," and during public

"You either see it or you don't" at London's Dennis Severs House.

Dennis Severs House, Photo by Lucinda Douglas-Menzies

hours, the house is full of wondrous "wow" moments. Fires smolder in the grates, candles illuminate interiors, vegetables stock the kitchen, plates of nibbled cake and half-drunk cups of tea in Georgian chinaware languish in the parlor.[23] Even urine is added to the bedroom chamber pots. The house smells of smoke, spice, and sweet musk. The clock chimes, the floorboards creak; listen carefully and you can hear the muffled voices of the Jervis family or the church bells pealing in the distance. This adds up to an immersive experience that is staged like a tableaux vivant of objects, rather than people—as if the Jervis family simply stepped out of the room for a moment.

Severs likened the experience to stepping over the threshold of a painting into a three-dimensional Baroque interior. From the moment the knocker strikes the door, and the host welcomes people into the house, there is strictly no talking or touching—the experience is highly visceral, and sensorial. Narrow, cluttered spaces mean movement up and down the stairs are carefully choreographed. The uneasy atmosphere creates uncertainty about what is around each corner. Compounded by the spatial silence, a small "shriek" or "wow" is amplified, and the perpetrator's stifled response adds to the tension. The story of the house is ambiguous, and guests must explore, observe, smell, and rely on their imagination. The experience is counterintuitive and relies on people losing themselves in the moment. There are no descriptive or interpretive signs to explain what things are, or what to do. Reality is suspended, while a narrative reveals itself and consumes the audience.

Design impact: Frustration to fervor

"You either see it or you don't" proclaims a cryptic message placed on a chair in the living room. The house elicits legitimate audience reactions that range from frustration to fervor. Some people willingly accept the ambiguity and self-exploration. Others express an inability to enter a quasi-meditative state and be transported to another time and place.[24] Do such contrasting reactions stem from people's overreliance on interpretive information? The Dennis Severs House is a world away from heritage sites that are strong on historic detail but weak on a sense of life. Severs, while not a professional designer, was motivated by a passion and determination to stage and create his home's history. The Dennis Severs House inspired historic house attractions to unhook their rope barriers, furnish their interiors, and invigorate their dull interpretation.[25] Many introduced greater context and feeling to connect with audiences, along with multimodal forms of communication that combine contemplative-, sensory-, discovery-, and participatory based exhibits.

The physical and accessible limitations of the house make the experience unavailable to all. The Dennis Severs House falls through the cracks. It is neither a conventional historic house nor an entertainment attraction. Judging by the minimal signage left on chairs and tables and according to Severs, it is *not* a museum. Part of its charm is that it defies classification. From one stifled "wow" moment to another, designers can learn from its theatrical presentation. Love it or hate it, the Dennis Severs House is a playful and irreverent interpretation of history.

Plates of nibbled food and half-drunk cups of tea in Georgian chinaware make for "still-life drama" at the Dennis Severs House.

Dennis Severs House, Photo by Lucinda Douglas-Menzies

Carrot Dangle: Rewards That Make the Audience Work a Little Harder for the Payoff

A collection of snapshots (memories) gives extra weight to the most intense and final moment of an experience. If memories add up to more than experiences, then designers need to provide a suitable ending—something big, a dramatic takeaway. The concluding "wow" moment should seduce and reward. Blockbusters, brands, celebrities, fandom, signature objects, lighting effects, obscure vantage points, being close up to something special for the first time—like stocking the essential items at the back of the supermarket—these rewards dangle a carrot and make the audience work a little harder for the eventual payoff.

Primary case study
The Reward

Hogwarts Castle Experience, The Making of Harry Potter, Warner Bros. Studio Tour, London, 2012–present
Principal Designer: Thinkwell Group

Design challenge: Guest as protagonist

Potter fans from around the globe flock to this behind-the-scenes mecca to tour the movie's back-lot. Exhibits feature authentic sets, concept art, scale models, costumes, and props associated with the original book series.[26] Tour guides lead people into an orientation theater to watch a film featuring the movie's key actors in Hogwarts Castle. Afterward, the screen rises to reveal the set of the Great Hall, and the one-way walking tour continues unguided. The designers at Thinkwell Group, who created the experience, consider the guest the main character and the protagonist in all their work.[27]

Design solution: Design manipulates the emotional journey

Near the end of The Making of Harry Potter tour people ascend a narrow switchback ramp to reach a doorway. The route is intentionally constricted. The doorway is standard size, uncharacteristic for an experience catering to hundreds of people every hour.

These deliberate design devices slow the progression of people and obscure the view ahead. People congregate around the doorway and into the room beyond. The entrance to the room is dark, and there is no information to tell guests what lies ahead. Before this point in the journey, people have marveled at many exhibits and themed environments. They may be tired, need a jolt, a change of rhythm. Rounding the corner, people enter the room, the light grows brighter, the soundtrack becomes louder, and the size of the space increases along with the noise of other people. The scale of the impending encounter is on the verge of consuming each person as they get a glimpse through the crowds to what lies ahead. Palpable gasps, uncontrolled shrieks, and many "oh my God"s can be heard. Everyone's gaze is strictly forward as they gather against a railing along the edge of an elevated viewing platform set back from the perimeter of the room. Then, the prize that people have been waiting for is revealed—it fills the entire space, pushing up against the edges of the viewing area, which exaggerates the scale and drama of the spectacle. The experience is the reward for people's patience—for Harry Potter fans, it is heaven.

Design impact: Shared social experiences

This dramatic reveal presents the impressive 35-foot-tall scale model of Hogwarts Castle that was used for fly-over footage when CGI would not suffice. Lighting effects transition from dawn to daylight to twilight to night every six minutes, and two thousand internal lights illuminate the interior windows of the castle as the guests circumnavigate the model.[28] The journey of discovery is designed to be a social experience. An evocative attraction, slow reveal, and a stunning reward lure guests to collectively confront the castle. The reward is a peak-ending that stands out because the elevated platform makes people feel like they are flying over Hogwarts. The designers chose to transition the experience, not give the game away immediately, and make the audience anticipate the payoff.

Evocative attracts, slow reveals, and stunning rewards lure guests to collectively confront Hogwarts Castle at The Making of Harry Potter, Warner Bros. Studio Tour.

Photo: RichART Photos / Alamy Stock Photo

Potent attraction, slow reveal, and stunning reward

The elements of attraction, reveal, and reward extend to a range of experience-based encounters. Who is not captivated by finding their way out of a maze, who does not shriek in surprise when a drop of water falls on their head during a darkened ghost ride, or who is not driven by the rewards associated with solving the mystery in an escape room? Alternatively, have people become too cool for surprise, saturated with visual stimuli, less responsive to attraction, and too accustomed to reward through the overmonetization of what used to be free? What is the future role of designers to create these enduring emotive experiences? Emotional impact is difficult to accurately measure, but people's visible reactions are unmistakable, and the signature "wow" moments of any experience are the ones that will be shared, immortalized, and memorized. The next chapter examines the designer contribution to creating a multisensorial atmosphere to support these "wow" moments.

Tips and Tricks

Implement spatial design and object placement methods that are behavior-based using the following design techniques:

1. Place striking objects on sightlines—create spectacle to pull people through a space.
2. See-through windows provide openness and mystery; place objects in walls and openings as teasers to the next space.
3. Entry response: All other things being equal, people go in the larger, better-lit opening.
4. People are attracted to bright color; not always a preference, but an instinct (chromaphilic behavior).
5. People are attracted to brightness and generally are averse to darkness (photophilic behavior).
6. People are attracted to largeness and gravitate to the biggest object in the room (megaphilic behavior).
7. Social species—people are attracted instinctively to other people.
8. Personal space—when violated, people react, are repelled, or move away.
9. Pace peak and "wow" moments at the beginning, middle, and end to keep people engaged.
10. Incorporate surprise—reveal content and make people work a little to make it stick.

Notes

1. "Do You Know About Mickey's 10 Commandments?" *DisneyFanatic*, December 30, 2022. https://www.disneyfanatic.com/do-you-know-about-mickeys-10-commandments-lh1/.
2. "The Eye of the Needle," accessed May 10, 2021, https://www.mjt.org/exhibits/hagop/hagop2.html.
3. John H. Falk and Lynn D. Dierking, *The Museum Experience* (Washington, D.C.: Whalesback Books, 1992).
4. "Duncan McCauley—Museumsplanung und Ausstellungsgestaltung—All," accessed May 10, 2021, http://www.duncanmccauley.com/en/projects/all.
5. Andreas Komninos, "Norman's Three Levels of Design," The Interaction Design Foundation, accessed May 5, 2021, https://www.interaction-design.org/literature/article/norman-s-three-levels-of-design.
6. Iris Bakker, Theo Van Der Voordt, Peter Vink, and Jan de Boon, "Pleasure, Arousal, Dominance: Mehrabian and Russell Revisited," *Current Psychology* 33, no 3 (2014). 405–21.
7. "User Memory Design: How To Design For Experiences That Last," *Smashing*, https://www.smashingmagazine.com/2016/08/user-memory-design-how-to-design-for-experiences-that-last/.
8. "Re-XD: Chaos at the Museum," accessed May 5, 2021, http://re-xd.org/.
9. Iris Bakker, Theo Van Der Voordt, Peter Vink, and Jan de Boon, "Pleasure, Arousal, Dominance: Mehrabian and Russell Revisited."
10. Ellen Lupton, *Design Is Storytelling* (New York: Cooper Hewitt, Smithsonian Design Museum, 2017), 79–81.
11. Takumi Toyama et al., "Museum Guide 2.0—An Eye-Tracking Based Personal Assistant for Museums and Exhibits," May 1, 2011.
12. "Do You Know About Mickey's 10 Commandments?"
13. Barbara Maria Stafford et al., *Devices of Wonder: From the World in a Box to Images on a Screen* (Getty Publications, 2001), 148–49.
14. "Science Museum's New Medicine Galleries Are Just . . . Wow," *Londonist*, November 15, 2019, https://londonist.com/london/science-museum-s-new-medicine-galleries.
15. David Dean, *Museum Exhibition Theory and Practice* (London; New York: Routledge, 2002), 42–53.
16. Daniela Sheinin, "Kookie Thoughts: Imagining the United States Pavilion at Expo 67 (or How I Learned to Stop Worrying and Love the Bubble)," *Journal of Transnational American Studies* 5, no. 1 (2013),

https://escholarship.org/uc/item/6c81k3t1#author.

17. "Expo 67 U.S. Pavilion: Historic Exhibit Design," CambridgeSeven, accessed May 5, 2021, https://www.cambridgeseven.com/project/expo-67-u-s-pavilion/.

18. "AD Classics: Montreal Biosphere / Buckminster Fuller," ArchDaily, October 7, 2018, https://www.archdaily.com/572135/ad-classics-montreal-biosphere-buckminster-fuller.

19. Peter Chermayeff, *Design for a Fair: The United States Pavilion at Expo '67 Montreal*, 2010, https://www.youtube.com/watch?v=6TnT2lSLHxo.

20. Sheinin, "Kookie Thoughts."

21. Dean, *Museum Exhibition Theory and Practice*, 42–53.

22. jamestheposh, *Dan Cruickshank—The House That Wouldn't Die* (1985 Original), 2013, https://www.youtube.com/watch?v=Q4fq1md2Z-Q.

23. Tennis Channel, *Destination Tennis London—Dennis Severs' House*, 2017, https://www.youtube.com/watch?v=kJXqk74Yyt0.

24. Based on anecdotal interviews and the author's frequent visits to the house with student groups (2010–2019).

25. Bill Adair, Benjamin Filene, and Laura Koloski, eds., *Letting Go? Sharing Historical Authority in a User-Generated World* (Philadelphia: The Pew Center for Arts & Heritage, 2011), 321.

26. "The Making of Harry Potter," Harry Potter Wiki, accessed May 19, 2021, https://harrypotter.fandom.com/wiki/The_Making_of_Harry_Potter.

27. "Theme Park Design: Thinkwell Group Brings Stories To Life," accessed May 5, 2021, https://creativecloud.adobe.com/discover/article/theme-park-design-thinkwell-group-brings-stories-to-life.

28. Joe Zenas. Correspondence with Timothy McNeil about the "Making of Harry Potter." Thinkwell Group, January 19, 2022.

Designer's Toolbox: **Atmosphere**

Designers release a range of atmospheres into the exhibition environment using a selection of sensory-based tools. Light, color, and sound combine with architecture and scenography to add thematic context for objects and stories. Open the designer's toolbox to reveal the ingredients and hidden spatial infrastructure required to deliver experiences and implement atmosphere.

Visualization: Roger Escalante Quintero is an architect and designer of learning experiences based in Medellín, Colombia

Sound and Light

Color and Texture

Smell and Taste

CEILING

1. HVAC ductwork/vents
2. House lights
3. Cable tray/Outlets
4. Sound system/wi-fi router
5. Light track with fixtures
6. Gobo/Spot light
7. Fire sprinkler system
8. Drop ceiling/anchor points
9. Smoke detector/
   Security camera

WALL

10. Steel/Wood stud framing
11. Plywood covering
12. Wall board
13. Paint/Finishes
14. Safety railing
15. Audio speaker
16. Insulation
17. Structural wall
18. Acoustic panels
19. Strobe
20. Exit sign
21. Light sensor/Controls
22. Wall and floor electrical outlets

FLOOR

23. Concrete footing
24. Concrete slab
25. Floor insulation/Acoustic
26. Sub floor/floating surface
27. Floor materials (wood, carpet, rubber, linoleum, polished/colored concrete)
28. Floor joist
29. Integral lighting
30. Seating

Temperature and Humidity

CHAPTER 6

Beyond the White Cube

Environments that engage the senses pull on a full range of the designer's palette.

Key message: Design creates the cohesive flavor and atmosphere of the exhibition experience.

Key word: atmosphere

The white cube is as synonymous with contemporary art installations as the black box is to theater—both are favored for their flexibility and neutrality. The term *white cube* refers to a display space characterized by its square or oblong shape, uncluttered aesthetic, with white- or gray-colored walls. Free from incursions, distractions, and personality, the space is perceived as an ambiguous context that recedes to place the audience's focus squarely on the exhibition content.

This chapter questions the trope's continued relevance as a display method, regardless of the context and origins of the material to be presented, and it positions the white cube as an introduction to the design of exhibition atmosphere. Changing exhibition environments for museums, expositions, and trade shows are specifically designed to be flexible, to use an open plan, with few spatial impediments. A high level of built-in infrastructure supports lighting and color changes, allows for electrical and data requirements, and secures exhibition furniture, props, and components. Beginning with this blank canvas, designers create different spatial configurations, alter the architectural features, control the visual backdrop to suit the objects and content, and add elements to engage the senses and impact the embodied experience and overall atmosphere.

White Cube: Framing the History of Exhibition Modernism

The *Artforum* essay series, *Inside the White Cube* (1976), gave a catchy new name to the mode of display dominant in museums and commercial galleries.[1] Artist and critic Brian O'Doherty confronted the technique's neutrality. He wrote that rather than serving the artwork, the exhibition space became the main event, and that the history of modernism is intimately framed by that space; or the history of modern art can be correlated with changes in that space and in the way we see it.[2] Little has changed since O'Doherty's criticism. Museum galleries have reached the apex of minimalism—integrated materials complement one another, sophisticated daylight and electrical light gently wash walls, the default wall color remains a shade of white—an aesthetic that is not comfortable for all audiences.

Perceived perfection and purity

Scholars and social/spatial justice advocates question the white cube's association with modernism and the international style in post-colonial Europe. In Western culture, color has often been treated as corrupting, foreign, or superficial, and the term *chromophobia* manifests itself in an aversion to the use of color, particularly in products and design.[3] This design aesthetic, developed by predominantly white male architects and designers, has little regard for people's cultural and indigenous backgrounds.[4] Future exhibition spaces on the African continent, like Ghana's Pan African Heritage Museum, are set to tell the story of Africa using African voices, tools, and culture as well as a distinctly African architecture and design aesthetic.[5]

Museum and exhibition atmospheres can be alienating and intimidating to enter, creating what Elaine Heumann Gurian termed "threshold fear."[6] People tend to prefer surroundings that emulate their domesticity, that foster a sense of belonging, are familiar, colorful, comfy, and welcoming.[7] In contrast, overly contextualized environments that invoke alienation and reinforce stereotypes and cultural appropriation are under scrutiny. Exhibition designers are partly responsible for injecting inclusive atmospheres into storytelling environments from the perspective of pluriversalism.[8] It is time for designers—and society—to move beyond the white cube.

White extended the frame

The white cube mirrored the abstraction of modern art in early-twentieth-century Europe and the subsequent professionalization of exhibition design practice. Artists and designers associated with groups like De Stijl and the Bauhaus school preferred to minimize distraction and display their works against simple, light-colored walls that served as an extended frame. Museums in the United States during the early 1930s, visual merchandising, and the commercial success of modern department store, all created the white cube as we know it today. The Museum of Modern Art in New York is the most celebrated example. Alfred Barr Jr. institutionalized the technique for the display of art and inspired modern museum exhibition design to do away with frivolity in favor of a focus on the objects.[9]

Design challenge: Beige cloth to white paint

Alfred Barr Jr. assumed the directorship at MoMA in 1929. His significant curatorial and design achievements accumulated quickly. Barr was inspired by his discussions about modernism and travels to Europe with MoMA colleague and friend, architect Philip Johnson. Initially, Barr manipulated the exhibition atmosphere by stretching a monk's beige-colored cloth over the walls to help neutralize the space for the artworks. With a new focus on short-term loan exhibitions at MoMA, this reusable method made installations quicker and patching wall holes easier. Eventually, the cloth became impractical, and Barr transitioned to white (or off-white) paint for future exhibitions. *Cubism and Abstract Art* was comprised of four hundred items, and it filled the museum with paintings, works on paper, sculpture, architecture, furniture, theater design, typography, and photography. The exhibition ignored any political or social context, instead establishing the chronology and development of Cubism and abstract art, and their influence on the more practical arts.[10]

Design solution: Hiding ornament

Barr wanted the visual impact of each work to speak for itself—typewritten cards (some of the first object labels) pinned to the gallery walls described how the objects related to each other. The gallery design removed any context in part to unify such

a wide range of media. Paintings were spaced out evenly and sparingly at accessible viewing heights to facilitate the appreciation of a singular artwork. Their aesthetic dimension took precedence over architectural and site-specific associations.[11]

The museum at this time operated out of the Manhattan townhouse owned by the Rockefeller family. Barr attempted to negate the decorative domestic interior by exposing the wood floors, painting the walls and ceilings white, and installing simple light fixtures to eradicate the house's ornamentation and elevate the artworks.[12] Look carefully, and the articulated baseboards, decorative moldings, and electrical outlets are still visible in the galleries.

Design impact: Elevating the art

MoMA's new building opened in 1939 with purpose-designed pristine gallery walls and surfaces made to Barr's minimalist specifications. This trend caught on quickly at other museums in the early twentieth century reflecting societies' modernization. The international style replaced overly ornate Beaux Arts and revivalist architecture. Audiences reacted positively, and curators hired designers like Herbert Bayer and Paul Rudolph to transform exhibition experiences. Their work still looks remarkably contemporary compared to today's exhibitions, making one wonder if museums and galleries will ever shake the white cube tradition.

Between Minimalism and Contextualism: Design Takes a Front or Back Seat

Exhibition makers and those who create immersive experiences wrestle with the appropriate amount of atmospheric context to infuse into their designs. Barr's minimalist mindset remains the favored tack for contemporary art museums. But what about exhibitions that embody a rich cultural history, or feature stories that would benefit from a contextual environment? Depending on the goals and content of the project, designers choose to either create display environments that sit back using a subtle palette to emphasize objects (museums) or come forward using a strident palette to underscore themes (branded environments). Many examples fall in between, and hybrid solutions let the atmosphere be both the driver and passenger.

Atmosphere matters

Placing objects and themes in modern or historical contexts is a matter of design semantics. It communicates values and meanings, and it draws on the designer's experience, training, and cultural perspective. Exhibition design transforms the meanings of objects from other cultures and periods within the framework of the current time, and the exhibition venue imprints their commentary and ideology.[13] Abstraction takes the essence of architectural styles or historical motifs and transforms them into decorative elements. Examples include ornate Korean moldings without the rich coloring, lattice work from Islamic architecture without the curves, or the distinctive roof lines found on Japanese temples. Is this re-creation of context authentic and appropriate for exhibition content, or does it verge on cultural appropriation? Does the embellishment begin to detract or fail to support the exhibition theme? When does it come between audience knowledge and experience? Designers should consider these questions before embarking on their creative journey.

The J. Paul Getty Museum in Los Angeles has debated these questions ever since the first museum was constructed as a re-creation of a Roman villa in a Malibu canyon (1974). The Getty Center (1997) extends this dichotomy to combine semi-authentic historical interior gallery settings, wrapped in a gleaming modernist outer shell designed by Meier Partners. Compare the Getty Villa's permanent collection galleries (2005) with those of the Louvre Lens (2012), a luminous outpost of the venerable Paris Museum.[14] The galleries at the Villa are a faithful reinterpretation of a Roman interior mixing patterned terrazzo floors, ornamented coffered ceilings, and casework replete with bronze trim and a mixture of materials. The antiquities feel at home in this intimate

Cubism and Abstract Art **was one of the first to expose wood floors and paint the walls and ceilings white to neutralize the gallery and elevate the artworks.**

Architects Machado Silvetti and the Getty design team staged objects from the ancient world in galleries adorned with patterned terrazzo and color at the Getty Villa.

The J. Paul Getty Museum, Villa Collection, Malibu, California

Designers Sanaa and Adrien Gardère staged objects from the ancient world in galleries washed with filtered daylight and white colored surfaces at the Louvre Lens.

Photo: Iwan Baan

spot-lit environment. The cavernous gallery spaces at the Louvre Lens position their ancient art collection in a wash of filtered daylight through simple louvres/blades on the ceiling. The aluminum walls create fuzzy reflections and a sense of infinity. The harmonious gray and white floors and object pedestals are barely perceptible in this white cube homage. Similar objects, two vastly different atmospheres, each with their merits—does one work better than the other?

What is the design saying silently?

Having established that the context of an exhibition venue imparts a design ideology, note the proliferation of museums, theme parks, and attractions that are created by architects and designers with a worldview and creative style that is nonindigenous to a site's geographic location. Pamela Erskine-Loftus points to research that identifies low-context cultures (Europe and North

The historic Sheikh Abdullah bin Jassim Al Thani's Palace nestled against Ateliers Jean Nouvel's contrasting addition sends a contrasting message at the National Museum of Qatar.

Photo © Qatar Museums, National Museum of Qatar, 2022

Exhibition spaces at the National Museum of Qatar shed the building's exterior oval curves and decorative references to the historic palace.

Photo © Qatar Museums, National Museum of Qatar, 2022

America) that prefer explicit, didactic, and singular experiences, and high-context cultures (Asia and Arab states) that gravitate to implicit, nonverbal, and social experiences.[15] This dichotomy may present barriers for exhibition audiences where the design orchestrator relies on atmosphere methods found in low-context cultures to communicate to people in high-context cultures. The Middle East is a good example where museum building has intentionally employed design expertise mostly from Europe and North America, which may not always be well suited to its high-context audiences.

The National Museum of Qatar in Doha (2019) celebrates Qatari culture and heritage.[16] The building's contrasting architecture is striking. The Qatari desert rose inspired the enormous inward-curving "spaceship-like" structures that appear to have landed from another planet. Nestled within the discs is the historic Sheikh Abdullah bin Jassim Al Thani's Palace, a traditional building at the heart of the Qatari national identity. The exhibition galleries' geometric volumes communicate yet another message—missing are the oval curves of the exterior and decorative references to the historic palace—large, immersive video projections and dioramas provide an experience that is spatial and sensory all at once.[17] The museum complex presents a dynamic set of contextual design semantics that are at once complementary and contradictory.

Exhibition Infrastructure

Temporary exhibitions and event spaces are designed to facilitate the insertion of exhibit structures using hidden infrastructure under the floor, behind the walls, and above the ceiling. Infrastructure provides designers with a platform to manipulate spatial layouts and reinvent the atmosphere using colors, textures, materials, and lighting effects. For the Burning Man festival to succeed in its desert environment, participants must bring in the infrastructure to create its nomadic encampment and support the appropriate atmosphere of shade, sand, and spiritual escapism. These environments are infinitely flexible, the anti-architectural space—the exhibitor's version of the black box.

Rides and attractions provide highly engineered environments because the risk of failure is too high, and they go to great lengths to conceal any evidence of infrastructure that gets in the way of complete guest immersion. Museums tend to be less accommodating. Exhibitions may contend with obstinate architectural features, natural light, slanted walls, floors that cannot be repaired, or a lack of available electrical outlets. Tensions between a building's architects and the team who designs, installs, and services the exhibition experiences inside are common.

Primary case study
Ultimate white cube

National Exhibition and Convention Center (NECC), Shanghai, 2015–present Designers: Ministry of Commerce of China/Shanghai Municipal Government

Design challenge: Space matters

Convention center exhibition halls epitomize the flexibility of infrastructure. The NECC in Shanghai is one of the largest single-block buildings and exhibition complexes in the world, with a total area of 1.47 million m². The main structure draws inspiration from the auspicious four-leaf clover and incorporates a symmetrical design concept, with the Commercial Plaza as the central hub and the surrounding exhibition halls as the four leaves. There are sixteen indoor exhibit halls that total 500,000 m². Each has its own delivery truck loading bay, which can be programmed to host multiple exhibitions and conventions simultaneously. The NECC is one of the landmark buildings in Shanghai.[18]

Design solution: Flexibility matters

The following infrastructural elements are built into exhibition halls to accommodate a range of exhibit booth designs, stands, and VIP lounges, and to add atmosphere.

Flexible floor: Anchor system/points to bolt structures; grid of electrical outlets; HVAC system meets guidelines for relative humidity, temperature, and filtration; changeable floor coverings like carpet tiles to dampen noise and refract sound; few structural columns to facilitate exhibit placement; concealed data points.

Open, clear walls: Wall board surfaces for ease of repair, plywood backer for secure anchoring/fastening of objects; discreet or hidden electrical wall outlets;

fire and safety controls near door; placement of exit signs, security sightlines, cameras, fire strobes, and extinguishers; acoustical materials and coverings to dampen noise and refract sound; option to change wall color.

High, accessible drop ceiling: Unistrut or suitable beams for hanging heavy objects; electrical outlets that can extend downward; fire suppression and sprinkler systems, smoke detectors; lighting track on multiple circuits, installation houselights; HVAC system meets guidelines for relative humidity, temperature, and filtration; acoustical foam, baffles, or banners absorb sound; concealed data/Wi-Fi routers.

***Design impact:* Turnaround matters**

Centers like the NECC are mini cities—the equivalent of an airport operation. The trade show industry has generous budgets, with rapid design and installation time frames, as each company wants to outshine the other. Advances in new materials, technologies, and exhibit construction inform other exhibition sectors. At the end of the day, it is still about coordinating all the specialist skills that need to come together to mount an exhibition, the ever-present audience experience, and placing the product front and center.

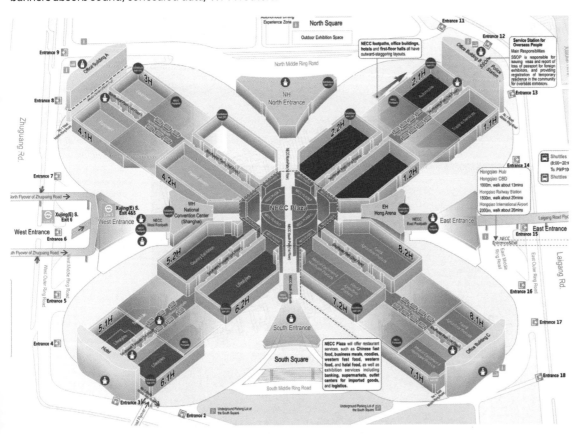

Shanghai's National Exhibition and Convention Center is one of the largest single block buildings and exhibition complexes in the world with 16 indoor exhibit halls.

NECC

Designing Atmosphere: Incorporating Color, Lighting, and the Senses

Avant-garde artists amped up the atmosphere in reaction to the white cube. Marcel Duchamp's installation at the Exposition Internationale du Surréalisme in Paris (1938) suspended simulated bags of coal from the ceiling, released smells from a coffee roaster, and added laughter via a loudspeaker to evoke a synesthetic experience and arouse desires.[19] El Lissitzky's infamous *Abstract Cabinet* (1927) was commissioned by exhibition protagonist Alexander Dorner, who fled his native Hannover during WWII, and later mixed things up at the Rhode Island School of Design Museum. Rather than isolating artworks against a white wall, Dorner plunged them into what he called the "atmosphere room."[20] Piped-in music, colored lights, mechanized display cabinets, and slide projections immersed people in the look and feel of the period. Dorner applied the latest media to amplify context, expand object resonance, and elevate multisensory engagement and audience participation—a key tenet of museum learning theory that expanded in the 1980s.

Open floors, walls, and tall, accessible ceilings provide a flexible infrastructure for exhibitions at the National Exhibition and Convention Center in Shanghai.

Photo: Xinhua / Alamy Stock Photo

Shanghai's National Exhibition and Convention Center exhibition halls are highly adaptable to accommodate rapid design and installation timeframes.

Photo: Xinhua / Alamy Stock Photo

Gesamtkunstwerk (total work or activating all the senses) aptly describes the creation of atmosphere tied to sensory-based, architectural, and theatrical experiences. Today, these are delivered through design choices and techniques that constitute a consistent, cohesive, and unifying language that serves the audience and exhibition content. Color and light are dominant, visceral atmospheric qualities. Texture, sound, temperature, smell, and taste are highly evocative and inclusive design elements that should not be overlooked.

Color

Empirical studies in the early twentieth century advocated against audience fatigue caused in part by the density of objects on display and the variety of colors found in newer museums. With less objects, a greater expanse of the wall surface was revealed, and the color of the walls became more central to the design of the galleries.[21] Exhibition makers have never looked back. Color is vital for engaging audiences, albeit highly subjective. The history, theory, and perception of color are well documented.

Color choice sends semiotic messages and implies cultural associations—white, for instance, is associated with marriage in Western culture, while in many parts of Asia it symbolizes mourning. Designers should be cognizant of cultural appreciation and not appropriation. The curving, interconnected galleries at Ghana's Venice Art Biennale pavilion (2019) were modeled on traditional Gurunsi earth houses and designed by Ghanaian/British architect Sir David Adjaye.[22] The display walls were plastered with earth as a backdrop for images celebrating Ghana's heritage and culture. Appropriately, the color selection is associated with the story, themes, and exhibition content.

Primary applications of exhibition color include *Context*—overall color that adds thematic, historical, or contemporary atmosphere; *Feature*—striking color to emphasize or draw attention to surfaces or areas; *Backdrop*—complementary color to contrast, accentuate, or harmonize with exhibits/objects; and *Control*—color to absorb (black) or reflect (white) light in a film theater or on a projection surface.

Color is not just about pigmentation, value, and hue. The level of finish determines aesthetics and durability. Eggshell and satin are easier to clean than matte finishes, gloss finishes more hard-wearing for hands-on and touch. Textured and faux finishes are used extensively in the themed entertainment industry. Architectural colors and finishes are better specified from paint manufacturers. Other formulas include RAL and Pantone, which can be matched or specified for exhibit components. Selecting color has never been easier, which the abundance of online tools and matching systems—for instance, Adobe Color—indicates.

Color implies cultural associations in galleries at Ghana's Venice Art Biennale pavilion which were modeled on traditional Gurunsi earth houses.

Ghana Freedom Pavilion. Photo by David Levene.

Light

Light is the unsung hero—often out of sight and left to the last—that can make or break the intended atmosphere. Lighting design is a highly specialized field, and this is a cursory overview. Light's primary goals are to create optimum conditions for viewing objects, dramatic effects, and ambiance, and visual comfort for the audience. Glare, and the inability of the human eye to quickly transition from light to dark spaces, means that understanding human perception and the science of light is important for designers.

Exhibition and theater share the same fundamental lighting techniques—bathe a scene in a wash of light or highlight a precise area with a spot of light. Lighting is particularly challenging for attractions and outdoor environments that work with a range of unpredictable light sources depending on the time of day or night. Museum lighting has very finite object conservation requirements, akin to the importance of acoustics in a performance space.

Basic exhibition light sources include two types of lighting: (1) artificial (ceiling-mounted, electrical track-based system with the ability to adjust light intensity, move fixtures, and change lamps), and (2) natural (daylight through windows or skylights that can be diffused, or blocked). Artificial light sources evolved from incandescent to fluorescent, halogen to light-emitting diode (LED). The control, longevity, and energy efficiency of LEDs has transformed exhibition lighting in the same way electricity supplanted the skylights and ceiling alcoves pioneered at Sir John Soane's Dulwich Picture Gallery in 1817.

Primary applications of exhibition lighting include: *Indirect/reflected*—reveals volume and scale; *Diffuse*—light passing through translucent materials, shadowless glow on surfaces; *Color and Texture*—provides drama, immersion by manipulating intensity, color, and texture using theatrical lighting hardware/projection systems (gobos); *Spotlighting*—provides focus and hierarchy by highlighting specific objects or areas; using narrow-beam luminaires/fixtures; *Integral*—lighting that is recessed/built into exhibit cases, components, or architecture; typically uses small-profile lighting hardware (i.e., miniature spotlights or linear strips, or flexible light sources that follow contours).

Available Light Inc. illuminated the U-505 Submarine exhibit at Chicago Museum of Science and Industry using a range of lighting design techniques, 2006.

Museum of Science and Industry, Chicago/Getty Images

Designers Muniz/McNeil introduced textured surfaces as a metaphor for domesticity in *Home Lands: How Women Made the West*.

Courtesy of Autry Museum of the American West

Texture/Materials

Architectural embellishment and the textures/materials that create exhibits are illustrated throughout this book. Choosing the appropriate material has ramifications for object conservation, safety, and the longevity of exhibition components and interactives (see chapter 8).

Successful designers understand materials, use them efficiently, and adapt them in surprising, inventive ways. Materiality and atmosphere are synergetic. A complementary palette of material choices makes the most striking impression. *Home Lands: How Women Made the West* (2008), at the Autry National Center in Los Angeles, wove a story of women, environmental history, and the American West through compelling object experiences. The exhibition's engaging material narrative used cornhusks, sackcloth, and indigo swatches to cover walls; as well as unfinished wood, metals, and rammed earth for display furniture—the design embraced texture as a metaphor for the environment and the domesticity of home.

Sound/Voice

Exhibitions are no longer quiet, contemplative environments. Buffering sound spill is still an important spatial consideration, but thanks to advances in sound delivery, mitigation, and performance, the acoustical experience of receiving, understanding, and responding to audio content (voice, music, noise) is a valuable component of atmosphere. Auditory volume can be controlled by listening devices or by sensors that ramp levels up and down depending on the ambient noise.

Primary applications of sound delivery include *Soundscape*—social, room-based experiences using multi-speaker surround-sound; *Ambient*—shared, exhibit-based experiences using directed, localized speakers; *Personal*—individual, exhibit-based experiences using listening devices, headphones, and wands.

Exhibitions also facilitate participatory forms of sound immersion and invite people to record their own stories or respond to audio prompts. Planet Word in Washington, D.C. (2020), is a voice-activated museum of language where audiences use their voices to interact and engage with exhibits while hearing from other people who share what language means to them.

Temperature/Humidity

The Antarctica climatic biosphere at Edinburgh's Dynamic Earth (1999) captures people's frozen handprints in a large block of ice. Atmospheric shifts in air temperature and humidity are highly sensorial because people's skin register the interpretive emotion. International object conservation

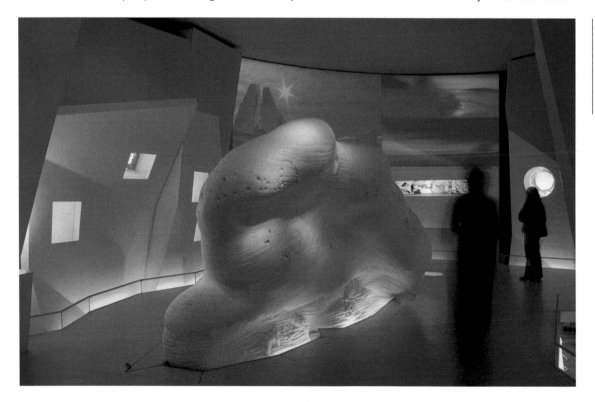

standards require stable display environments. These prevent exhibitions from drastically turning the dial. When possible, atmospheric transitions from hot and cold, to dry and muggy, are exceptionally evocative. They reinforce climatic and geographic experiences at attractions, natural history museums, gardens, zoos, and aquaria.

Smell/Taste

According to scent historian Caro Verbeek, each day people breathe about twenty-two thousand times, and all that time we smell. Strong scientific evidence links smell to memory. Verbeek is part of a growing movement in museums to associate smell with art and heritage. She re-creates the scents of the past and introduces them to groups, including blind and nearsighted people, during tours at the Rijksmuseum in Amsterdam.[23] Science centers, theme parks, and festivals manipulate people's olfaction functions with odors that are both fabulous and foul, across a range of hands-on exhibits and themed rides.

Closely related to the lasting resonance of smell is taste. York's Chocolate Story (2012) introduces audiences to the mouthwatering history of chocolate, its growth, and its manufacture. Audiences are guided through a multisensory experience that is, thankfully, punctuated with opportunities to sample the wares—from the cacao nibs, which are yuck, to the fondant-filled candies, which are yummy—it is like Willy Wonka's Chocolate Factory.

Atmospheres at attractions like York's Chocolate Story are diametrically opposed to the white cube. One seeks to hide any context; the other accentuates it though all the senses. Parallels can be drawn with zoos and aquaria, where, like a painting, the context should not override the animal experience—except those tigers, toucans, and tapirs are not an obedient medium to work with.

Audiences smell and more importantly sample the wares at York's Chocolate Story designed by MET Studio.

York's Chocolate Story

Primary case study
Complete atmosphere

**Bioclimatic Zones, San Diego Zoo, Balboa Park, CA, 1985–present
Designers: Louis John Gill (original cages and animal grottos); Jones & Jones (bioclimatic zones)**

Design challenge: Cageless exhibits
Zoos are increasingly immersive experiences for both humans and animals. More than four million people visited the San Diego Zoo in 2018.[24] One of the largest and most progressive zoos in the world, the San Diego Zoo pioneered cageless, open-air habitats, where wildlife care specialists look after more than 12,000 animals and 650 species.

Design solution: Third-generation enclosures
Bioclimatic exhibit design closely replicates nature and shows how wildlife and plants cohabit in their native habitats. These immersive "third-generation" habitats consider the needs of wildlife—both physical and psychological—removing cages (first generation) and moats (second generation)—to provide people with a clearer picture of interspecies relationships.[25]

Within the Zoo's current one hundred acres, bioclimate zones ranging from desert to lush tropical areas are dotted with numerous habitats and connected via meandering paths that conform to the site's dramatic and complex topography. Approximately seven hundred thousand plants located throughout the grounds form a dense, well-shaded botanical garden that is integrated into the guest experience and provides food for many of the Zoo's herbivores.[26] The Lost Forest is one of the most ambitious bioclimates, demonstrating how these zones serve the Zoo's education purposes and contextualizing the plants and animals for Zoo audiences. Interpretive experiences and signage convey a consistent, solution-oriented conservation message of how San Diego Zoo Wildlife Alliance works with conservation allies to save wildlife and how guests can help.

Design impact: Totally inclusive
Bioclimatic habitats facilitate social experiences between wildlife and guests. They activate an entire sensorial range to make wildlife encounters accessible and inclusive. Zoo guests traverse water features, lush aviaries, a myriad of exotic landscape textures, dappled light through the tree canopy, animal sounds and smells, and shifts in temperature and humidity—the ultimate contextual and atmospheric experience.

Guests at San Diego Zoo traverse a myriad of exotic landscape textures, the ultimate atmospheric experience.

San Diego Zoo Wildlife Alliance

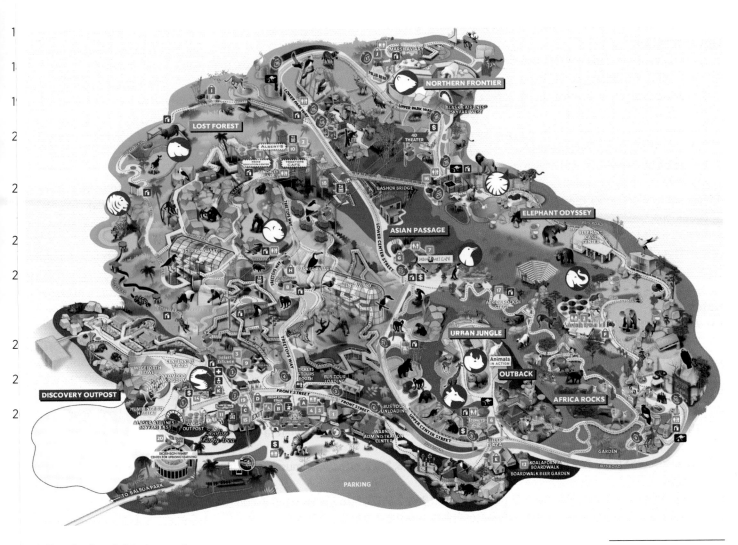

Dialing in the right atmosphere

The white cube's contentious association with neocolonialism and elitism brings into question its future legitimacy and relevance. There is no solid evidence to suggest an exhibition atmosphere that responds to the context and cultural origins of the material presented, detracts from the objects on display—in fact, judging by the success and inclusivity of themed entertainment environments, it is quite the opposite, and it is about dialing in the right measure. Perhaps the solution lies with the viewer? Advances in LED technology mean entire wall colors can change on demand, offering one way to truly put atmosphere in the hands of the audience.

Bioclimatic habitat design at the San Diego Zoo closely replicates nature and how animals and plants cohabit in their native habitats.

San Diego Zoo Wildlife Alliance

Designer's Toolbox: **Staging**

Placing exhibits and arranging display environments is driven by narratives, objects, and themes. Designers consider these relationships and respond with engaging and appropriate exhibition layouts (staging), and organizational structures for the placement of specific elements (composition). Unlock the designer's toolbox and release the principles of balance, rhythm, contrast, emphasis, and unity.

Visualization: Evan Yang is an exhibition designer at Gallagher & Associates.
He is based between Washington D.C., U.S.A., and Shanghai, China

Hanging
Salon
Style

BALANCE   CONTRAST   UNITY   RHYTHM   EMPHASIS

CHAPTER 7

Hanging Salon-Style

Composition and staging in the exhibition space should be as varied as the viewers who see them.

Key message: Design advocates for the visual variety and arrangement of the exhibition elements.

Key word: staging

People go to great lengths to stage their personal space. From arranging furniture in living areas, to selecting family photographs to display on a desk at work, they rely—albeit unwittingly—on the same compositional instincts that professionals use to stage exhibition and experience environments. Depending on the story or message to be conveyed, the arrangement of items, props, and elements in exhibitions oscillate from dramatic floor-to-ceiling arrays, to discreet, solitary objects arranged in a single row.

This chapter makes visible the *salon-style*, one of the most common and understated exhibition design tropes. The style originates from a dense method of hanging paintings popular in the eighteenth century. Subsequent stylistic versions diversified object content, toyed with spatial perception, and activated people's eye movements using complex compositional design theory. This popular staging technique continues unabated, with striking results in today's exhibition and experience environments.

Field of Vision: Activating the Exhibition Plane

Herbert Bayer described the emerging language of exhibition design as the apex of all media and powers of communication and of collective efforts and effects.[1] Bayer is one of the founding proponents of exhibition design. He theorized a fledgling discipline that straddled two primary areas of his practice—the design of human spaces, for which Bayer is also celebrated through his large environmental projects, and visual communication, the area in which he excelled in his graphic design work.[2]

Total application

Bayer's *Fundamentals of Exhibition Design*, first published in 1937, introduced extended vision techniques that challenged compositional conventions, particularly the balanced proportions and symmetry of the prevailing Beaux Arts style.[3] His theories are cited by those researching, teaching, and critiquing exhibition design, and employed extensively by contemporary exhibition design practitioners. Bayer categorized *exhibition design* as the "total application" of graphics and architectural structure, with psychology and concepts of light, color, motion, and sound.[4] He honed his methodology through collaborations with notable colleagues from the Bauhaus school in Germany, and by observing the work of Russian designer El Lissitzky, whose towering super-graphic structures for the *Pressa* exhibition in Cologne (1928) inspired modern exhibition design practice.[5] It is probable that László Moholy-Nagy used Bayer's theories to formulate the exhibition design curriculum at the *New Bauhaus* in Chicago (1937). Bayer revisited his "fundamentals" in *Erberto Carboni: Exhibitions and Displays* (1955), a book about the work of the gifted and prolific Italian exhibition designer, as well as *The Curator* journal in 1961.

Herbert Bayer's original 180-degree field of vision diagram from the 1929–1930 Deutscher Werkbund exhibition catalogue.

Herbert Bayer © 2022 Artists Rights Society (ARS), New York / VG Bild-Kunst, Bonn. Digital Image © The Museum of Modern Art/Licensed by SCALA / Art Resource, NY.

Diagram of field of vision

Spatial perception, extended vision, and compositional asymmetry epitomized Bayer's signature exhibition design style. Central to this philosophy was the perspective of people and their movement through space. Unlike other mediums of communication, such as books and film, he argued, it is the object that remains fixed while the individual is in motion.[6] The spatial organization of elements should guide the succession of eye movements beyond the horizontal plane and activate the viability of the vertical axis.

180 and 360 degrees

Bayer crafted two field-of-vision diagrams. The first was printed in the 1929–1930 Deutscher Werkbund exhibition catalogue. It depicts a standing, scale person, with an oversized eye as their head, viewing multiple elevated and angled rectangles that span 180 degrees. Each eye movement is represented by a dashed line with an arrowhead, and demonstrates that moving the eye, the head, or the body extends the field of vision, and increases with greater distance between the eye and the object.[7]

The second diagram, produced in 1935, develops the principle further. This version affords the person a 360-degree field of vision by elevating them on a platform. The rectangular planes circle them like the numbers on a clock and activate every available surface. Bayer's later installations for the Building Worker's Union, Berlin (1931), and the Bauhaus Exhibition at the Museum of Modern Art, New York (1938), included elevated walkways and bridge-like structures to vary the audience's vantage point and guide their intellectual curiosity.

Fundamentals of Exhibition Design indicates Bayer's desire to share his theories beyond an expert audience. The field-of-vision diagram in the Werkbund catalogue marks an intentional gesture to educate members of the public about the exhibition's design.[8]

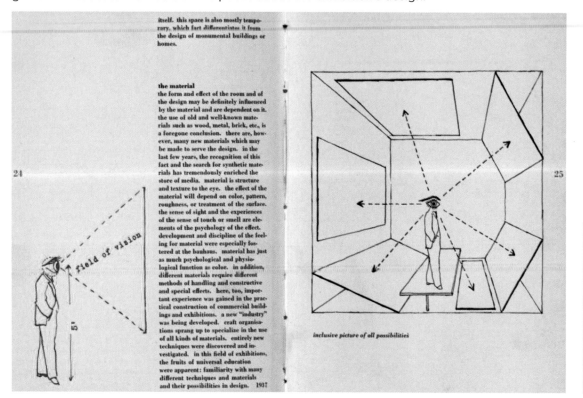

itself. this space is also mostly temporary, which fact differentiates it from the design of monumental buildings or homes.

the material
the form and effect of the room and of the design may be definitely influenced by the material and are dependent on it. the use of old and well-known materials such as wood, metal, brick, etc., is a foregone conclusion. there are, however, many new materials which may be made to serve the design. in the last few years, the recognition of this fact and the search for synthetic materials has tremendously enriched the store of media. material is structure and texture to the eye. the effect of the material will depend on color, pattern, roughness, or treatment of the surface. the sense of sight and the experiences of the sense of touch or smell are elements of the psychology of the effect. development and discipline of the feeling for material were especially fostered at the bauhaus. material has just as much psychological and physiological function as color. in addition, different materials require different methods of handling and constructive and special effects. here, too, important experience was gained in the practical construction of commercial buildings and exhibitions. a new "industry" was being developed. craft organisations sprang up to specialize in the use of all kinds of materials. entirely new techniques were discovered and investigated. in this field of exhibitions, the fruits of universal education were apparent: familiarity with many different techniques and materials and their possibilities in design. 1937

24

25

field of vision

5'

inclusive picture of all possibilities

The Fundamentals of Exhibition Design (1937) developed Herbert Bayer's principle further to a 360-degree field of vision and an elevated platform.

Herbert Bayer © 2022 Artists Rights Society (ARS), New York / VG Bild-Kunst, Bonn. Rare Book Division, The New York Public Library. "Fundamentals of Exhibition Design" New York Public Library Digital Collections. Accessed June 12, 2022. https://digitalcollections.nypl.org/items/90f2757f-0c82-18e9-e040-e00a18064bc0

Beyond the horizontal plane

Generations of temples, churches, and mosques are adorned from head to toe in ornamentation and iconography. Vertical motifs spiritually elevate people's plane of vision upward into their vast spatial volumes. These decorative architectural traditions fell out of favor with modernism in the early twentieth century. Avant-garde artists associated with Surrealism and Dadaism reacted to the prevailing style of harmonious composition. Psychologists identified theories of visual perception celebrating irregularity and compositional imbalance (Gestalt principles). Frederick Kiesler's science of relationships, or "Correalism," advocated for the continual interaction between people, art, and environments.[9] His installation of paintings on the curved walls of Peggy Guggenheim's *Art of This Century* gallery (New York, 1942) removed the artwork's frames and pedestals. He designed arms and brackets to cantilever works from the wall, tilting paintings to their preferred viewing angles. Mary Anne Staniszewski's book *The Power of Display* captures in detail this nascent period in the history of exhibition design.[10]

Italian architect and museum designer Carlo Scarpa was an expert in materials, asymmetrical composition, and object placement. He influenced a generation of postwar exhibition creatives with his imaginative elegance.[11] Scarpa worked intermittently between 1957 and 1975 on the Castelvecchio Museum in Verona. The project is celebrated for its skillful and holistic approach and integrates sculpture within a building that has a complex architectural history. Described as his most extraordinary compositional achievement, Scarpa's display of the equestrian statue of Cangrande is perched precariously on an elevated outcrop of cast concrete, and visible from multiple vantage points, it is one of the most remarkable settings for a single work of art ever made.[12]

The Sultan Ahmed Mosque (1616) uses vertical motifs to elevate people's plane of vision into its upper spatial volumes.

Frederick Kiesler's design for Peggy Guggenheim's _Art of This Century_ gallery, New York (1942).

Artists: Max Ernst, "Various Works" © 2022 Artists Rights Society (ARS), New York / ADAGP, Paris. Paul Delvaux, _The Break of Day_, 1937 © 2022 Foundation Paul Delvaux, Sint-Idesbald – ARS/SABAM Belgium. Hans Arp, _Head and Shell_, c. 1933 © 2022 Artists Rights Society (ARS), New York / VG Bild-Kunst, Bonn. Joan Miró, _Dutch Interior II_, 1928 © Successió Miró / Artists Rights Society (ARS), New York /ADAGP, Paris 2022. Victor Brauner, _Fascination_, 1939 © 2022 Artists Rights Society (ARS), New York / ADAGP, Paris. Rene Magritte, _The Voice of the Air_, 1931 © 2022 C. Herscovici / Artists Rights Society (ARS), New York. Leonor Fini, _The Shepherdess of the Sphinxes_, 1941 © 2022 Artists Rights Society (ARS), New York / ADAGP, Paris. Joan Miró, _Seated Woman II_, 1939 © Successió Miró / Artists Rights Society (ARS), New York /ADAGP, Paris 2022. Henry Moore, _Reclining Figure_, 1939. Image © 2022 Austrian Frederick and Lillian Kiesler Private Foundation, Vienna.

Carlo Scarpa's placement of the statue of Cangrande at the Museo di Castelvecchio in Verona is described as his most extraordinary compositional achievement.

Photo: Arcaid Images / Alamy Stock Photo

Access and inclusive design

Bayer's field-of-vision method is ubiquitous. The Lascaux International Center for Cave Art in Montignac in France (2018) relies on facsimiles (for preservation reasons) of the famous prehistoric cave paintings, enhanced by digital learning experiences. Bayer's technique is used to display changing images that unfold around people in a cavernous chamber on the walls and ceiling.

Lascaux's example offers a cautionary tale. Staging objects and exhibit elements high on walls and ceilings is acceptable if the content, or objects—in this case, images—do not need to be studied in detail. Asking people to excessively crane their necks defies inclusive design. Objects and readable exhibit content placed on a wall within a range of 42–68 inches (or 56–60 inches to center) from the floor, at an average viewing distance of 72 inches, is recommended by the Smithsonian Guidelines for Accessible Exhibition Design.

Herbert Bayer's field of vision method was effectively employed by designers Casson Mann at the Lascaux International Center for Cave Art.

Photo: Hemis / Alamy Stock Photo

Primary case study
Extended vision

Room 5, Section Allemande: Deutscher Werkbund, Exposition de la Société des Artistes Décorateurs, Paris, May 14–July 13, 1930
Designers: Herbert Bayer, Walter Gropius, Marcel Breuer, and László Moholy-Nagy

Design challenge: Machine Age prowess

The Werkbund exhibition was an opportunity to demonstrate German design efficiency and Machine Age prowess in Paris the bastion of good taste. Walter Gropius and the other co-organizers, including Herbert Bayer, had left the Bauhaus school two years earlier. The exhibition embodied distinctive Bauhaus themes in the guise of a community center. While a group "Bauhausler" effort, Gropius and Marcel Breuer took responsibility for designing a gymnasium and pool, bar, and dance floor, reading room, and furnished apartment. László Moholy-Nagy presented a photography exhibition and a display of light fixtures. The last two rooms of the Section Allemande included mass-produced household objects, fabrics, kitchenware, architecture, and furniture, and it fell to Herbert Bayer to resolve.

Design solution: Magically bodyless

Without the architectural backdrop and singular theme of the other spaces, Bayer was tasked with creating an appropriate atmosphere for a section on utilitarian German craft and industry. The architecture and furniture room integrated design and industrial production and included Gropius's scale model for the Bauhaus Dessau building. For the first time, Bayer tested his field-of-vision display principle for an audience.

Rising floor to ceiling, angled architectural photographs float off the wall at one end of the room and directly correlate to Bayer's diagram. The large, frameless images are suspended from indiscernible wires. They appear magically bodyless, as if a gust of wind had picked them up and tossed them toward the wall, only to freeze them in mid-action. Architectural models placed on thin tubular steel pedestals protrude outward and continue the line of vision across the floor. Columns of chairs and small tables climb to the ceiling on the other side of the room. Invisibly attached to the wall surface, they defy gravity. The ephemeral installation emphasized the furniture's lightweight modernity—directing the audience to consider household items as objects of elegance and beauty in the growing age of the machine.

Design impact: Timeless technique

Bayer's dynamic staging encouraged people to fully participate. Making their eyeballs work harder shifted the emphasis from the display to the viewer.[13] Bayer was an influential exhibition designer who integrated field-of-vision techniques throughout his career (see *Airways to Peace* in chapter 9). The Eames Office's multiplicity of stacked screens in the *Information Machine* at the 1964/1965 New York World's Fair is another good example (see chapter 10). *David Adjaye: Making Memory* at London's Design Museum (2019) featured a wall of inspirational architectural landmarks linked to ongoing projects by the architect. The frameless photographs and angled composition directly pay homage to Bayer's 1930 field-of-vision diagram.

Rising floor to ceiling, angled photographs at Paris' Deutscher Werkbund exhibition float off the wall and correlate to Herbert Bayer's field of vision diagrams.

Hang to the Line: Staging, Composition, and the Salon-Style

Consider for a moment the multileveled shopping mall. Stores on the lower level are visited more than those on the top levels because of their proximity to the main entrance, and they are the first to catch an eager shopper's eye. Each storefront is positioned hierarchically akin to an object

The angled composition of photographs in *David Adjaye: Making Memory* at London's Design Museum is an homage to Herbert Bayer's field of vision diagrams.

Photo by Ed Reeve

The demand to display work at London's Royal Academy in 1787 resulted in a stunning hierarchical composition dubbed the "salon-style" hang.

British Museum/Library

in an exhibition. While Bayer's diagrams encouraged an extended plane of vision, placement did matter, and the most essential elements were at eye level, within an average person's 60-degree cone of vision, and not at the periphery.

Salon-style

Nefarious motives were at play behind the frenetic scenes of establishment artists installing their paintings in fashionable eighteenth-century galleries. A hidden agenda called "on the line" referred to the eight-foot-high wall cornice that aligned with the top of the picture frame. Below this line was considered the primo viewing spot, and a point of distinction for artists exhibiting

Salon-style describes the massing of multiple objects or elements like this imposing wall of cars created by designers Event for the Riverside Museum in Glasgow.

Photo: David Ridley / Alamy Stock Photo

Using the principles of salon-style a breathtaking display of diversity dances in every direction at the American Museum of Natural History.

Photo: American Museum of Natural History Library, AN1163059 at London's Royal Academy salons.[14] The demand to display work resulted in paintings above the line skied cheek-by-jowl until they were halted by the ceiling molding—and a stunning hierarchical composition ensued, dubbed the "salon-style" hang. This term is used today to describe the massing of multiple objects or elements, and compelling riffs on the salon-style proliferate in contemporary exhibition design. The imposing wall of cars at the Riverside Museum in Glasgow (2011) is irrefutable evidence that the style also extends to weighty, non-flat objects.

Less is more

Hanging pictures using the salon-style dates to the Académie des Beaux-Arts Paris Salon in the mid-eighteenth century, and the method was standard in Western museums and galleries until the late-1900s. Once audiences voiced their indignation at having to crane their necks and crouch awkwardly, the National Gallery of Art in London, under the directorship of Charles Eastlake, took steps to remedy this criticism with a "less is more" approach, and hang fewer pictures, with the majority at eye level.[15] Benjamin Ives Gilman's pioneering 1918 study into museum fatigue at the Boston Museum of Fine Arts led to object display improvements, where people could see things without bending over.[16] Alexander Dorner's reinstallation of Gallery 44 at Hannover's Landesmuseum in the late 1920s was one of the first to reject the salon-style legacy and introduce a spare aesthetic, staging pictures in single, neat, horizontal rows.[17]

Today's professional design practitioners compose exhibitions that are resplendent in staging effects. Derivative of the salon-style, tightly packed objects interpret stories that touch on both the wonder and the fragility of life and human existence.

Primary case study

Compelling object staging using the principles of salon-style

Tower of Faces, **United States Holocaust Memorial Museum, Washington, D.C., 1993–present;** *Habitat Wall*, **American Museum of Natural History, New York, 1998–present**
Principal Designer: Ralph Appelbaum Associates

Design challenge: Difficult content

Previous chapters introduced exhibition design consultancy Ralph Appelbaum Associates (RAA). This case study compares critically acclaimed, signature work for two specific exhibits, which cemented RAA's storytelling reputation and design style. Together, they illustrate the impact of exhibition composition and object staging.

The United States Holocaust Memorial Museum's permanent exhibition was one of RAA's first major projects and is arguably their most famous. The museum team leaned fully into difficult content to create an emotional encounter about modern genocide, its methods, and its effects. The audience experience is theatrically organized into three chronological "acts" on three floors. Large-scale objects and architectural structures provide context and convey the magnitude of the Holocaust.[18]

The American Museum of Natural History combines permanent and changing exhibition areas and the Rose Center for Earth and Space. The Hall of Biodiversity, the museum's first "issues" gallery, conveys the role humans play in Earth's massive loss of biodiversity. Specimens from the museum's collection introduce audiences to the twenty-eight major groups of life, their beauty, and the benefits humans derive from them.[19] The installation references natural history displays like the Gallery of Paleontology and Comparative Anatomy in Paris (1898), where over one thousand animal skeletons are packed literally floor to ceiling and wall to wall, occupying every architectural nook of this classic nineteenth-century gallery.

Grand gestures are made from the massing of smaller parts and the impact of the overall narrative supersedes individual elements at the _Tower of Faces_ (the Yaffa Eliach Shtetl Collection).

United States Holocaust Memorial Museum, Photo by Max Reid

Design solution: Multiplicity

Crossing the elevated walkway in the *Tower of Faces* reverberates with emotional resonance—the multiplicity of over one thousand tightly packed, uncropped, and frameless photographic reproductions (designed with Dr. Yaffa Eliach) envelop audiences and continue upward to culminate in a translucent lightwell. The images are residents from Eisiskes, a small settlement in Eastern Europe where a Nazi-led massacre in 1941 killed the entire Jewish population.[20] The composition resembles a family album, each photograph floating off the wall surface as if mounted to a page suspended in a tower of spatial infinity.

Audiences standing in front of the Natural History Museum's sixty-foot-long *Habitat Wall* survey the Earth's nine major biodiversity habitats and learn about ecological threats through interpretive media. From shell dwellers to shark swimmers, the diversity of fauna is breathtaking as it dances in every direction and flies off the wall toward the viewer.

Design impact: Grand gestures

Both installations are grand gestures made from the massing of smaller parts—like the salon-style hang—the impact of the overall narrative supersedes the individual elements. This method works effectively when objects share characteristics and connect by theme, type, size, or shape. A concentrated massing of elements often precludes individual object labels. Hence the interpretative rail along the front of the *Habitat Wall* and the availability of a smartphone AR application to reveal captions for the photographs in the *Tower of Faces*.

Even the scale model for the design of the *Tower of Faces* reverberates with emotional resonance as the tragic multiplicity of photographs envelope audiences.

United States Holocaust Memorial Museum, Photo by Arnold Kramer

Staging and Compositional Theory: Proportion to Proximity, Scale to Symmetry

There are no rules to design, only guidelines, or so the adage goes. Theories, techniques, and frameworks do exist to make understanding design composition easier. These are the material of long-standing foundation courses across the traditional design disciplines. However, exhibition design's multidisciplinarity makes their comprehension harder because the laws of physics, rules of architectural proportion, and perceptual theories of visual communication are all at play. The following methods may seem intuitive to the well-trained eye, but they are associated with tried-and-tested practice and theoretical reasoning.

Grids to Gestalt

Grids establish a set of guidelines for how elements should be positioned within a spatial layout. They provide the rhythm for a design and define the reoccurring patterns. Grids set expectations, define the rules, and streamline decision-making to save time during an exhibition installation. The *Habitat Wall* at the American Museum of Natural History uses a visible grid structure that becomes part of the design voice, to organize and categorize the plethora of biodiversity and related interpretative materials. A grid makes content accessible and helps people understand where to find the next piece of information within the exhibit layout. Think of a grid as providing the road map along which the audience travels.[21]

Golden Ratio is a mathematical ratio used to create harmonious and structured compositions. Closely related to the Fibonacci Sequence, commonly found in nature, it describes the perfectly symmetrical relationship between two proportions.[22] Equal to approximately a 1:1.5 ratio, the formula translates to the Rule of Thirds applied in photographic and graphic design composition.[23] Meier Partners designed the museum buildings at the Getty Center in Los Angeles using a 30-inch square module—highly visible in the iconic travertine stone cladding. This module guided the gallery proportions and informed the dimensions of furniture, exhibits, and graphics, using exponential multiples or fractions of this number. For example, the standard pedestal deck measured 15 inches square and brochures 7.5 inches in height.

Mauk Design's tile exhibit for the American Institute of Architects and Italian Trade Commission (2007) is a classic example of symmetrical balance.

Design, Mitchell Mauk, Mauk Design; Client: Ceramic Tiles of Italy; Photography: Andy Caulfield Photography

Gestalt means "unified whole." Gestalt principles refer to the way in which people, when looking at a group of objects, see the whole before the individual parts. Many of the previous salon-style examples are exemplary of this theory. Applying the six Gestalt principles—similarity, continuation, closure, proximity, figure/ground, symmetry/order—can make the staging of exhibition elements feel connected, coherent, and complete.[24]

Thinc Design's beautifully staged *Infinite Variety: Three Centuries of Red and White Quilts* (2011) organized by the American Folk Art Museum, sends 600 objects spiraling skyward in rhythmic repetition and motion.

Photography: Gavin Ashworth, Tom Henne; Design: Thinc Design

Designer Barbara Stauffacher Solomon's signature supergraphics emphasize the entrance to *The Sea Ranch* (2018) at the San Francisco Museum of Modern Art.

San Francisco Museum of Modern Art, photo by Matthew Millman

Compositional theory and principles

In the context of this chapter, two interchangeable terms are used to describe the arrangement of exhibition spaces. *Composition* refers to the methods used to place specific elements into their spatial relationships (paintings on a wall). *Staging* denotes the overall method/rationale for organizing larger elements in a space (exhibit stands at a trade show). Regardless of the scale or content, exhibitions rely on balance, rhythm, contrast, emphasis, and unity to add visual variety, activate attention, and engage audiences.[25]

Balance occurs when all the design elements are equally distributed throughout the design. Symmetrical elements are arranged equally on both sides of a composition to suggest stability, affinity, and peacefulness (formal balance). Asymmetrical elements create a deliberate imbalance to suggest motion, activity, and tension (informal balance).

Rhythm is a pattern created by repeating elements next to each another by a standard or uniform distance. Rhythm denotes movement in the way that elements direct our gaze to other elements. The term *sequence* is used to refer to the viewing order and determines the flow between elements.

Contrast stresses the differences in size, shape, color, and texture between the elements to enhance visual perception. Contrast draws and directs the viewer's attention to specific areas or elements.

Emphasis indicates the most important—the focal point of a design—the element that stands out and gets noticed first. Emphasis can be created by taking an element and making it bigger, bolder, or brighter, setting it in a contrasting color, or surrounding it with empty space.

Unity is reached when all elements look like they belong together. The concept of unity describes the relationship between the individual parts and the whole of a composition. It investigates the aspects of a given design that are necessary to tie the composition together, and it stems from Gestalt theories of visual perception.

Lastly, never underestimate the importance of using *negative space* in exhibition design. The negative space is as important as the positive space of the object.[26]

A feeling of unity—when all the elements come together—in *El círculo caminaba tranquilo* at the Museo de Arte Moderno de Buenos Aires.

Artists: Otto Dix. Big City (Draft for a Big City Triptych), 1926 © 2022 Artists Rights Society (ARS), New York / VG Bild-Kunst, Bonn. Works by Jörg Immendorff, Jakub Julian Ziolkowski, Linda Matalon, Eva Hesse. Courtesy of the Museum of Modern Art of Buenos Aires, Argentina. Photo: Josefina Tommasi.

Salon-style meets white cube-version 2.0

El círculo caminaba tranquilo (The Circle
Walked Casually), Museo de Arte Moderno
de Buenos Aires, September 10, 2014–
January 18, 2015
Principal Designers: Daniela Thomas and
Felipe Tassara

Design challenge: **Space and line**

Argentine curator Victoria Noorthoorn collaborated
with Brazilian stage designer Daniela Thomas, and
the architect Felipe Tassara, to create an exhibition
of objects from the Deutsche Bank's collection at
the Museo de Arte Moderno de Buenos Aires. Over
180 artist works on paper were chosen to tell a story
that traveled along an imaginary horizontal path. A
metaphor for experiencing the two main qualities
was found in the act of drawing, space, and line.[27]

Design solution: **Virtual reality salon-style hang**

El círculo caminaba tranquilo is a magical experience—a contemporary mashup of infinity room,
white cube, and salon-style hang. Rounded and
non-perceptible, the room's edges dissolve where
the walls meet the floor. Gleaming overhead light
reflects off the white, glossy floor and walls to illuminate the drawings and bleach out the gallery
perimeter. The illusion removes the architectural
context, and the framed objects are suspended
midair, in a virtual salon-style hang. The drawings

rhythmically follow an eye-level sightline, which
dances through the space. People gingerly navigate between the back and the front of the framed
drawings—a wonderful way to encounter objects
usually anchored firmly to the wall.

Design impact: **Unanimous unity**

The exhibition achieves symmetrical balance using asymmetrical arrangements. The drawings are
installed in a deluge of twisting patterns, and their
compositional rhythm encourages people to weave
through the space. Bold, colored objects are strategically positioned on sightlines to pull people
through the composition, allowing emphasis to take
the stage. Unanimous unity is at play—audiences
are magnetized when they enter the exhibition, and
once they digest the whole, they are attracted to
the individual drawings. The drawings then release
their own compositional intensity. The surrounding
negative space is as important as the positive space
of the object.

Compositional conclusion

El círculo caminaba tranquilo moves Herbert Bayer's field of vision from the vertical to the horizontal plane in what is an eye-catching and exquisite exhibition experience. Bayer's 1929 diagram
of extended vision established the beginnings of a theoretical framework for designing experiences. It has been cited in every contemporary book on exhibition design. There is a direct correla-
tion between Bayer's diagrams, the salon-style, and the signature object wall designs employed
by Ralph Appelbaum Associates and many other designers. Upcoming chapters will reveal why
Bayer's "total application" advanced the display of exhibition information in the same way nineteenth-century cycloramas fueled total immersion in theme parks and attractions.

Tips and Tricks

Compositional theory is understanding spatial relationships. The following design techniques keep audiences engaged and focused:

1. Typical object hang height is 56–60 inches to its center from the floor. Perhaps lower to meet the needs of the audience—accessible for children and people using wheelchairs.
2. Keep corridors, spaces, and widths between floor elements accessible—greater than 60 inches.
3. Activate the full plane of vision but keep the vital information/elements within a person's average cone of vision and eye level.
4. Consciously use the full suite of compositional basics to disrupt and engage audiences, as simple as two frames double-hung rather than all in a row.
5. Consider the object's original context—a fresco fragment on a wall, floor tile on the ground, airplane hanging from the ceiling.
6. Create tension and variety between elements— stage big against small, densely packed with sparsely spaced.
7. Mass objects of the same type for spectacle—a wall of masks, a ceiling of taxidermy seabirds, a floor of shoes.
8. Establish staging grids to place objects, bring unity, and save decision-making time.
9. Access the tools of atmosphere to add emphasis and make elements stand out or recede.
10. Rather than the spice of life, *variety* adds compositional pep for fatigued audiences.

Notes

1. Herbert Bayer, "Aspects of Design of Exhibitions and Museums," *Curator: The Museum Journal* 4, no. 3 (1961): 258, https://doi.org/10.1111/j.2151-6952.1961.tb01561.x.
2. Gwen Finkel Chanzit and Daniel Libeskind, *From Bauhaus to Aspen: Herbert Bayer and Modernist Design in America* (Boulder [Colo.]: Johnson Books, 2005), 111.
3. "Fundamentals of Exhibition Design," Rare Book Division, *The New York Public Library Digital Collections*, 1940-01 1939, https://digitalcollections.nypl.org/items/90f27111-9714-4fc1-e040-e00a18064ba4.
4. Bayer, "Aspects of Design of Exhibitions and Museums," 258.
5. Arthur A. Cohen, *Herbert Bayer: The Complete Work* (Cambridge, Mass.: MIT Press, 1984), 283.
6. "Fundamentals of Exhibition Design."
7. "Fundamentals of Exhibition Design."
8. Chanzit and Libeskind, *From Bauhaus to Aspen*, 142.
9. Thyr Björnson, "Frederick Kiesler's Correalism in Contemporary Art | Designblog," accessed July 19, 2021, https://designblog.rietveldacademie.nl/?p=64207.
10. Mary Anne Staniszewski, *The Power of Display: A History of Exhibition Installations at the Museum of Modern Art* (Cambridge, Mass.: The MIT Press, 2001).
11. John Harris, *Alan Irvine: Architect Designer: Exhibitions, Museums, Interiors* (London: Royal Institute of British Architects Heinz Gallery, 1989). Foreword citing Scarpa's influence on Alan Irvine.
12. Richard Murphy et al., *Carlo Scarpa and Castelvecchio Revisited* (Edinburgh, UK: Breakfast Mission Publishing, 2017), Introduction.
13. Cohen, *Herbert Bayer*, 289.
14. K.W. Luckhurst, *The Story of Exhibitions* (London and New York: The Studio Publications, 1951), 18.
15. Niklas Maak Demand Charlotte Klonk and Thomas, "The White Cube and beyond: Museum Display— Tate Etc," Tate, accessed July 1, 2021, https://www.tate.org.uk/tate-etc/issue-21-spring-2011/white-cube-and-beyond.
16. "Benjamin Ives Gilman," in *Wikipedia*, June 8, 2021, https://en.wikipedia.org/w/index.php?title=Benjamin_Ives_Gilman&oldid=1027589053.
17. Staniszewski, *The Power of Display*, 16.
18. "Ralph Appelbaum Associates," accessed July 21, 2021, http://www.raany.com/commission/united-states-holocaust-memorial-museum.

19. "Ralph Appelbaum Associates," accessed July 21, 2021, http://www.raany.com/commission/hall-biodiversity/.
20. "*The Tower of Faces* (the Yaffa Eliach Shtetl Collection) in the Permanent Exhibition at the United States Holocaust Memorial Museum—Collections Search—United States Holocaust Memorial Museum," accessed February 27, 2022, https://collections.ushmm.org/search/catalog/pa1116002.
21. Sam Hampton-Smith, "The Designer's Guide to Grid Theory," Creative Bloq, accessed July 22, 2021, https://www.creativebloq.com/web-design/grid-theory-41411345.
22. "Fibonacci Number," in *Wikipedia*, July 15, 2021, https://en.wikipedia.org/w/index.php?title=Fibonacci_number&oldid=1033704237.
23. "A Designer's Guide to the Golden Ratio | Creative Bloq," accessed July 22, 2021, https://www.creativebloq.com/design/designers-guide-golden-ratio-12121546.
24. Sam Hampton-Smith, "The Designer's Guide to Gestalt Theory," Creative Bloq, accessed July 22, 2021, https://www.creativebloq.com/graphic-design/gestalt-theory-10134960.
25. " Sheena Tu—Design Principles & Gestalt: The Basic Tenets of Design Can Be Grouped into Two | Course Hero," accessed July 22, 2021, https://www.coursehero.com/file/18297944/DES001-Tu-Design-Principles-Gastalt/.
26. "Who designed this? Signe Mayfield on the exhibition designer Ted Cohen—ARCADE Magazine," *ARCADE*, accessed April 18, 2022, https://arcadenw.org/journal/who-designed-this-signe-mayfield-on-the-exhibition-designer-ted-cohen.
27. "Deutsche Bank—ArtMag—83—on View—The Power of Images—The Circle Walked Casually in Buenos Aires," accessed July 1, 2021, https://db-artmag.com/en/83/on-view/the-power-of-images-the-circle-walked-casually-in-buenos-aires/.

Designer's Toolbox: **Constraints**

Exhibition furniture facilitates the display of precious or living collections, their safety, and preservation. Design constraints dictate the display of contents, and access for audiences. See what is trapped in this section of the designer's toolbox; there is more to exhibition furniture than meets the eye.

Visualization: Sayaka Koike is an exhibition designer producing projects that frequently break out of the box at ATELIER BRÜCKNER in Stuttgart, Germany

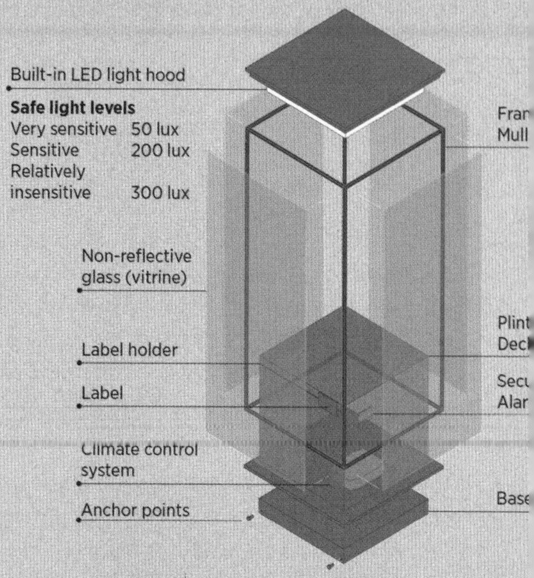

Built-in LED light hood

Safe light levels
Very sensitive	50 lux
Sensitive	200 lux
Relatively insensitive	300 lux

Fram
Mull

Non-reflective glass (vitrine)

Label holder

Label

Climate control system

Anchor points

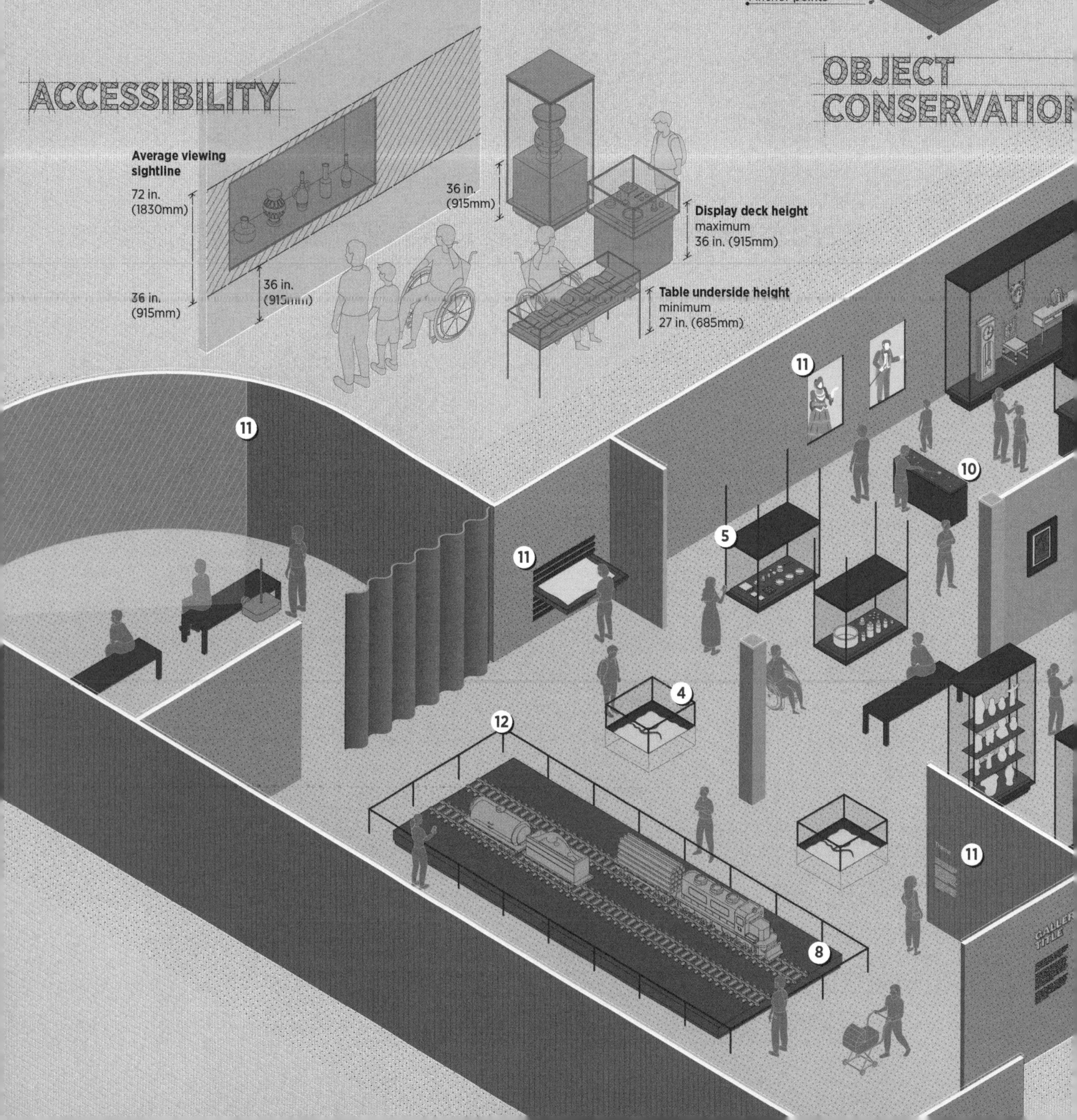

Plint
Dec

Secu
Alar

Base

ACCESSIBILITY

OBJECT CONSERVATION

Average viewing sightline

72 in. (1830mm)

36 in. (915mm)

36 in. (915mm)

36 in. (915mm)

Display deck height maximum 36 in. (915mm)

Table underside height minimum 27 in. (685mm)

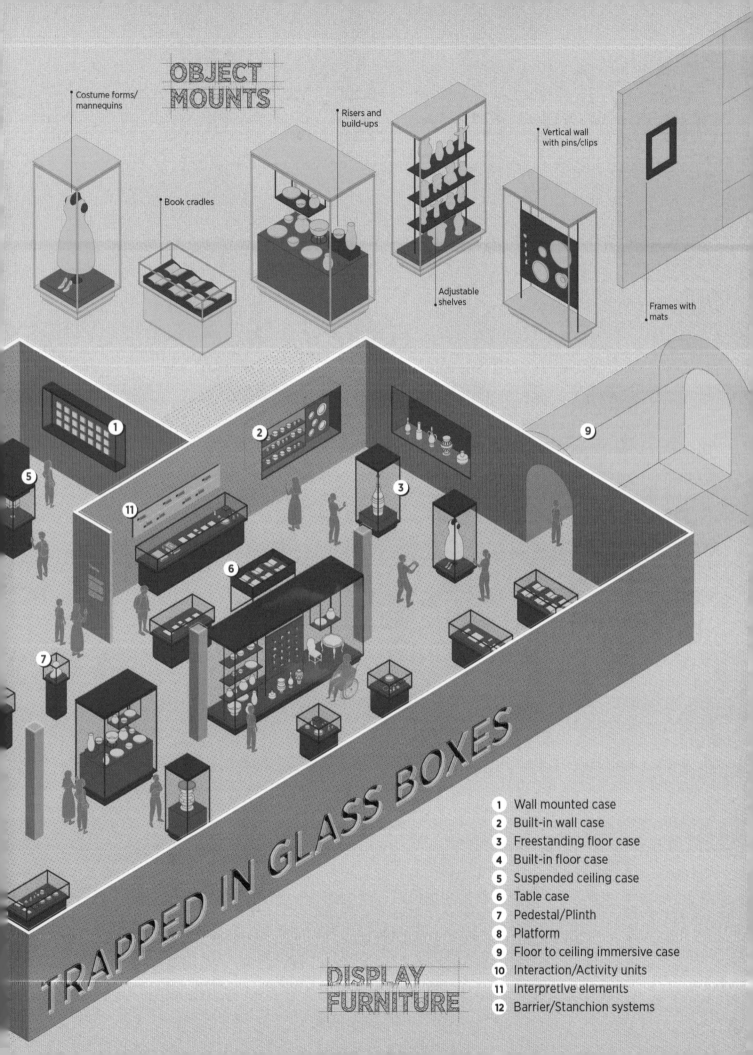

OBJECT MOUNTS

Costume forms/mannequins

Book cradles

Risers and build-ups

Vertical wall with pins/clips

Adjustable shelves

Frames with mats

TRAPPED IN GLASS BOXES

DISPLAY FURNITURE

1. Wall mounted case
2. Built-in wall case
3. Freestanding floor case
4. Built-in floor case
5. Suspended ceiling case
6. Table case
7. Pedestal/Plinth
8. Platform
9. Floor to ceiling immersive case
10. Interaction/Activity units
11. Interpretive elements
12. Barrier/Stanchion systems

CHAPTER 8

Trapped in Glass Boxes

Designed exhibitions and experiences must protect objects
and people.

Key message: Design responds proactively to the constraints inherent in creating a
safe exhibition environment.

Key word: constraints

Picture the stereotypical exhibition gallery, and it contains rows of sturdy
display furniture, crammed with old artifacts in glass boxes to protect
them from the overly curious public. This visceral image is burned into
people's consciousness through nineteenth-century museum display.
"Dead things trapped in glass boxes" is a trope associated with these
stuffy and staid museums. In this chapter, it provides a metaphor for object conservation, security, accessibility, fabrication, and tight budgets—
the constraints presented to exhibition designers delivering quality, safe,
and people-centered solutions. Indeed, the glass box is symbolic, a microcosm of the challenges and constraints audiences face while navigating a
multitude of exhibition environments.

Objectification of the Artifact: Role of Exhibition Display Furniture

Designing containers to house objects (dead or alive) is highly specialized, and solutions come
in multiple forms. Aquaria have perfected large, immersive glass box enclosures where people
press up against the ocean experience. Museums prefer less nose grease and more distance. Their
exquisite showcases attempt to strike a balance between protecting irreplaceable objects and
promoting viewer interaction, but the message is "hands off."

Placing an object inside a glass box (vitrine) transforms its relationship with the viewer.
Isolated and out of context, it is objectified, attains new meaning, and assumes a jewel-like quality.[1] The designer adds the display ingredients to this metaphorical glass mixing bowl—a backdrop
and elevated buildup to accentuate the object, information extolling the object's significance,
and the icing on the cake—theatrical lighting—to illuminate the object from every angle. Creating
display furniture is akin to designing a mini exhibition: The deck becomes the space, the glass box
the walls, and the objects inside the exhibits to be staged.

Bringing objects to life

Objects in glass boxes do not have to be life-less, nor are their voices muted. *Resonant Bodies*, commissioned for the London Design Festival (2018) and hosted by the Victoria and Albert Museum Research Institute (VARI) in their Asian art galleries, invited sound art-ist and composer Caroline Devine to create a unique, site-specific installation that provided playful and unexpected encounters with mu-sic. Devine added sound to accompany several Indian musical instruments arranged in a large, glass-fronted showcase. Compact speakers, pressed up against the case rather than fac-ing the room, delivered sound to audiences through the glass surface. The glass performed as a large resonant soundboard. Sitars sang and drums pulsated in an agreeable ensem-ble. For a time, the glass barrier disappeared, the objects offered up their musical secrets, and an immersive ambient sound experience reverberated beyond the silent, text-based in-terpretation.[2]

The glass box became a musical soundboard for Caroline Devine's *Resonant Bodies* at the Victoria and Albert Museum.

Photo: © Victoria and Albert Museum, London

Display furniture evolved along with World's Fairs, expositions, and the first public muse-ums in Europe and the Americas, deepening further with the installation of period rooms where entire galleries became display cases that audiences viewed from the outside. Aisles of glass box-es, packed with objects, were the product of research expeditions facilitated by colonial collecting practices at museums, libraries, and universities. Much can be gleaned from the design of these original furniture systems, and in many ways, little has changed in contemporary display practices.

Primary case study
Trapped and constrained

The Court, Pitt Rivers Museum, University of Oxford, 1884–present
Designer: T.N. Deane

Design challenge: Furniture fundamentals

A cacophony of crowded casework delights people as they enter the Court at the Pitt Rivers Museum in Oxford. Resolutely fixed in time, the arrange-ments of stupefying ethnographic objects from all over the world adhere to their nineteenth-century origins. Despite its dated appearance, this museum of anthropology addresses head-on its checkered colonial past and dubious collecting practices, and it embraces a multiplicity of viewpoints to diversify audience engagement.[3]

From vantage points on mezzanine levels, overstuffed glass boxes can be studied from every angle. Each glass-fronted case is like a stopped clock, offering a rare place to witness an evolution in exhib-iting styles, and compare past with contemporary display methods.[4] The museum is a lesson in furniture fundamentals, truly an exhibition designer's dream.

Design solution: Construction, conservation, and access

The Pitt Rivers is a playful reminder of cabinet of curiosities compositions. Grouped by theme, the taxonomy of object types contends for space and attention. The *salon-style* massing is clearly about the collective whole rather than the individual item.

Objects in the glass boxes are stacked on buildups (or risers) like wedding cake tiers rather than relegated to a single deck or attached to the backwalls with object mounts. These packed arrangements make installing these mounting devices challenging. Today, the preference is to stage objects with breathing room to encourage individual focus.

Solid and long-lasting, the display furniture at this museum is a glorious counterpoint to contemporary versions fashioned from lighter composites, acrylic, and aluminum. Local cabinetmakers dressed up oak carcasses with lacquered wood trim and ornate legs that resembled domestic Victorian furniture. Fabricated from segmented sheets of glass, seamed at the corners with visible edge mullions like the windows in a house, the glass boxes keep dust and wandering hands from touching the objects. These mullions create viewing blind spots, and light from the ceiling causes shadows on the case interior. In contrast, modern vitrines are seamless, with tighter joints to create micro-climates, and they often use internal case lighting to avoid shadows interfering with the objects.

In some instances, the furniture contains objects in glass boxes close to the floor. This makes it hard for people to view without bending over. Short distances between furniture elements negate the five-foot-minimum wheelchair turning radius and make it awkward for people to comfortably view standing back-to-back. Contemporary exhibition furniture designs acknowledge accessible viewing heights and activity surfaces and incorporate recessed bases for everyone to maneuver closer to exhibits.

Display furniture at the Pitt Rivers includes pull-out drawers that reveal even more objects for curious visitors. These preempt the "closer look" open storage at exhibitions like the Smithsonian's *Q?rius* (see chapter 12). Charming by today's standards, interpretive signs on the top of the furniture introduce themes, and descriptive labels jostle for available space inside the glass box. For ease of installation, current practice often places these elements outside the glass box on rails attached to the front of the display case, or as vinyl lettering applied directly to the glass surface.

Design impact: **Modularity**

The display furniture at Pitt Rivers is a multimodal typology of table cases, enclosed pedestals, and platforms in a systematic range of sizes. While not the only intact historical example, this modular kit of furniture parts launched the design vernacular for exhibition display furniture still in use and modified in numerous exhibitions today.

Furniture Typologies: Inventories, Vocabularies, and Display

Museums are not the only environments that utilize exhibition furniture. Theme parks provide sheltered seating and accessible areas for people to stand in line; trade shows and festivals require places to store products and giveaways; sports stadiums show off trophies; and zoos and aquaria require railings to contain animals and protect guests (or is it the other way around?). Exhibition furniture is much more than a safe platform for presenting objects; it is necessary wherever there is a public interface and crowds to manage.

Furniture inventories

The design possibilities and the variety of exhibition furniture are as expansive as the objects they display—ranging from high-end, metal-and-glass showcase systems found in permanent museum galleries, to inventive displays using repurposed shipping crates, and cardboard storage boxes in temporary exhibitions.

Fewer resources are required if exhibition furniture systems are modular and reusable. Fabrication time is reduced if the elements can be reconfigured and refinished to complement changing exhibition aesthetics. Storing any inventory is an ongoing constraint; therefore, furniture systems should be specified and designed for disassembly, and flat-packed for stowage and shipping (a necessity for the trade show industry)—consider IKEA's methods and their impact on the design industry.

The typology of casework at the Pitt Rivers Museum helped launch a design vernacular for contemporary exhibition display furniture.

Photo: adam eastland / Alamy
Stock Photo

Furniture typologies

Margaret Hall wrote extensively about the technicalities and complexities of designing exhibition furniture based on her experiences at the British Museum. *On-Display: A Design Grammar for Museum Exhibitions* (1987) documents installation methods for every conceivable object type, from armor and textiles to stamps and sculpture.[5] The following is a glimpse into the ever-expanding range of exhibition furniture types and related fixtures (see Designer's Toolbox).

Display furniture (protecting objects)—Dramatically different in design, scale, and function, display furniture can be custom, off-the-shelf, or repurposed. Forms include table, wall, pedestal, platform, or floor-to-ceiling types either built-in, against walls, or floating and visible in the round. Each one consists of four layers: base, deck, vitrine (optional), and light hood (optional). The base is either solid, set back to reduce the mass, or open with legs. Display decks are horizontal or vertical (backboard) or angled for one-way viewing. Vitrines vary in the number of see-through facets from one (single sheet) to five-sided (glass box).

Display mounts (securing objects)—Whether for security or seismic shifts, object mounts are an integral part of the exhibition furniture language. Build-ups or riser blocks elevate or tilt objects off the deck to make them easier to view; fasteners, shelves, and clips attach objects to decks and surfaces; cradles support and protect book bindings and keep pages open; mannequins create body forms to fit costumes and textiles; frames hang paintings, and mats sandwich works on paper. Invisible, mounts are carefully crafted and finished by skilled makers to blend with their surroundings and not to impede the object experience.

Transactional furniture (distributing content)—Tickets, T-shirts, and takeaways are distributed using furniture that facilitates the sale, rent, and loan of exhibition items. Examples include desks and booths for meet-and-greets, information, audio devices, handheld and VR headgear pickup, retail and merchandising units, brochure/map dispensers, and card racks. This furniture is designed to be portable, and it includes storage, signage, wiring for power and data, and attendant seating.

Safety furniture (protecting people)—Hygiene and health are relative newcomers to what is already an extensive list of security and safety components for designers to specify and consider. Entry checkpoints to exhibitions with alarm systems now sit alongside hand sanitizer stations. Portable stanchion systems control lines of eager people. Post and rope/wire barriers, and low extended platforms in front of objects send a subtle, but more welcoming message, to keep a safe distance without using vitrines and overt security measures.

Welcome furniture (resting people)—Providing a place to sit builds positive people-centered experiences and provides for creature comforts. It seems obvious, but many exhibition spaces fail to offer enough seating.[6] Whether it is lolling on loungers, benches, or beanbags, or a quick stint on a stool, seating takes a myriad of forms. Circular sofas date back to nineteenth-century salons; portable chairs and stools offer a contemporary repose. Rather than resorting to off-the-shelf options, specify seating that reflects the exhibition theme and is consistent with the design of the display furniture.

Activity furniture (facilitating discovery)—Designed to be robust and resilient, and built to facilitate hands-on exhibits, activity furniture expands beyond the traditional touch table. Discovery-based actions, manipulating objects, and opening draws compete with dynamic new media surfaces that respond to movement and gesture, and fixed and free-standing kiosks that accommodate interactive screens. All these examples require power and data access embedded into the furniture structure that is easily updated.

Interpretive furniture (dispensing information)—Didactic content and exhibit interpretation have evolved from handwritten to computer driven. Embedded graphics, text, images, and digital media require supporting furniture. Signage pylons situated in weighted bases, object label rails mounted to display cases, projection units suspended from ceiling armatures, are examples of these often-overlooked details.

Auxiliary furniture (stuff everyone forgets)—Designers, promise you will never use these in the exhibition space: plastic office trash bins; empty buckets as an umbrella stands; handwritten signs taped to doors; outdoor crowd control stanchions to protect indoor objects and exhibits. Design for purpose, research and acquire the right fixture for the right job, and create a superior public impression.

fischer Z architekten challenged the traditional glass box display furniture by using the ceiling and floor surfaces at the Kelten Römer Museum Manching, 2006.

kelten römer museum manching / Foto: Michael Heinrich.

Architects Hariri & Hariri's elegant, raised platforms elevate display mannequins, and serve as barrier and object label surface in *Contemporary Muslim Fashions* at San Francisco's de Young Museum, 2018.

Copyright Hariri & Hariri Architecture DPC. Photographer: Eric Laignel. Courtesy Fine Arts Museums of San Francisco.

Comfort is lolling either on loungers, benches, or bean bags as in the installation ICEBERGS at the National Building Museum, Washington, D.C., 2016.

ICEBERGS at the National Building Museum, by James Corner Field Operations. Photo by Timothy Schenck.

Designed to be robust, resilient, and built to facilitate
hands-on, activity furniture
designed by Gagarin for the
Eldheimar Museum, Iceland,
2014.

© studio: Gagarin / photo: Magnús
Elvar Jónsson

Breaking the glass box barrier

In Rotterdam, the Depot Boijmans Van Beuningen (2021) challenges the notion of display furniture as a barrier between objects and observers. Rather than hiding 94 percent of its collection
in storage, the building is utterly democratic and makes everything visible to the public in thir-
teen giant exhibit cases suspended in the atrium.[7] Audiences at the Depot immerse themselves in
the behind-the-scenes aspects of a museum and experience what maintaining and caring for an

Depot Boijmans Van
Beuningen was designed by
architects MVRDV as a glass
box container for people
as well as accessible open
storage for objects.

Depot Boijmans Van Beuningen.
Fotos: Aad Hoogendoorn

art collection actually entails, independently or with a guide.[8] The building resembles a massive spherical, mirrored display case turned inside out, where the glass box becomes the container for people as well as the objects.

Sixty years earlier, architect and exhibition designer Lina Bo Bardi questioned the relationship of exhibition furniture to people, learning, and object experiences. Materials and modern production methods will replace primitive methods; preserving not the forms, but the underlying structure of those possibilities, was a driving force throughout her career.[9]

Primary case study
Scene but not seen

Galleries, Museu de Arte de São Paulo, Brazil, 1968–present
Designers: Lina Bo Bardi; refurbished by Metro Arquitetos, 2015

Design challenge: Rethinking display furniture
Lina Bo Bardi experimented with floor-to-ceiling aluminum poles, cables, and supports before unveiling designs for the installation of paintings and sculpture at the new Museu de Arte de São Paulo. Her 1968 glass and red-beam building is now celebrated as a brutalist masterpiece. Bo Bardi ported the same aesthetic to the exhibition display furniture, which transitioned from an original concept sketch featuring a glass ceiling and opaque walls, to a building design with glass walls and a solid ceiling.[10]

Design solution: Rethinking the easel
Paintings from the museum's collection are mounted to a system of "crystal easels" made from large glass panels inserted into concrete support bases and anchored using wooden wedges. The free-standing easels allow audiences to walk around them, and they face forward so the entire gallery of works can be experienced from a single viewpoint. The frames are attached to the front of the glass panel, and the backs of the paintings are revealed to show a rarely seen surface. Interpretive labels are placed on the reverse so that reading does not interfere with viewing.[11]

Bo Bardi's radical display furniture deliberately sought a reaction from the audience. Paintings became liberated from the walls. Free-standing and sculptural, the easels created new and unusual juxtapositions between the artworks and a labyrinth of surprising spatial relationships. Copasetic material choices between the easels and the gallery space reinforce the cohesive visual language. The easel's glass support structure offers little distraction as the focus is *on* the object and the *design* appears to disappear.

Design impact: Art to audience relationship
The studio easel rarely graces the museum gallery. Bo Bardi explicitly chose this form because it is a working instrument where the painting is born in the air; she wanted paintings to be seen as works and strip them of their sacred character.[12] The lack of hierarchy between artworks of stature was novel and uncompromisingly democratic. It rethought the relationship between art and audience and probed the prevailing cultural and learning experience.

Metro Arquitetos refurbished the easels and updated the main gallery of the Museu de Arte de São Paulo according to Lina Bo Bardi's original vision.

Photo: Eduardo Ortega, Collection of Centro de Pesquisa do MASP - Museu de Arte de São Paulo Assis Chateaubriand

Lina Bo Bardi's system of "crystal easels" form a labyrinth of surprising spatial relationships between artworks at the Museu de Arte de São Paulo.

Photo: Collection of Centro de Pesquisa do MASP - Museu de Arte de São Paulo Assis Chateaubriand

Structure and Function: Conservation, Accessibility, and Materials

Constraints make design better. They focus scope, fine-tune solutions, and flirt with fabrication methods that are cost effective and doable (well, not always). Designers themselves often feel trapped in a glass box at multiple stages of an exhibition project. Practitioners stress the challenges of working within constraints, particularly the equilibrium between quality, time, and budget.[13] Blue-sky design thinking is imperative, but there is never enough available funding to act on every concept. During the design process, measure creative and practical solutions against the constraints that hem in a project.

Metaphorical glass box

Designing exhibition furniture for the display of objects presents a set of unique constraints and ethical considerations. These include caring for culturally sensitive objects; the exhibiting of indigenous artifacts, sites of consciousness, and live animal encounters; object safety, conservation, and building preservation; accessible viewing heights, human-scaled proportions, accommodations, and the health and well-being of the exhibition's participants; and environmental concerns associated with waste, toxins, and energy consumption. Thankfully, teams of exhibit professionals are involved to advise on these challenges and safeguard artifacts.

Sacred, culturally restrictive, or holy pieces used in ritual are considered culturally sensitive; for example, objects seen or handled only by specific people such as initiates or medicine keepers, or by one gender only. Respect is the keyword when it comes to exhibiting sacred or culturally sensitive objects. Approaches to display, conservation, and care should be defined by the objects originating community to form a partnership that protects the object's both tangible and intangible attributes.[14] Some of these factors may conflict with museum or exhibition practices and impact placement, access, display duration, lighting, visibility, the proximity and relationship to other artifacts, level of interpretation, and what is said about an object.

Conservation—Designer friend or foe?

Stringent conservation requirements and limitations when working with treasured objects and museum collections can frustrate designers. Conversely, those charged with protecting and documenting objects (conservators, registrars, and security staff) can feel the same way about exhibition design solutions that adversely push established object-display boundaries.

Contaminants in the exhibition atmosphere can be harmful to objects. Light contains ultraviolet (UV) and infrared waves that weaken and fade materials, airborne pollutants and humidity alter surfaces and distort chemical balance, rogue insects find textiles and wood particularly tasty, and the ground tends to vibrate (especially in a seismic zone). Light mitigation, air handling, and climate control help, but the ultimate line of defense is the glass box.

International guidelines that govern object conservation strive for a "do no harm" approach through stable, consistent, exhibition environments that prevent new or ongoing damage, particularly as objects are loaned from one venue to another. Scholarship and practice in the conservation field is deep and varied. Exhibition makers require a basic understanding of the subject to specify appropriate designs for many exhibition environments.

Conservation basics

Guidelines recommend stable environments of 70 degrees Fahrenheit ± 2 degrees, 50 percent relative humidity (RH), and HVAC systems that filter circulated air to reduce dust and contaminants. Because stone, wood, metal, and paper require different light and humidity levels, caution should be used when mixing object media in the same display zone. To avoid damage, materials near objects should release zero-low VOCs (Volatile Organic Compounds) and be acid-free.

Lighting objects

Light sources for exhibition spaces were discussed in chapter 6. Typical exhibition lighting relies on *focusable* light sources: either crisp, shadow-producing spotlights and/or diffuse wash sources mounted to flexible ceiling tracks. Constraints are introduced by the specific illumination requirements (both technical and aesthetic) of objects on pedestals, on platforms, and inside glass display

Oil and Acrylic	diffused daylight/artificial light (200 lux); avoid direct sunlight
Works on paper	artificial light (50 lux); susceptible to fading: instability of pigments; keep flat and avoid touch; use acid-free paper mats
Stone and marble	daylight/artificial light (300 lux); touch leaves oils on surfaces
Textiles, dyed leather	artificial light (50 lux); susceptible to fading and instability of dyes; support to avoid stretching and stress; avoid touch; insect free
Wood	artificial light (50 lux); susceptible to fading and darkening; avoid touch; insect free
Metal	daylight/artificial light (300 lux); bronze disease requires zero RH and micro-climate; avoid touch
New Media	cool temperature; backup original version

Exhibition makers should understand the basic conservation display requirements for object media.

Diagram: Timothy J. McNeil

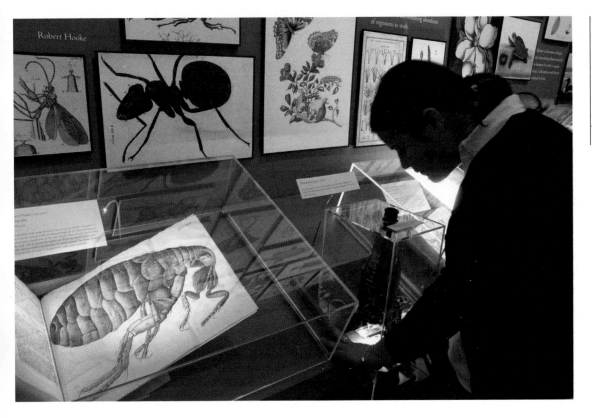

Glass boxes in *Beautiful Science* at the Huntington Library (2008) were designed by Gordon Chun Design and Karina Whlte for close-up viewing, minimal light exposure, and the rotation of objects.

Image by Lisa Blackburn, courtesy Huntington Library, San Marino, California

cases. The glass tops on five-sided display vitrines transmit overhead light from outside the case with mixed results, potentially creating hotspots, shadows, and unwelcome reflections. Incorporating light sources (either LED or fiber optic) inside vitrines and closer to the objects allows more flexibility over light levels, fixture placement, and ultimately lighting composition. Objects in cases can be illuminated from below (fixtures mounted on the bottom of the case), from the edge or side (fixtures mounted to vertically oriented rods), and/or from above (but inside) the top (hood) of the case. With integral case lighting, distracting shadows caused by external impediments (i.e., people standing between the light source and the case) are significantly reduced. Size the glass box to provide an adequate distance between the objects and illumination source to maximize the light spread and avoid hotspots. Keep a six- to seven-foot distance from the floor to the underside of a light hood so people looking into the case are offered an unobstructed view with reduced perceived glare from the light source. Whenever possible, do a lighting mockup/test before a case is built; the lessons learned will be invaluable.

LED light sources offer excellent beam control, electrical efficiency, small form factor, and unlike their predecessors (i.e., halogen) generate little heat released into the glass box to potentially damage the contents. For designers seeking to eliminate heat generated by the light source, consider employing a fiberoptic system with a remote light source (which would also typically be LED-driven) located outside of the case. The best type of light for looking at objects is diffused or simulated daylight. In all cases, harmful light in the UV spectrum must be eliminated. Objects such as works on paper are extremely susceptible to fading from both the amount of and prolonged exposure to light; even a few weeks can make a difference! Whenever possible, consult with a conservator when tasked with illuminating delicate objects. Color rendering index (CRI), correlated color temperature (CCT measured in Kelvin), beam spread (or angle), and light intensity (measured in lux or foot-candles) are factors that must be carefully considered, calibrated, and monitored.

Designers WilkinsonEyre's lengthy prototyping process resulted in an agile system of display furniture for a diverse range of object types at the Medicine Galleries, Science Museum London, 2019.

Photo: © Science Museum Group

Materials and fabrication

Imagine trapping a rare fourteenth-century illuminated manuscript in a glass box filled with formaldehyde. Many construction materials and finishes deemed safe for building purposes release trace amounts of toxins/acids (VOCs) over time that affect fragile artifacts. Specify inert materials and/or design display furniture with nonpermeable barriers between materials that off-gas and the object zone. The Oddy Test is a simple method to make sure materials are safe for objects.[15] Reassuring to conservators, it does expand the creative constraints for designers.

Designers crave the latest and greatest materials. Exhibition furniture substrates have not changed significantly since the introduction of tempered glass, aluminum, stretch fabrics, laminates, plywood, and particleboards in the 1930s, acrylics/plastics in the 1960s, and lead-free paints in the 1970s. Innovations have made materials and finishes lighter, less toxic, and easier to work with. Composite products like Corian are widely available; bioderived material sources such as mycelium offer promise; and three-dimensional printing, CNC milling, and laser cutting make rapid prototyping and construction possible.[16]

Vitrines are fabricated from one-quarter to half-inch laminated safety glass (anti-reflective) or acrylic panels that are mitered and glued together to form a box. While specialized glass products are robust and reduce unwanted reflections, clear acrylic is less expensive, but it warps and scratches easily. Acrylic is favored for temporary exhibitions, and glass for long-term installations, for these reasons. Vitrine designs also use visible frames/mullions (see Pitt Rivers Museum case study), or clips (L-brackets) to join glass panels together. Glass boxes that contain certain objects, like ancient bronze, need to be airtight. Known as micro-climates, they operate independently from the external exhibition space. Gaskets seal the glass edges from temperature fluctuations, and desiccants regulate the relative humidity inside.

Security and safety

Vitrines protect objects, and mounts position or secure them to the internal display surfaces. Vitrines are usually lowered into place over the deck and secured. Some have hinged doors, locks, and alarm systems if the display furniture must be accessed regularly. Display furniture must be designed with the ability to remove or rotate objects during the run of an exhibition or installation.

In certain instances, this step is preceded by fixing the display furniture to a wall or the floor using existing anchor points or drilling and bolting into a subsurface. This is necessary where earthquakes, ground vibrations, or sudden movements (i.e., near to train tracks) are prevalent. The furniture then moves in synch with the building and not independently. Museums in Japan and California, for example, use sophisticated isolator bases inside their large sculpture display pedestals. These bases move independently of the building and counteract seismic shocks.

Primary case study
Accessible, adaptable, and agile

Being Human, Wellcome Trust, London, 2019–present
Principal Designer: Assemble Studio

Design challenge: Design for all
Located on London's busy Euston Road, this free exhibition space was inspired by the medical objects collected by pharmaceutical entrepreneur Henry Wellcome to challenge how people think about health.[17] *Being Human* is a permanent exhibition exploring what it means to be human in the twenty-first century. Drawing on the Wellcome collection and artist commissions, Assemble Studio was invited to rethink the public gallery with accessible design at the forefront.

Design solution: Co-design
Assemble's Joseph Halligan describes their design response as a reaction to the previous gallery, which was like a laboratory or a hospital, with traditional vitrines and draws in Corian-faced MDF.[18] Their design brings a natural, anti-clinical feel to the space by introducing tempered natural light, soft oak flooring, and walls lined with knotted-pine paneling stained with white, green, and blue pigmented oils.

The exhibition's furniture design was developed in consultation with local disability groups. Accessible features include overhanging display deck surfaces (lower than 36 inches from the floor, they accommodate wheelchair users and up-close viewing); audio, Braille, and tactile interpretive text; white-washed, cross-laminated wood platforms and pedestals, with darkened bases visually contrast with the floor; and benches placed off-center allow equal media viewing opportunities for people in wheelchairs.

Design impact: People-centric
Generous spacing between the exhibit elements, inclusive viewing heights, and people-scaled proportions come together in *Being Human*. Like the glass boxes at Pitt Rivers, and Bo Bardi's glass easels, this exhibition's furniture seeks to reduce the barrier between object and audience experience. The difference was the furniture emerged from placing people, rather than objects, at the center of the design process.

Benches placed off-center allow equal media viewing opportunities for people in wheelchairs in *Being Human* at London's Wellcome Trust.

Work by Heather Dewey-Hagborg, *T3511* (2018). Courtesy of the artist and Fridman Gallery. Photo © Steven Pocock

***Being Human* at London's Wellcome Trust was developed with local disability groups who advocated for tactile object interpretation to be incorporated into the display furniture.**

Works by Tamsin van Essen.

Escape from the box

Striking a balance between object safety and viewer interaction is nothing new—but how do designers transcend the glass box barrier? Technology is one answer. Three-dimensional scanners can produce virtual representations or tactile object reproductions, making content more accessible for people with sight or mobility impediments, and those who would gain from closer object interaction. Industrious designers strive to devise imperceptible methods to keep audiences at arm's length, making barriers implied rather than explicit. The glass box then becomes invisible and less intimidating; in the same way, technology integration works when people do not realize they are using it, and designers lose track of the constraints inherent in exhibition making.

Tips and Tricks

Lean into exhibition constraints by embracing the following design techniques:

1. If people can touch, they will. Use low-key barriers with a minimum distance of 42 inches to the object if there is no vitrine.
2. Exhibition furniture pulls content off the walls, creates spatial divisions, and causes unexpected object encounters.
3. Specify cohesive, multimodal furniture systems that are easy to store and transport, and that respond to the existing exhibition/building module (fit through doors, in elevators, etc.).
4. Consider the glass box a mini-exhibition environment—stage using buildups, light internally, integrate interpretive methods.
5. Incorporate graphics into the furniture exterior and not inside the glass box to make object installation/changes easier.
6. Make a good impression. Consider all exhibition furniture, even the humble trashcan.
7. While not experts, designers need a basic knowledge of conservation best practices.
8. Protecting objects does not always require a glass box. Work within conservation and security constraints and challenge conventional display methods to heighten learning and audience experiences.
9. Unethical design is exhibit furniture that is not inclusive and accessible for everyone.
10. Unsustainable design is exhibit furniture that dismisses longevity, modularity, and reuse.

Notes

1. James Putnam, *Art and Artifact: The Museum as Medium* (Thames & Hudson, 2001), 15.
2. "Resonant Bodies—A Sound Installation Commissioned by the V&A Research Institute (VARI)," accessed July 30, 2021, https://www.youtube.com/watch?v=OhQvexmOWSg&t=60s.
3. "How UK Museums Are Responding to Black Lives Matter," *BBC News*, June 29, 2020, sec. Entertainment & Arts, https://www.bbc.com/news/entertainment-arts-53219869.
4. "The Future of Museums, Past and Present: Pitt Rivers AD 2065," *Museum-ID* (blog), March 22, 2019, https://museum-id.com/the-future-of-museums-past-and-present-pitt-rivers-ad-2065-by-dan-hicks/.
5. Margaret Hall, *On Display: A Design Grammar for Museum Exhibitions*, 1st ed. (London: Lund Humphries, 1987), 127–210.
6. Kathleen McLean and Wendy Pollock, *The Convivial Museum* (Washington, D.C.: Association of Science-Technology Centers, 2011).
7. "MVRDV—Architects," accessed July 29, 2021, https://www.mvrdv.nl/projects/10/depot-boijmans-van-beuningen.
8. "MVRDV—Architects."
9. "Lina Quotes," Lina Bo Bardi Together, September 18, 2012, https://linabobarditogether.com/2012/09/18/lina-quotes/.
10. "Lina Bo Bardi," Art on Display 1949-69, March 11, 2020, https://art-on-display.hetnieuweinstituut.nl/en/case-studies/lina-bo-bardi.
11. Condé Nast, "Examining Lina Bo Bardi's Exhibition Design at São Paulo's Museum of Art," *Architectural Digest*, November 8, 2016, https://www.architecturaldigest.com/story/lina-bo-bardi-exhibition-sao-paulo-museum-of-art.
12. "Lina Bo Bardi."
13. Clare Brown and design team at Gallagher & Associates. Interview by Timothy McNeil about design constraints and working process, March 6, 2020.
14. Canadian Conservation Institute, "Caring for Sacred and Culturally Sensitive Objects—Preventive Conservation Guidelines for Collections," September 22, 2017, https://www.canada.ca/en/conservation-institute/services/preventive-conservation/guidelines-collections/caring-sacred-culturally-sensitive-objects.html.

15. "Oddy Test," in *Wikipedia*, March 30, 2021, https://en.wikipedia.org/w/index.php?title=Oddy_test&oldid=1015021002.

16. Maria Saxton, "Mycelium Fungi as a Building Material," Rise, February 13, 2020, https://www.buildwithrise.com/stories/mycelium-fungi-as-a-building-material.

17. "Wellcome Collection | A Free Museum and Library Exploring Health and Human Experience," Wellcome Collection, accessed July 30, 2021, https://wellcomecollection.orgundefined.

18. Wallpaper* Magazine, "Assemble Designs New Wellcome Collection Gallery in London," Wallpaper*, September 3, 2019, https://www.wallpaper.com/architecture/assemble-new-wellcome-collection-gallery-london.

Designer's Toolbox: **Immersion**

Immersive experiences take many fanciful forms from full
(panoramic) to partial (dioramic) environments and employ
a variety of media and sensory-based design techniques.
Borrowing from theater and cinematic arts, designers choose
from a range of props to construct exhibition settings and
facilitate wraparound experiences. Escape into the designer's
toolbox for inspiration.

Visualization: Lorem Ipsum create immersive experiences across physical and digital environments in New York,
London, and Moscow

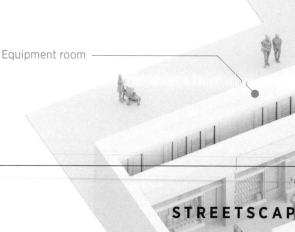

PLAZA

Equipment room

Fixed Mural

STREETSCAPE

Soundscape

Dynamic Mural

DOME

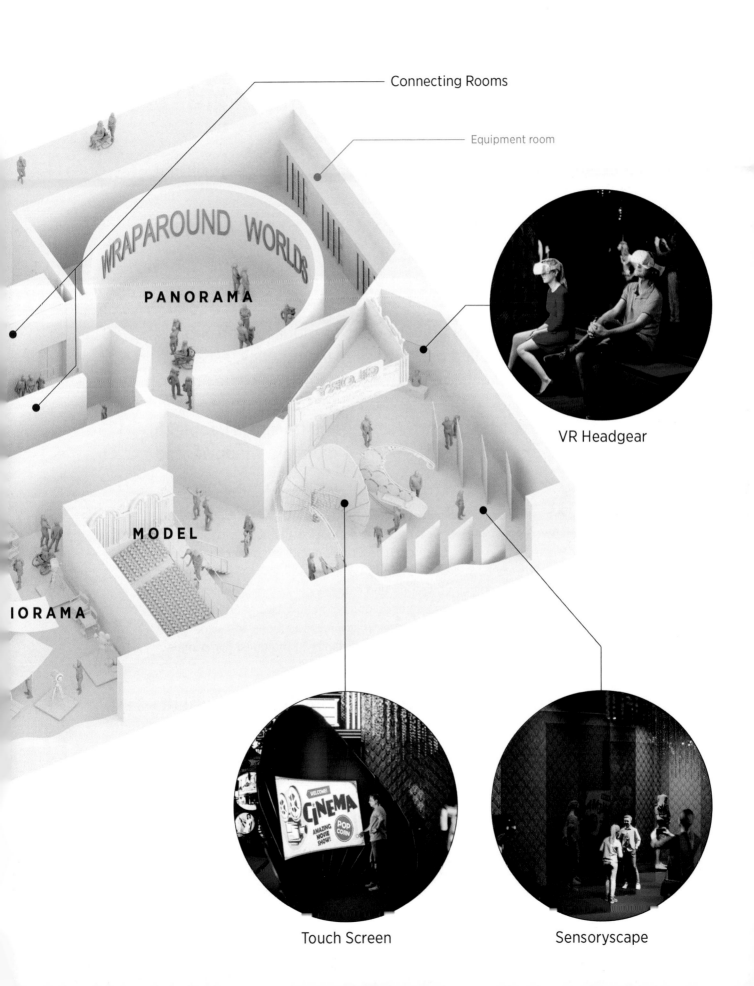

Connecting Rooms

Equipment room

WRAPAROUND WORLDS

PANORAMA

MODEL

IORAMA

VR Headgear

Touch Screen

Sensoryscape

CHAPTER 9

Wraparound Worlds

Immersive environments captivate people through the design of physical and virtual experiences.

Key message: Design captivates an exhibition audience and facilitates an experience that is not everyday.

Key word: immersion

From handheld sixteenth-century prayer books to mobile smartphones, people have always had an innate desire to seek reassurance, escapism, and immersion in alternate realities. This trope acknowledges the numerous wraparound experiences in the exhibition environment, their historical trajectory, and their ability to convey stories and transport people to another time or place using panoramic scenes, dioramic windows, and digital portals.

This chapter explores how designers reinvent the tools to deliver wraparound worlds, relying on precedent set by some of the earliest public experiences. Panoramic paintings in nineteenth-century cycloramas and dioramas captivated and thrilled audiences long before cinema and the moving image. Mid-twentieth-century World's Fairs and amusement parks offered designers plenty of opportunities to implement wraparound experiences using large-scale models, rides, photographs, super-graphics, film, image, and light projection. Designers for today's immersive encounters employ sophisticated large-format image reproductions and experiment with digital projection, gaming, virtual reality, and augmented reality in the quest for complete audience immersion.

Immersive Spaces: Escapism, Engagement, and Entertainment

Immersion is currently trending. Escaping into fantasy spheres has never been easier with twenty-first-century technologies that extend reality. Locate an empty warehouse, power it up, and instantaneously teamLab or a myriad of creative and artist experiences spread their luminous tentacles. People's quest to escape reality goes back centuries. Escapism ranges from spiritual (meditation, viewing beautiful art) to hedonistic (bungee jumping, riding Twisted Colossus at Six Flags Magic Mountain). The joys of distraction and going down rabbit holes started with stupefying painted domes of religious and devotional sites all over the globe.[1] Fifteenth-century French artist Jean Fouquet painted pocket-sized prayer books (book of hours) for wealthy aristocrats to consult "on-the-go" for divine enlightenment and immersion. They were the equivalent of today's smartphones and handheld devices.

Real and "make-believe" immersion

Immersion is a quadrant in Pine and Gilmore's *Four Realms of Experience*. It is woven into the work of exhibition and experience designers, where museums are equated to cathedrals for the twenty-first century, nature centers are gateways to rejuvenating outdoor experiences, and trade shows use brand immersion to tempt their customers. Once across the experience threshold, design transforms places from real to imaginary, enveloping people in fantasy worlds for moments or several days.

Total guest immersion is central to "make-believe" experiences encountered at theme parks, festivals, and attractions. Main Street, U.S.A. at Disneyland Park re-creates an urban landscape. The Immersive Digital Galleries at the National Museum in Seoul (2020) take the experience indoors with an unforgettable journey through some of Korea's most famous paintings.[2] Digital, high-resolution videos projected onto massive panoramic screens create an immersive experience as contemplative and absorbing as the artworks themselves. Janet Cardiff's *Forty-Part Motet*, at the Cleveland Museum of Art (2013), and countless other enchanting environmental soundscapes by the artist, illustrate how listening, acoustics, and music are vital wraparound components.

Immersive Digital Galleries at the National Museum of Korea are devoted to wraparound encounters.

Courtesy of National Museum of Korea

360-Degree Panoramic Experiences: Cycloramas, Immersive Rooms, Moving Panoramas

Panorama, or "all sight," is a method of wraparound immersion that, for good reason, has captivated and entertained exhibition audiences for centuries.[3] Travel to Scotland in 1792, and the industrious artist and entrepreneur Robert Barker used "The Panorama" to describe his almost-2,700-square-foot, 360-degree painting of Edinburgh housed in a cylindrical exhibition hall. Barker took his invention to London and with Robert Mitchell built the first permanent panorama building in Leicester Square in 1793. The building had multiple viewing platforms at various levels, and each of the paintings—typically historic patriotic naval battle scenes—occupied ten thousand square feet. Audiences must have been spellbound by the spectacle as they entered a dark subterranean corridor and up a spiral staircase to suddenly emerge and find themselves transported to a faraway place, as if by magic.[4]

Janet Cardiff's 40-track audio installation *Forty-Part Motet*, at the Cleveland Museum of Art, demonstrates how soundscapes are vital wraparound experiences.

Cyclorama

Panoramas gained worldwide popularity in circular buildings that were known as cycloramas. Spectators stood on central platforms to view 360-degree panoramic scenes. Skylights ensured an even light across the painting's face (before electrical light), which meant the availability of daylight was important. Props such as hanging tree branches, and sand/rocks on the floor, hid the painting's edges and provided visual depth.[5] Few of the thousands of panoramas and the

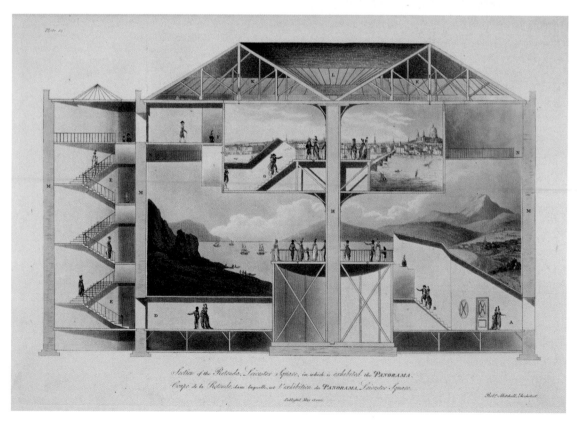

Cross-section of the Panorama building in Leicester Square designed by Robert Mitchell to exhibit the panoramic paintings of Robert Barker who patented a method of painting that allowed for the curvature and perspective.

Skylights (before electrical light) at cycloramas like the Panorama Mesdag enhanced the illusion with an even wash of daylight across the painting's face.

Courtesy of Museum Panorama Mesdag

Hugo d'Alesi's *Maréorama*, at the 1900 Paris Exposition, had the qualities of a modern flight simulator powered by electric motors and hydraulics.

Illustration of the *Maréorama* at the 1900 Paris Exposition, 29 September 1900, Scientific American, provided by Wikimedia Commons. CC-PD

cycloramas that housed them exist today. The Panorama Mostag (1881) in Den Haaq, Netherlands, and the Gettysburg Cyclorama (1884), a 27-foot-high, 359-foot-long painting depicting Pickett's Charge, with synchronized lighting effects, continue to be open for public view.

Moving panoramas

Throughout the nineteenth and early twentieth centuries, panoramas entertained crowds with new inventions and immersive technologies. At the 1900 Paris Exposition, Hugo d'Alesi's *Maréorama (or pleorama)* transported audiences using a moving panorama and a simulated spectacular sea voyage powered by electric motors and hydraulics. A one-hundred-foot-long replica steamship accommodated up to seven hundred people standing on its deck. Two immense painted canvases (42 feet high by 2,500 feet long) unfurled from port to starboard like scrolls.[6] These encircled the ship, and their movement revealed a journey from Nice to Constantinople. To the delight of audiences, the vessel pitched and rolled as if on the high seas, funnels belched, whistles howled, light effects transformed the journey from night into day, air was blown through kelp to simulate fragrant sea breezes, and captain and crew actors kept things shipshape.

Modalities of immersion

The *Maréorama* epitomizes the three interrelated modalities of immersion: envelopment (wrapped in image and/or sound), saturation (adding all the senses), and participation (people are part of the action).[7] Hugo d'Alesi offered a prelude to later multimodal technologies like Morton Heilig's *Sensorama* (1962) and modern flight simulator rides such as *Soarin' Over California* (2001) at Disney California Adventure Park.[8] Here, guests are strapped into banks of seats that ascend upward to simulate a bird in flight. This airborne adventure envelops people in a projected flyover film and equally uplifting musical score from surround-sound speakers.

Virtual panoramas

Panoramic immersion in the physical space has now met its digital nemesis with the rapidly advancing medium of virtual reality.[9] *Mona Lisa*'s smile (see chapter 3) went virtual at the Louvre Museum's *Leonardo da Vinci* exhibition (2019). Headgear wearers entered a VR wraparound world to meet the "real" Lisa del Giocondo, the Florentine silk merchant's wife who posed for Leonardo da Vinci in 1503—an actor whose face was digitally altered to resemble the *Mona Lisa*.[10] Yet, the cyclorama, with its long history, remains popular with contemporary audiences and an enduring immersive device.

Primary case study

Long live the panorama

Cyclorama, English Heritage Stonehenge Visitor Centre, Salisbury, UK, 2013–present
Principal Designers: Haley Sharpe Design (hsd), exhibition design; Centre Screen, video/CGI; Electrosonic, media integration

Design challenge: 360-degree CGI

With a history spanning about five thousand years, Stonehenge has many different meanings to people today. It is a wonder of the world, a spiritual place, and a source of inspiration.[11] A walk around the monument is the highlight of any visit. At one time, people entered the stone circle for the full experience, but conservation concerns for the fragile iconic symbol of Britain meant access was eventually restricted. English Heritage opened a much-anticipated revamp of the Stonehenge experience in 2013. Exhibition designers Haley Sharpe Design (hsd) developed exhibits that included an immersive CGI cyclorama experience at the heart of a new visitor center. An ambitious film was created entirely using computer-generated 3D imagery, which wraps around audiences to capture the experience of standing within the ancient stone circle.[12]

Design solution: Making the invisible, visible

The cyclorama's (33 feet diameter x 10 feet high) film and soundscape transports audiences to key points in the development of the ancient site. A masterpiece of engineering, the stone circle was built by hundreds of people using only simple tools and technologies. Every chisel mark is visible in the imagery and captured using minutely detailed laser scans of the stones. The film's narrative transitions audiences through millennia and conveys the unique quality of this prehistoric monument at pivotal moments in the seasonal year.[13]

Unlike the experimental multislide projections in the 1950–1960s, which struggled with image registration and synchronization, today's immersive technologies seamlessly stitch together several images originating from multiple digital projection units. Media integration is vital to the success of contemporary cycloramas, and companies like Electrosonic are adept at creating the back-end systems that run these large-scale audiovisual installations.[14] Credit should also be given to Centre Screen for the success of this piece.

Design impact: Reality inside-out

Virtual reality is turned inside-out at Stonehenge's cyclorama, where audiences participate in a physical, 360-degree VR-type experience without the cumbersome headgear and controller. Painted, printed, or projected onto a cylindrical surface, wraparound images crop up in countless contemporary exhibitions and still successfully deliver stories and contextual experiences.

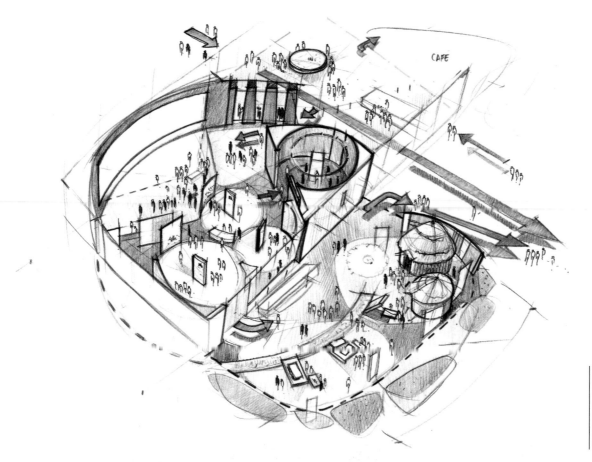

Cylinder to Sphere: Domes, Planetariums, and the IMAX Experience

Panoramic experiences laid the foundation for a generation of twentieth-century immersive experiences that broke from the cylinder and into the sphere. Electric lights replaced skylights, and there was less to impede the above-head experience. Switching natural light for night sky, the popularity of planetariums attests to this development, where reclined seating focuses the audience's attention on the ceiling as the primary presentation surface. Spherical structures superimpose themselves in a litany of exposition and World's Fair examples such as Buckminster Fuller's Montreal 67 biosphere (chapter 5). IMAX (Image MAXimum) theaters are a later iteration. The Smithsonian National Air and Space Museum in Washington, D.C., was one of the first to feature a dedicated IMAX film when it opened its doors in 1976. *To Fly* wowed visitors with wraparound higher-resolution film images, so good was the feeling of immersion that people experienced vertigo and a loss of balance.[15]

Globes and spheres

On a smaller scale, a sphere placed within an exhibition offers a room-within-a-room. An immersive detour that reengages people before releasing them back into the general exhibition flow. Designer Herbert Bayer employed this technique for *Airways to Peace* (1943), an exhibition at New York's Museum of Modern Art that traced the evolution of flight and how air dominance was crucial to winning WWII. According to the press release, "the most striking and unusual feature of the exhibition . . . will be an immense sphere into which the visitor can walk."[16] The sphere was suspended from the ceiling by aircraft cable; its wooden frame and plywood cladding resembled the internal structure of an airplane. Painted on the interior was a map of the world. The lower land masses were fret-cut. People playfully dodged continents to navigate entry to the sphere. Bayer turned the globe inside-out. Okay, Antarctica gets short shrift, but the immersive experience allowed the viewer to comprehend the entire world, compare flight distances, and grasp geopolitical dynamics quickly. Bayer employed his extended field-of-vision technique to a spherical form—thirty years later, it met its match in Japan.

Before wallpapered vinyl and direct-to-substrate inkjet printing, the sphere's interior global map in *Airways to Peace* had to be painstakingly painted by hand.

Photo by Samuel H. Gottscho © Gottscho-Schleisner. Digital Image © The Museum of Modern Art/Licensed by SCALA / Art Resource, NY

Primary case study

Hacking the dome

Pepsi Pavilion, Osaka Expo, Japan, 1970
Principal Designers: Tadashi Doi (architect); E.A.T. (exhibition), Bob Breer, Frosty Myers, David Tudor, and Robert Whitman

Design challenge: Creative havoc

Pepsi commissioned Experiments in Art and Technology (E.A.T.) to design the interior of their Expo '70 pavilion—a 120-foot diameter-faceted dome designed by Japanese architect Tadashi Doi.[17] E.A.T. was formed in 1967 to foster collaborations between artists, architects, and engineers and dissolve these disciplinary boundaries, *experimental* being the operative word.[18] E.A.T. was at odds with Pepsi's corporate philosophy and the building's architecture right from the get-go. Their exhibition design hack transformed the pavilion into a multisensory and immersive experience in the spirit of 1960s radicalism, media experimentation, and Marshall McLuhan's "the medium is the message."

Design solution: Optical effects

E.A.T. considered the pavilion's architecture omnipresent. They dematerialized the building's form, making it disappear in what they referred to as a "living responsive environment." Fog-emitting nozzles were installed on the pavilion exterior to cloak the dome in a cloud of mist and blur the architectural boundaries, sometimes six feet deep depending on the wind and climatic conditions. People entered the pavilion through a subterranean tunnel and emerged into an audiovisual extravaganza of reflections and light play. The domed interior was covered with mirrored mylar (like being inside an enormous birthday balloon), suctioned against the perimeter shell with negative vacuum pressure. The reflective surfaces and lack of corners created mesmerizing optical effects with a boundless sense of infinity. People appeared holographic, upside-down. Adding to the sensory overload, whale calls reverberated through a surround-sound speaker system. Bird songs (heard via handheld sound sticks) were triggered by interactive floor surfaces made from varied materials. Laser beams bounced around the interior, and hands-on props made the audience experience even more performative.[19]

Fog-emitting nozzles were installed on the exterior of the Pepsi Pavilion at Expo '70 in Osaka, Japan, to cloak the dome in a cloud of mist and blur the architectural boundaries.

Photo: Shunk-Kender © J. Paul Getty Trust. Getty Research Institute, Los Angeles (2014.R.20)

The domed interior of the Pepsi Pavilion at Expo '70 in Osaka was covered with mirrored mylar that transformed the performative space with boundless infinity.

Photo: Shunk-Kender © J. Paul Getty Trust. Getty Research Institute, Los Angeles (2014.R.20)

Sounds reverberated through the interior and bird songs played via hand-held sound sticks in the Pepsi Pavilion at Expo '70 in Osaka, Japan.

Photo: Shunk-Kender © J. Paul Getty Trust. Getty Research Institute, Los Angeles (2014.R.20)

Design impact: Audience as actors

The pavilion proved too radical for Pepsi; citing a lack of accessibility for the average person, they turned it into a music venue for the remainder of the Expo. E.A.T.'s open-ended, sensorial experiment resonates with today's participatory exhibition environments and selfie museums. Their wraparound world of sound, light, and performance predates highly immersive installations by artists like Olafur Eliasson, and community participatory events organized by groups like Artichoke. Today's audiences would lap up their work.

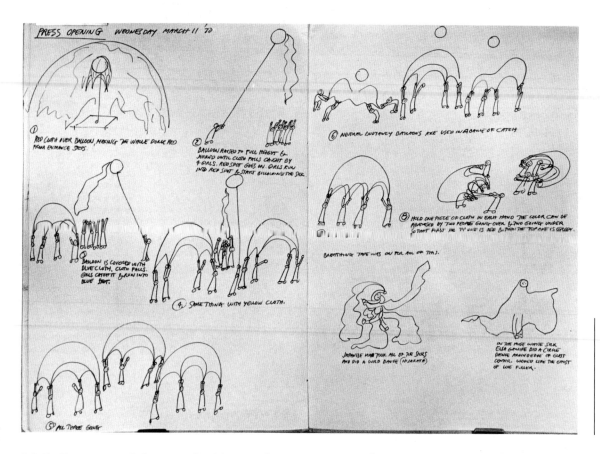

Napkin sketches depict an array of performative props (balloons and colored cloth) that accentuate the dome for the opening of the Pepsi Pavilion at Expo '70 in Osaka, Japan.

180-Degree Dioramic Experiences: Landscape Immersion and Windows to the World

Before audiences were plunged into panoramic and spherical immersive encounters, there were dioramic experiences to occupy people's peripheral vision. Like windows into other worlds, dioramas started small in seventeenth-century viewing boxes, transitioned to stage-like presentations, and then found a fitting place in the habitat halls of natural history museums and the landscape dioramas that envelop audiences at attractions and theme parks.

Large viewing boxes

The earliest dioramas, like Barker's panoramas, were created as a source of commercial entertainment. In 1822, Charles Marie Bouton and Louis-Jacques-Mandé Daguerre (inventor of the daguerreotype) built the Diorama Theater in Paris to display paintings that, thanks to some clever light and sound effects, and the occasional wandering animal, seemed to come alive. Audiences stood on a circular stage and looked down a long tunnel to a large translucent, linen canvas (70 feet wide x 45 feet high) with pictures painted on both sides. A team of stagehands would carefully choreograph incoming sunlight onto the canvas using screens, shutters, and colored gels. This revealed the painting on either side of the canvas and created the illusion of movement or the passage of time. The stage would then revolve to redirect the audience's view to another tunnel and diorama, to complete the theatrical experience.[20]

Habitat dioramas

Dioramic representations of animals, plants, and people in specific geographic and cultural land-scapes are an enduring interpretive technique. A product of expertise and skills aligned with conservation specialists and teams of scientists, sculptors, taxidermists, carpenters, and muralists, rather than exhibition designers. Museum habitat dioramas are associated with innovations in animal taxidermy, and a rethinking of sterile animal displays in nineteenth-century glass boxes. Since the 1970s, museums have augmented, renovated, and re-envisioned diorama halls in tandem with developments in educational/learning theory, technology, science, and visitor studies.[21]

The first habitat diorama created for a museum was constructed by taxidermist Carl Akeley for the Milwaukee Public Museum in 1889. Akeley set taxidermy muskrats in a three-dimensional re-creation of their wetland habitat with a realistic painted background. Akeley's exhibits went on to influence science and art institutions worldwide.[22]

Like the display windows in a department store, these portals into the natural world combine composition, illusion, lighting, and seductive backdrops to absorb audiences. Frozen in time, these static vignettes were the closest people came to observing exotic animals in their native habitats. Object Theater is an exhibit technique that animates dioramas using programmed lighting—as the story unfolds, areas of the diorama illuminate and gain prominence in synch with a recorded narration. Today, live action dioramas using animatronics bring people even closer to reality, not unlike how Daguerre's Diorama Theater anticipated mixed reality.[23] London's Natural History Museum's Darwin Centre (2009) combined naturalist Sir David Attenborough's telling of the evolutionary story with a portable handheld device and brought to life one of the first habitat dioramas using augmented reality.[24]

Diorama halls

A hall of dioramas contains a series of glassed-in habitat vignettes in one cohesive gallery environment. Later design iterations enhanced the immersive experience and strategically placed obstacles—wooden logs and vegetation—to imply barriers. Positioned centrally in the Grande Galerie de l'Évolution, the Noah's Ark procession of African animals at the Museum of Natural

Le Musée de la Chasse et de la Nature in Paris gives rise to delightful object juxta-positions and unexpected dioramic encounters.

Photo: Hemis / Alamy Stock Photo

Local Project's Immersion Room at the Cooper Hewitt, Smithsonian Design Museum is a romp through the history of surface design where the dioramic encounter is in the hands of the audience.

Cooper Hewitt Design Museum. Photo: Allison Hale.

History in Paris (1994) is an exquisite example of taxidermy liberated from the glass box. Cross the Seine River, and Le Musée de la Chasse et de la Nature (founded 1967) commissions exhibits that release their collection of taxidermy animals into seventeenth-century room settings, giving rise to delightful object juxtapositions and unexpected dioramic encounters.

Landscape immersion

Habitat dioramas waned in popularity in the 1950s.[25] Audiences preferred new hands-on exhibits installed in other parts of the museum. The "diorama dilemma" meant that many institutions removed or closed their taxidermized treasures. Around the same time, "landscape dioramas" were designed into theme parks, zoos, and museums. Here, audiences entered the diorama and participated in re-created built or natural environments.

Traditional dioramas are enjoying a technological renaissance. Even the stalwart period rooms in historic houses and museums (often overlooked as dioramas) are being reimagined. The *Immersion Room* (2014) at the Cooper Hewitt, Smithsonian Design Museum in New York allows people to select patterns from the museum's virtual wallpaper collection. Using an interactive touch table, they make their choices, which are then digitally projected onto the room's wraparound wall surfaces. This romp through the history of design allows audiences to program the rooms interior décor and evaluate their selection—a dioramic encounter in the hands of the audience.

Miniaturized Worlds: Streetscapes, Models, and Flyover Experiences

Strolling along Kirkgate in York's Castle Museum, you can smell the candy in the sweetshop, greet costumed guides, and marvel at the austerity of the local police jail. In the 1930s, Dr. John Lamplugh Kirk donated his collection of Yorkshire life to the local history museum and purposefully set about displaying these artifacts as part of an indoor Victorian streetscape against a backdrop of salvaged authentic buildings.[26] His architectural assemblage constituted one of the first multimodal wraparound environments—part museum and part themed attraction.

Across the Atlantic, thirty years later, the Milwaukee Public Museum developed what became known as the "Milwaukee style," immersive exhibits where audiences step into the sights and sounds at the turn of the twentieth century by strolling through a three-quarter-scale reconstruction called *The Streets of Old Milwaukee*. Updated to heighten the sensory experience, both examples remain popular areas of their museums—some of the first indoor walk-through dioramas in the world.[27]

Streetscapes

Living history museums, like Skansen in Sweden (1881), reenact history and heritage, and predate walk-through dioramas and streetscapes. Las Vegas casinos and themed shopping promenades like The Grove in Los Angeles offer commercial streetscapes that re-create historical experiences. Walking Cinema is an immersive audio and AR experience that reinvents the streetscape by leading audiences step-by-step through a particular theme or narrative. The museum around you is unlocked through a mobile app, where real outdoor streetscapes become the visuals for a series of fascinating historical stories.[28]

Models

Designers use scale models to plan exhibitions and communicate their vision—who does not like to play dollhouse? Tactile models are also great interpretive tools for communicating content with exhibition audiences. Since the 1930s, model villages and leisure towns have captivated both the young and the old.

The Battle of Bannockburn experience in Scotland (2014) immerses people in medieval warfare using state-of-the-art technology.[29] The visitor center's battle room gathers participants around a central topographical model to choose a side (Scots or English) and reenact the famous conflict. Warfare commences when the model is activated by object theater-like projected digital overlays, facilitated by the Battle Master. Blending multiple interpretive methods, the school groups that visit Bannockburn for their Scottish history education find the "gaming" experience far more familiar and engaging than the adjacent grassy field where the real battle played out.

Warfare commences when object theater-like projected digital overlays activate the model at the Battle of Bannockburn Experience designed by White Light Studios.

Courtesy of National Trust for Scotland. Photo: Timothy J. McNeil.

Primary case study
Flyover experiences

Futurama, GM's *Highways and Horizons* exhibit, New York World's Fair, 1939 Designers: Norman Bel Geddes (exhibit); Albert Kahn (architect)

Design challenge: Magical flight

Inspired by entertainment and popular culture, World's Fairs opened themselves up in the early twentieth century to larger sections of society. Less preoccupied with static object displays, the focus shifted to people's attention span and managing their expectations. The 1939 New York World's Fair General Motors

pavilion was part of this transformation, introducing state-of-the-art exhibit making, a multimedia environment, and a dramatic buildup.[30] Up to twenty-eight thousand people a day waited eagerly to enter the transportation world of tomorrow. The pavilion exterior—in the streamlining style—shrouded a complex of companion exhibits connected by elevated pedestrian walkways. The star attraction was the *Futurama* ride, a magical flyover of 1960s America. General Motors commissioned theatrical and industrial designer Norman Bel Geddes to create this futuristic vision, aptly calling him "the man behind the spectacle."[31]

Design solution: Mechanical diorama

Bel Geddes set to work on a lifelike scale model diorama/panorama that even today defies comprehension. City blocks, schools, skyrises, an airport, factories, farms, trees, and mountains were gridded and bound together by sprawling roads and multilane, elevated highways with autonomous cars that were moving. *Futurama*'s mechanical diorama extended for a third of a mile. In addition to a half million model buildings, there were more than fifty thousand scale-model automobiles, all approved by Bel Geddes for form, color, realism, good taste, human interest, and dozens of other measuring standards.[32]

Audiences described *Futurama* as "just mind-boggling."[33] Seated side by side, they looked through a glass window down onto the miniature metropolis below from the "carry-go-round," which took about sixteen minutes to snake around the vast scale model using a Westinghouse conveyor system traveling at approximately 102 feet per minute. The traveling sound-chairs had built-in speakers that delivered a series of accompanying voice-overs to describe the various sections of the futuristic landscape.

Design impact: Enchanting audiences

Futurama ticks the boxes of multiple exhibition design tropes, where simply entering the pavilion wowed audiences. Described as "more than a collection of sleek predictions," the exhibit provided an experience that was visceral and believable, total immersion that offered a "tangible example of the potential of the future."[34] *Futurama* foretells how the design of miniature worlds and people movers can successfully enchant audiences and convey stories, anticipating what was to take place in Anaheim, California, fifteen years later.

Futurama's mechanical diorama extended for a third of a mile, included half a million scale-model buildings and 50,000 automobiles.

Photo: Bettmann/Getty Images

Illusion of infinity

Early immersive installations were limited to large-scale static panoramic paintings presented as reverse theaters in the round where the audience occupies the stage. Providing 360-degree views was the closest approximation to simulating the real world, and an illusion of infinity. While primarily a visual medium, panoramic and dioramic exhibits evolved to incorporate movement, smell, light, objects, and sound, with the help of itinerant entertainers and their illusionary use of smoke and mirrors.

Tips and Tricks

Allow audiences to temporarily escape to other worlds using the following design techniques:

1. Consider every design detail and viewpoint just enough to immerse people in another world and suspend disbelief.
2. Accommodate wheelchair users and children and provide seating or leaning rails in 360-degree viewing theaters.
3. Digital projection is a high-spectacle and minimal-impact (reversible) solution, with a good cost-to-impact ratio.
4. Stitching together images from multiple projection units requires back-end media integration to achieve synchronization.
5. Total immersion is as much about sound quality as image scale.
6. Methods of immersion range from large-scale images to digital projection, to handheld and headgear-activated experiences.
7. There is no singular definition for the term *diorama*. Its main purpose is to re-create a specific moment in time or an illusionary setting.
8. Creating immersive experiences involves a team with a range of specializations and skills.
9. Traditional dioramic techniques like object theater can be transformed using digital tools.
10. Scale models captivate audiences and provide a high-tactile and accessible experience.

Notes

1. Alison Griffiths, *Shivers Down Your Spine: Cinema, Museums, and the Immersive View* (New York: Columbia University Press, 2008), 17.

2. "Immersive Digital Gallery 1," National Museum of Korea, accessed August 18, 2021, https://www.museum .go.kr/site/eng/content/https%3A%2F%2Fwww.museum.go.kr%2Fsite%2Feng%2Fcontent%2Fdigital _realistic_1.

3. "Rama-O-Rama: A Guide to 5 Visual Extravaganzas!" April 8, 2013, https://www.mentalfloss.com/ article/49894/rama-o-rama-guide-5-visual-extravaganzas.

4. Stephan Oettermann, *The Panorama: History of a Mass Medium* (New York: Zone Books, 1997).

5. "Rama-O-Rama."

6. "Rama-O-Rama."

7. Laurent Lescop, "360° Vision, from Panoramas to VR," *Envisioning Architecture: Space/Time/Meaning* (Mackintosh School of Architecture, Glasgow School of Art, 2017), 230–32.

8. "Sensorama," in *Wikipedia*, July 26, 2021, https://en.wikipedia.org/w/index.php?title=Sensorama&oldid =1035510271.

9. James Martin Charlton, "A Desire for Immersion: The Panorama to the Oculus Rift," September 10, 2015, https://www.academia.edu/22443751/A_Desire_for_Immersion_The_Panorama_to_the_Oculus_Rift.

10. "More Than *Mona Lisa*: Louvre's Leonardo Da Vinci Is a Blockbuster with Brains," *Guardian*, October 21, 2019, http://www.theguardian.com/artanddesign/2019/oct/21/mona-lisa-leonard-da-vinci-louvre -exhibition.

11. "Stone Circle," English Heritage, accessed August 25, 2021, https://www.english-heritage.org.uk/visit/ places/stonehenge/things-to-do/stone-circle/.

12. "Stonehenge Visitor Centre | Centre Screen," accessed August 25, 2021, https://www.centrescreen.co .uk/project-post/stonehenge-visitor-centre/.

13. "New Stonehenge Visitor Centre Finally Opens," *Guardian*, December 17, 2013, http://www.theguardian .com/culture/2013/dec/17/stonehenge-visitor-centre-opens-english-heritage.

14. "Electrosonic, The First 50 Years | PDF | Computing And Information Technology," Scribd, accessed August 25, 2021, https://www.scribd.com/document/496325490/Electrosonic-the-First-50-Years.

15. "IMAX—Not the First, but Close!" accessed August 19, 2021, https://airandspace.si.edu/stories/editorial/ imax%E2%80%94not-first-close.

16. MoMA, "Press Release: Museum of Modern Art to Open Large Summer Exhibition, Airways to Peace" (MoMA, June 14, 1943), https://www.moma.org/calendar/exhibitions/3138?.

17. Jimmy Stamp, "When PepsiCola Allowed a Team of Artists to Wreak Creative Havoc," *Smithsonian*, accessed August 16, 2021, https://www.smithsonianmag.com/arts-culture/when-pepsicola-allowed-a -team-of-artists-to-wreak-creative-havoc-109661/.

18. "E.A.T.—The Story of Experiments in Art and Technology," accessed August 19, 2021, https://www.fondation-langlois.org/html/e/page.php?NumPage=236.

19. Dartmouth, "E.A.T.—Experiments in Art & Technology, 1960–2001," accessed August 19, 2021, https://www.youtube.com/watch?v=B0coC9CxER4.

20. "Rama-O-Rama."

21. Marjorie Schwarzer and Mary Jo Sutton, "The Diorama Dilemma: A Literature Review and Analysis," OMCA report, final draft November 25, 2009, accessed June 29, 2021, https://www.academia.edu/6727013/The_Diorama_Dilemma_A_Literature_review_and_Analysis_MS_and_MJS_The_Diorama_Dilemma_A_Literature_Review_and_Analysis?email_work_card=title.

22. "Gallery: The Art and Science of Museum Dioramas," *Ideas.Ted.Com* (blog), July 13, 2017, https://ideas.ted.com/gallery-the-art-and-science-of-museum-dioramas/.

23. Stephen C. Quinn, *Windows on Nature: The Great Habitat Dioramas of the American Museum of Natural History* (New York: Harry N. Abrams, 2006), 10.

24. "Attenborough Studio," SHADOW INDUSTRIES, accessed August 23, 2021, https://www.shadowindustries.co.uk/ifilm-1.

25. Condé Nast, "The Making of the American Museum of Natural History's Wildlife Dioramas," *New Yorker*, February 15, 2016, http://www.newyorker.com/culture/photo-booth/the-making-of-the-american-museum-of-natural-historys-wildlife-dioramas.

26. York Museums Trust, *York Castle Museum: Souvenir Guidebook* (Jigsaw Design & Publishing, 2018), 23–29.

27. "Streets of Old Milwaukee | Milwaukee Public Museum," accessed August 23, 2021, https://www.mpm.edu/plan-visit/exhibitions/permanent-exhibits/first-floor-exhibits/streets-old-milwaukee.

28. "Walking Cinema," Walking Cinema, accessed August 23, 2021, https://www.walkingcinema.org.

29. National Trust for Scotland, "Battle of Bannockburn Experience," National Trust for Scotland, accessed August 23, 2021, https://www.nts.org.uk/visit/places/bannockburn/highlights/battle-of-bannockburn-experience.

30. Herman Kossmann, Suzanne Mulder, and Frank den Oudsten, eds., *Narrative Spaces: On the Art of Exhibiting* (Rotterdam: 010 Publ, 2012), 178.

31. "Biblion: WORLD'S FAIR | STORY: GM/Futurama," accessed August 23, 2021, http://exhibitions.nypl.org/biblion/worldsfair/enter-world-tomorrow-futurama-and-beyond/story/story-gmfuturama.

32. "Biblion: WORLD'S FAIR | STORY: GM/Futurama."

33. "Remembering Futurama at the 1939 New York World's Fair," accessed August 23, 2021, https://sites.utexas.edu/ransomcentermagazine/2012/11/13/remembering-futurama-at-the-1939-new-york-worlds-fair/.

34. "Remembering Futurama at the 1939 New York World's Fair."

Designer's Toolbox: **Wonder**

Experience makers use projection, reflection, and mechanical devices to deceive, engage, and inform audiences. The art of illusion transports people into other worlds where escapist, emotional, and spiritual encounters transcend the everyday. Today's tools are packed with pixels and advanced artificial intelligence. Delve into the designer's toolbox and choose your method of deception.

Visualization: John Haden is part of a multidisciplinary team designing attractions, events, and entertainment at the Thinkwell Group in Burbank, U.S.A.

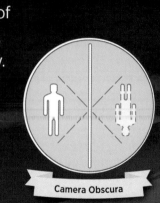

Camera Obscura

Mirrored Room

Ribbon Ride

Pepper's Ghost

SMOKE &

MIRRORS

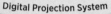

Digital Projection System

Rear Projection

Gobo Projection

Human Robot

Animatronic Dinosaur

Animatronic Human

Projected Face

Solid/Fabric Projections

Water Projection

Projection Mapping

Vapor Projection

CHAPTER 10

Smoke and Mirrors

The arts of illusion and deception are powerful tools in the exhibition designer's box of tricks.

Key message: Design inspires and transforms exhibition audiences.

Key word: wonder

Bamboozle, beguile, humbug, hornswoggle, and *hoodwink*—the lexicon of synonyms for the act of deception is long and wondrous. Those who develop, build, and design events, theme parks, and museum exhibits play tricks on us as they magically turn fantasy into reality using sleight-of-hand. Using the pragmatic to phantasmagorical, the designer's task is to provide people-centered, accessible, and inclusive solutions that leave audiences inspired and transformed.

From the weird to the wonderful, this chapter takes a journey through visual perception, what is real and what is not, and how the trope "smoke and mirrors" is central to the history of illusion resulting in today's mind-blowing technologies that blend art and engineering, where themed attractions, advanced animatronics, rides, and robotics are preceded by automata and clockwork systems. They are now joined by exhibits that apply machine learning using artificial intelligence with the potential to read and respond to audiences and provide customized experiences. Techniques of deception have a rich history and have stood the test of time, and many are now in the hands of social media users, allowing them to capture, manipulate, and share their own illusions.

Parlor to Performative: Origins of Illusionary and Deceptive Exhibition Experiences

Exhibition and experience design tends to be associated with the practice of architecture and museology. Philosophically the field aligns more closely with theater and dramaturgy, where objects and stories are the actors on the exhibition stage, and designers are the performers, acting out audience engagement scenarios as highly interactive designs are fine-tuned and take shape.[1] Disney understood the role of entertainer—"storytelling and showmanship"—was Walt's way and method of persuasion.[2] P. T. Barnum was the consummate performer. Barnum's American Museum (1841) displayed a controversial range of attractions that exploited humans and animals. Objects on display had questionable origins, and exhibits were not all they were made out to be.

Audiences nonetheless visited in droves and seemed happy to pay the admission price to participate in the art of illusion and delight in this deception.

Barnum, like Disney, employed a range of stagecraft technicians to design and build their deceptive apparatus. These forebears of exhibition design practice are descended from a lengthy line of itinerant entertainers, escape artists, sideshow carnies, and stagecraft technicians who developed spectacular illusions, commercial expositions, and immersive encounters to bamboozle audiences. While the precursors of exhibit techniques owe their origins to such entrepreneurial exploits, many of these deceptive practices evolved from parlor games and magic tricks, marketed as amusement activities to be played in the domestic setting, or they owe their origins to broader advances in science, electricity, exploration, and the arts.[3]

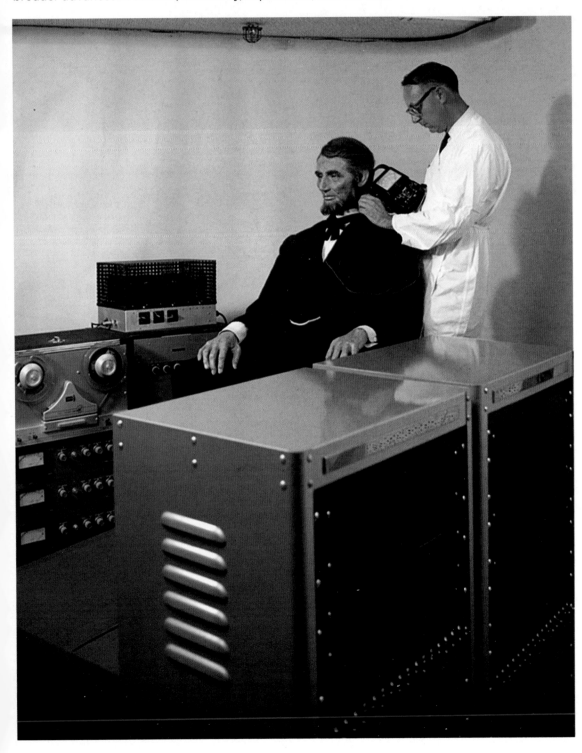

Wathel Rogers working on Audio-Animatronics replica of President Abraham Lincoln from the Disneyland Story Presenting Great Moments with Mr. Lincoln attraction.

© Disney

P. T. Barnum's American Museum (founded 1841) displayed a controversial and deceptive range of attractions.

"Barnum's Museum, Broadway and Ann Street, 1853; from BV Francis' Old New York; XI #1489. New-York Historical Society, 84190d."

Reflection, Projection and Pixels: Experiences That Alter Visual Perception

Imagine an entire exhibition space that becomes an alternative reality with the flick of a switch. Advanced projectors and sensors, interactive surfaces, sound and light effects, generative patterns, and animated creatures drawn by you, the audience, are released into the space to be chased and caught. This is the work of the international art collective and interdisciplinary group teamLab, which creates immersive sound and light spaces that are responsive to people and rooted in the exploration of logical structures of spatial perception in premodern East Asia.[4] This section delves into the exhibition designer's box of tricks to demonstrate how reflection and projection alter people's visual perception. These deceptive tools include mirrors and optical devices, projectors and lighting effects, pixels, screens, surfaces, and sounds.

Mirrors—reflecting society

The teamLab collective is following a fascination with infinity that goes back to the mirrored rooms of Louis XIV's palaces in France. The mirror is the earliest gadget of deception and reflects the allure of visual perception. People of the ancient world fashioned mirrors from obsidian rock and used polished metals. The most immediate association between exhibits and mirrors is the distorting kind found at fun fairs and amusement parks. One of the earliest forms of exhibition apparatus that projected an image was the solar microscope invented in 1740. The sun's rays fall on a plane mirror placed outside of a darkened room and are reflected toward a condensing lens and then to a second lens by which they are concentrated and focused to produce highly magnified images—preceding the magic lantern slide viewer, slide projectors, and today's sophisticated projection units.

teamLab's *Graffiti Nature: Lost, Immersed and Reborn* (2018) uses projectors, sensors, interactive surfaces, sound, and light effects to conjure up an alternate reality.

teamLab, *Graffiti Nature: Lost, Immersed and Reborn*, 2018, Interactive Digital Installation, Sound: Hideaki Takahashi © teamLab, courtesy Pace Gallery

Artists such as Lucas Samaras and Yayoi Kusama, and experience designer Es Devlin, have used mirrors and the concept of infinity in their work. The Cyber Infinity Room at the International Spy Museum (2019), designed by Gallagher & Associates, is a mirrored room that creates an endless digital landscape that tells the story of cyberwarfare. The mirrored surface as an experiential method and backdrop reflects the twenty-first-century obsession with sharing oneself on social media platforms. Artists like Olafur Eliasson are feeding this obsession, catering to a generation raised on Instagram, allowing people to infiltrate their artwork and record/make their own shared social media exhibitions, just as the fun fair mirrors have done at carnivals for years.

Phantasmagoria

Madame Dupont had to be resuscitated with smelling salts when she fell to the floor in fear during a showing of *Fantasmagorie* at Étienne-Gaspard Robertson's ghostly magic lantern performance in 1797. Paris loved it, and so did the world, wherever Robertson traveled with his horror show. The authorities at first shut him down because audiences thought the ghosts were real, but his spectacular shows continued and evolved for years. Others in the audience lashed out with swords, guns, and sticks in disbelief at winged skulls, devils, and frightening creatures that flew overhead. Long interested in the supernatural, Robertson's love of art and physics merged into *phantasmagoria*, meaning a gathering of ghosts.[5] He built a magic lantern on wheels called the *Fantoscope*, which projected layers of images all at once and moved around to make the figures appear to approach the audience. To heighten the drama, the images were projected onto a cloud of smoke made from nitric and sulphuric acid, combined with spooky candlelight, an introduction by Robertson on the afterlife (a successful ingredient of these shows was the dynamic live narration), and an eerily monotonous harmonic accompaniment and ventriloquism for the ghouls. Combined, this made for a most unsettling evening.

Preceding the magic lantern slide viewer, slide projectors, and today's sophisticated projection units was the solar microscope.

Source: Adam Wolfgang Winterschmidt (German, 1733–96). Etching and watercolor from *Microscopic Amusement Both for The Mind and For the Eyes: Containing Fifty Engravings Drawn from Nature and Illuminated, With Their Explanations, 1768*, via HathiTrust Digital Library

Primary case study
Projection deception

London Mithraeum / Bloomberg SPACE, Bloomberg UK Headquarters London, 2018–present
Principal Designers: Local Projects (Lead Designer/ Media); Studio Joseph (Exhibition Architect); MOLA (Museum of London Archaeology); Bloomberg Team

Design challenge: Reimagining history

The use of vaporized acid during Robertson's startling performance posed an obvious and more sinister threat to his audience. Dry ice, the staple of contemporary theater and music festivals, had yet to be invented and enter the exhibition designer's box of tricks. A visit to London Mithraeum / Bloomberg SPACE reveals another not-so-dissimilar, but safer use of smoke and mirrors. The ancient ruins of the Roman Temple of Mithras (about 240 AD) were carefully replicated at their original site beneath the office building, with the original ruins being moved to the archives of the Museum of London Archeology. The design team was commissioned to conjure up an experience that explained the significance of the site, reimagined how audiences engage with archaeology, and evoked an immersive encounter with this ancient mystery cult about which so little is known.

Design solution: Dramatic buildup

The experience unfolds over three levels. It begins with a display of over six hundred Roman artifacts, including personal effects, glassware, wooden writing tablets, and ceramics, unearthed during the construction of the Bloomberg UK headquarters. From there, visitors descend to the mezzanine level flanked by granite walls etched with stratigraphy—the layers of history from modern times to the original ancient Roman street elevation. Here, they encounter detailed interpretive media insights into the history and meaning of the temple and its occupants. The journey continues to the temple ruins, located on the bottom level of the subterranean museum. After a timed entry and a period of dramatic buildup, visitors enter a large, darkened room, where walls of structural light rise over the foundation remnants of the temple to reveal its original form. The ghostly reconstruction uses a harmless theatrical fog mix of glycol and water to give the light beams their physicality.

Design impact: Leaving no trace

The intervention disappears as soon as it arrives, leaving no perceptible trace and impact on the ancient site. The light is projected to a series of mirrors and refining apertures to increase the density and intensity of the beam.[6] More than two hundred years later, it is significant that Étienne-Gaspard Robertson's smoke-and-mirrors illusion continues to deceive, but mercifully not to poison its audiences.

People enter a darkened room where walls of structural light rise over the foundation remnants of the temple to reveal its original form at London Mithraeum / Bloomberg SPACE.

Photo: Local Projects

Prototyping the theatrical fog mix of glycol and water that give the light beams their physicality at London Mithraeum / Bloomberg SPACE.

Photo: Local Projects

Multi-projection

Smaller magic lantern projectors were a popular nineteenth-century form of home entertainment. Painted images and photographs on glass slides were inserted into the projector depicting well-known scenes. Magic lanterns predate the invention of 35mm slide projectors, a display method used extensively until the advent of digital projection systems at the end of the twentieth century. Inspired by creative design exploits at commercial expositions in the 1960s, museums embraced projection as a medium, and it proved pivotal for an emerging exhibition design field and signaled a bright future for projection as an illusionary mode.

Static and moving images using fourteen projectors and nine screens wowed audiences in the *Information Machine* at the 1964/1965 New York World's Fair IBM Pavilion.

Pepper's ghost illusion created using light projected from a magic lantern onto a performer and reflected in a sheet of glass on the stage.

Le Monde Illustré, 1862, published in *The World of Wonders*. Wikipedia Commons, CC-PD.

In 1961, the Eames office worked with architect Eero Saarinen (continued with Roche Dinkeloo and Associates after Saarinen's death) on what was their most impressive project to date, IBM's Pavilion at the 1964/1965 New York World's Fair.[7] Design polymaths Charles and Ray Eames reveled in the multidisciplinary medium of exhibition design. Their brief was to design an experience about the influence of computers in contemporary society, and the similarity between how humans and machines process and interpret information. The pavilion consisted of a gigantic Ovoid Theater floating one hundred feet above the heads of the people below. Stadium seating magically transported audiences upward into the *Information Machine*, a multiplicity of static and moving images consisting of fourteen projectors and nine screens. The experience was facilitated by an emcee dressed in formal attire who arrived by elevator to introduce and describe the more complex parts of the show. The extravaganza used rapid-image transitions and a rousing musical score to pull people into the narrative, like Etienne Gaspard Robertson had 150 years earlier, but with IBM's vision of U.S. exceptionalism rather than the darker ghosts and devils of the Parisian back streets.

Pepper's ghost

Magic lantern projection was originally used for one of the most enduring theatrical illusions called Pepper's ghost. Named after the English scientist John Henry Pepper, who demonstrated the technique for the first time in 1862, the illusion requires a brightly lit figure placed out of sight and reflected in a pane of transparent material (typically glass) placed between the performer and the audience. To the viewer, it appears as if the ghost is on the stage.

Primary case study
Pepper's ghost illusion

Haunted Mansion, Disneyland Park, Anaheim, 1967–present
Principal Designers: Yale Gracey and Rolly Crump, Walt Disney Enterprises (WED)

Design challenge: Introducing Imagineers

Who can forget a visit to Disneyland and the holographic ghosts dancing together in the Ballroom at the Haunted Mansion? The attraction was designed by a notable team of Walt Disney Imagineers, led by the technical talents of expert illusioneer Yale Gracey. Apparitions of swirling and twirling mechanical mannequins instead of live performers remain popular with audiences, who wonder how the illusion is achieved.[8] The attraction had been in the works for several years before it opened with a single-day attendance record of 82,516 in August 1969.[9] It was delayed due to WED's involvement in the 1964/1965 New York World's Fair and due to Walt Disney's death two years before its completion.

Design solution: Ghostly apparitions

The Haunted Mansion's elegant Antebellum-style exterior was originally designed to look in a state of disrepair, like the interior. Walt Disney, however, had a different vision and said that he'd keep up the outside and let the ghosts take care of the inside.[10] Guests enter the hallway, which is disguised as an elevator, and are spirited to the second-floor ride. Initially planned as a walk-through attraction, the delayed opening proved to be advantageous, allowing Imagineer Bob Gurr to perfect the Omnimover, an efficient method of moving many people in automated pods traveling on tracks. The clamshell Doom Buggies were the ideal solution, swiveling to turn and tilt the audience's attention to key illusions and parts of the story. Distinctive theme music accompanied by a spectral narration enthrall guests as they travel through a series of rooms where special effects defy explanation and scenes unfold.

Pepper's ghost activates multiple ghoulish scenes. People in portraits come alive, ghostly guests dine in the dining room, and couples cavort around the ballroom. The act of illusion centers on the intermittent appearance and disappearance of these apparitions. As guests look down from their Doom Buggies to scenes below, moving figures, some on large turntables, in the darkness under the elevated track (out of audience sight) are illuminated with light. Their translucent reflections are cast on a wall of glass separating the viewer from the scene below, making them appear to occupy the room and interact with the scenery. Turn off the light and instantaneously they vanish. Pepper's ghost delivers a proven, old-school technique that

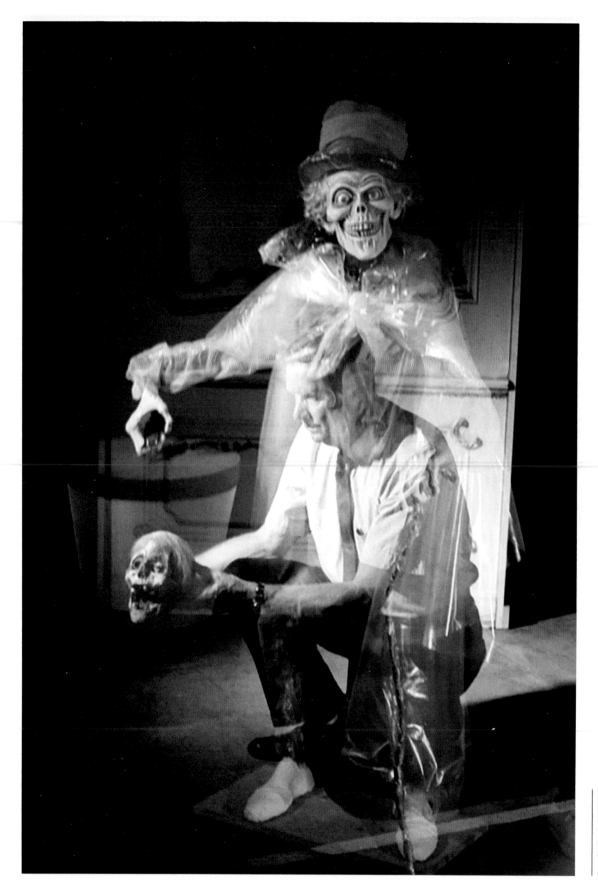

Designer Yale Gracey experiments with a Pepper's ghost illusion for the Hatbox Ghost from the Haunted Mansion attraction at Disneyland Park at the Disneyland Resort.

© Disney

can be relied on for an attraction that operates year-round for millions of people—simple and clever!

Design impact: Tinkerers and inventors

Animators Yale Gracey and Rolly Crump were recruited from the Walt Disney Productions to WED Enterprises in 1959. They designed late into the night in their second-floor studio. Imagine their active, messy studio and childlike antics as they shared scary stories and perfected illusions and gadgets of deception for the Haunted Mansion. While classed as experience makers, they were tinkerers and inventors; inspired by nineteenth-century illusions and magic tricks featured in magazines like *Popular Mechanics*, their experiments and devices left an indelible mark on Disney attractions and the world of themed experiences.

Oldest trick in the book

The proliferation of tools in today's digital design kit has not replaced the Pepper's ghost technique. The illusion continues to deceive audiences at attractions, museums, theaters, festivals, and concerts with holographic apparitions. It is used very effectively at the Grachten Museum (2011, refurbished 2020). The former dwelling communicates the history of seventeenth-century canal houses in Amsterdam through a series of cleverly designed exhibits, including a scale replica of the museum, which can be viewed in the round. Like a dollhouse, people peer into the windows to see how the rooms have been decorated and furnished over time. Using small-scale Pepper's ghost projections, the home's inhabitants move through the rooms in conversation. Museum audiences eavesdrop via headsets and inadvertently learn the history of the house. The exhibit's voyeuristic nature captivates onlookers with small domestic dramas that unfold in each vignette.

The advantage of Pepper's ghost is that it does not alter objects or leave a trace. A multitude of miniature dioramas at the Museum of Jurassic Technology in Los Angeles use this technique effectively to make rare books appear to open and their illustrations come alive. Founders David Hildebrand and Diana Drake Wilson would freely admit that their masterpiece of museology owes much to the history of illusion (plausible and implausible) and those who deceived audiences, as their displays challenge people's perceptions of what is real and what is not.[11]

Projection mapping

Increased lumens, smarter pixels (resolution), and design software that enables precise masking, animation, and real-time rendering have spawned outdoor light festivals and traveling exhibitions that use projection mapping in cities all over the world. The medium's temporality and scalability, combined with the potential of any surface in the built environment to become a screen, makes this a popular device with designers and for audiences.

Projection mapping re-creates what was invisible and lost in time. The exhibition *Leonardo: Experience a Masterpiece* (2019) at London's National Gallery of Art told the story of da Vinci's altarpiece painting, *The Virgin of the Rocks*, which was started in the 1480s and never installed in its intended Milanese church setting. Four distinct exhibition spaces interpret the painting from new perspectives. In the final space, people come face-to-face with the original masterpiece set in an imagined chapel—it is not only a lovely reward, but a deceptive moment. The media developers and designers at 59 Productions used tightly registered and vivid projection-mapping techniques to reveal what *The Virgin of the Rocks* might have looked like in its original setting as part of an elaborate altarpiece. Viewers are taken through a mesmerizing time-lapse journey with accompanying liturgical music, as the panels flanking the painting spring to life and reveal the under-drawing, carving, and fully painted subject matter. The result is visually stunning, the perfect use of this temporal, do-no-harm medium to tell a complex story—da Vinci becomes the magician.

Machines, Movement, and Bots: Experiences That Utilize Machine Learning

The exhibition designer's box of tricks contains spellbinding illusions that have struggled to find acceptance in the museum sector but are fully embraced in the attraction industry. Animatronics, rides, and robots use automated movement to deceive audiences by altering reality or simulating human or animal form. Originally powered by clock mechanisms, then hydraulics and electronics, these forms are now manipulated digitally and optimize machine learning. Yet, they remain beguiling because of their mechanical ingenuity.

Ghost in the machine

Human forms that seem to move spontaneously and of their own free will using levers, counterweights, ratchets, gears, and turbines have fascinated inventors and artists for centuries. Early mechanical automata developed in the sixteenth and seventeenth centuries for houses and gardens of the wealthy were modeled in the style of classical statues coming to life. Later versions of automata depicting all forms of flora and fauna reached their height of popularity in the eighteenth century and entertained the elite and the public.

Cornelis Jacobus van Oeckelen built and repaired organs, but his real interest was his automaton inventions, which played wind instruments using bellows and other mechanical techniques

popular in his trade. The Android Clarinetist, built in 1838, is the only one of his inventions that still exists. This six-and half-foot-tall man is holding a pseudo-clarinet and was dressed as a medieval troubadour. The android was brought to life by a complex mechanical infrastructure of cogs and linkages powered by two clockwork motors that operate his body motions, and bellows that force air through the clarinet. In addition, the clarinetist's head and eyes would move. Following in the footsteps of the other itinerant performers and entertainers discussed in this chapter, van Oeckelen and his android toured internationally playing for audiences in large concert halls. The duo performed so skillfully they duped people into thinking the automaton was real. At the end of

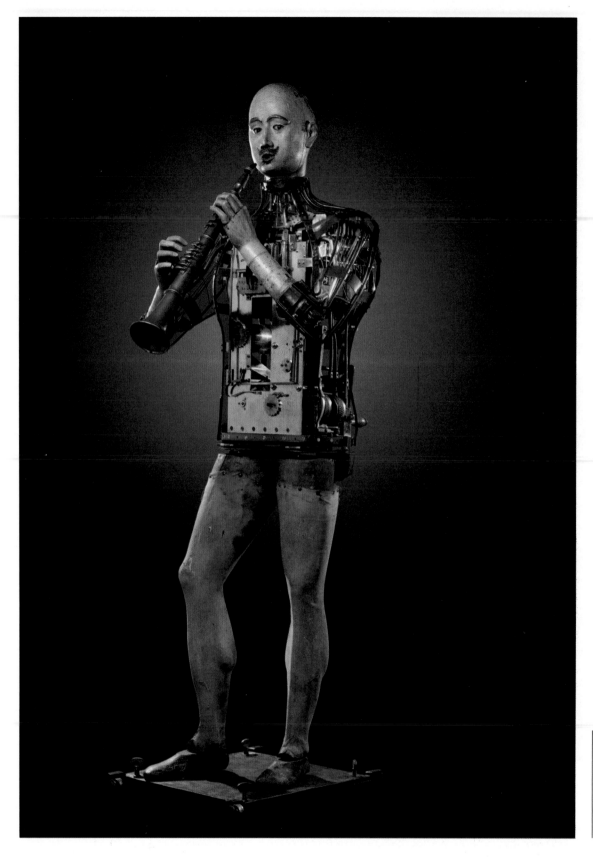

The Android Clarinetist's mechanical dexterity and repertoire of music was greater than comparable 19th century automata and his movements anticipated animatronics.

A GREAT
MECHANICAL, ANATOMICAL
—AND—
MUSICAL WONDER
THE
AUTOMATON MUSICIAN
FROM THE ISLAND OF JAVA.

The following description is taken from the Boston Transcript:—

It is the invention and production of Mynheer Van Oeckelen, who has recently arrived from the Island of Java, and is in the form of a full-sized anatomical figure of a man, the body of which is filled with many thousand parts of machinery, by which it plays quite artistically upon the Clarionet, &c. The illusion is so perfect in all respects that at a short distance the figure might well be mistaken for a living artist.

This automaton, being seven feet in height, and dressed in a very elegant troubadour's costume, is indeed worth seeing, as an extraordinary production of genius and labor, both by its playing on the clarionet and its various bodily motions. Acting entirely by the force of its own springs, it produces by internal wind, every tone upon its instrument; on which it plays with its fingers in such a graceful, life-like manner, that nothing could be preferred to its execution of a rondo of Weber, a fantasy concertante from the Frieschutz, a varied andantino of Beethoven, an introduction with the variations of Beriot, &c., and it is not exaggeration to say that the performance of every piece is united with such a tasteful expression as has hitherto been peculiar to highly cultivated artists alone. The crescendo, diminuendo, affectuoso, &c., are applied with so much accuracy, that the inspired musician can hardly surpass this inanimated image.

As soon as Mr. Van Oeckelen sits down at the piano to accompany the obligato of the player on the clarionet, the automaton begins to act, turning its head and eyes in different directions, while the whole body follows these motions in an easy and natural manner. After looking round a moment or two, it turns its face to the pianist to give the signal of commencement; it then brings its instrument to its lips to wet the reed; this it repeats twice, and then begins its solo with all that peculiar motion of the head, eyes, mouth and body, either each separately, or in such a happy combination that the most accomplished musician on the clarionet could have no more accuracy, neither better expression of feeling, nor higher energy; in a word, no more efficacious and delightful handling of an instrument.

By its elaborate and artistic construction, this curious figure can give 38 tunes, and adapt every motion with the greatest ease by blowing and fingering. Sometimes the piano having several measures of solo, the automaton not only follows its pauses, but also marks them softly with its lips. It has been the labor of a lifetime.

Exhibiting daily at Dr. Chapin's Church, No. 548 Broadway, from 11 A. M. to 10 P. M. Especial Evening performances commence at half-past 7 P. M.

ADMITTANCE - - - - 25 CENTS
Young persons under 15 years of age .... Half-price
☞ WILL CONTINUE ON EXHIBITION DURING THE MONTH OF OCTOBER.
HERALD PRINT.

Broadside of a concert featuring the Android Clarinetist who performed so skillfully people believed the automaton was real.

the concert, van Oeckelen made a point to reveal to audience members the wind-up hand crank, bellows, and barrels in the clarinetist's body just in case there was any doubt that he was not operated mechanically.[12]

Early animatronics

The Android Clarinetist is a remarkable feat of mechanical dexterity whose size and repertoire of music was far greater than any comparable automata that are known to have existed.[13] The talent of van Oeckelen to design something of such complexity and to replicate the human form as an object of exhibition and musical interpretation predates Disney's classic Audio-Animatronics figures.

Hanging from the ceiling in WED Enterprises, a bird in a cage would sing and move when its mechanism was wound up, Walt Disney had acquired it on a vacation trip to New Orleans.[14] This robotic bird and other mechanical toys captivated Walt and his team and are credited as the inspiration for the first Audio-Animatronics bird installed in the Enchanted Tiki Room that opened at Disneyland in 1963. Imagineer Lee Adams had been fiddling with Audio-Animatronics figures for several years, using frequencies and switches developed by the NASA space program to control faces and hands operated by pneumatic and hydraulic actuators.

One of the early prototypes was an Audio-Animatronics figure of President Lincoln that would eventually become part of *Great Moments with Mr. Lincoln*. This commission for the Illinois Pavilion at the 1964/1965 New York World's Fair was the catalyst Disney needed to step up the design complexity. Their new, patented Audio-Animatronics robotic creations blinked, smiled, and made other lifelike movements as they talked and sang. The reproduction of Lincoln offered people an intimate glimpse of the president as he stood from his chair, moved his head and hands, and gave a speech. The face was sculpted from a copy of Lincoln's actual life mask. The realism of Disney's Mr. Lincoln caused a five-year-old boy to exclaim to his father, "Daddy, I thought you said he was dead!" and other fair audiences were convinced the Audio-Animatronics figures were live performers.[15]

Animatronic family playing hnefatafl at the JORVIK Viking Centre which successfully straddles archeological site, attraction, and object-based museum.

York Archaeological Trust / The JORVIK Group

Primary case study
Real-life animatronics

JORVIK Viking Centre, York, UK,
1984–present
Principal Designers: RMA Themed
Attractions, Life Formations

Design challenge: Iterating history

The pungent smell of smoke, rotting food, and human waste cause kids and adults alike to have a visceral reaction to their time-travel experience when they visit the JORVIK Viking Centre. It is a multisensory and memorable experience that people take away with them lodged in their nose follicles.

Five years of excavation by the York Archeological Trust concluded in 1981 and unearthed the thousand-year-old remains of York's Viking city. With great public interest, the JORVIK Viking Centre opened in 1984 to interpret the historical finds on the very site where the excavation took place. The attraction has been updated three times since it opened and as a result makes for a great case study. The first design was led by designer John Sunderland, who started in film and television and introduced the time-car concept. RMA Themed Attractions handled redesigns in 2001, 2010, and 2016.

Design solution: Reconstructing history

Re-creations and some real remains of timber-framed and wattle houses, workshops, and the backyards can be seen under a glass floor where people begin their journey. A people mover suspended from a track in the ceiling, known as a ribbon-ride because of the way it snakes through the experience, transports people back in time to a reconstructed Viking neighborhood that is built on top of the original. The archaeological dig on this site unearthed a wealth of information about how the Vikings in this part of northern England lived, and the design of the street tableaux reflects this discovery. JORVIK uses animatronics to represent the street vendors, travelers to York, and residents. A number are modeled on human remains found at the dig, and others are based on historical records and research. A Viking eel flips around on a table waiting to be cut up and served for dinner. Several of the animatronics on the ride talk to each other in Old Norse and Old English, nearly lost languages that were voiced for the animatronics and interpreted by scholars and students at the University of York.[16] The final experience introduces audiences to many of the objects found at the site through traditional museum displays augmented by media, handling collections, and costumed guide interpretation.

Design impact: Popularizing history

The design of the JORVIK Viking Centre represents the middle ground between high audience appeal mixed with plenty of engagement and learning opportunities; it successfully straddles archaeological site, attraction, and object-based museum. Before migrating to online prebooking, lines of people waiting outside attested to its popularity. This groundbreaking project has been widely recognized as heralding the start of the heritage industry in the UK and for shamelessly making archaeology accessible.[17] Director Sarah Maltby considers JORVIK a learning experience; for her, "the attraction versus museum thing comes down to authenticity."[18] Indeed, everything is based on what was found and discovered during this Viking period, from the houses to the positioning of the objects to the design of the animatronics.

Contemporary animatronics

Animatronics today are less likely to stun contemporary audiences as they did in the 1960s, although natural history museums commonly deploy robotic dinosaurs to strike fear into people using their sheer scale and ferocity. While an expensive proposition for most museums and rarely used, designers value the medium of animatronics as an interpretive tool to lure audiences into experiences. The infrastructure required to operate animatronics has shrunk considerably, and their movement has become smoother, more lifelike, and more reliable. The latest versions have silicone rubber skin and cosmetics that appear more authentic than their predecessors. Their voice and audio narrative has benefited from improved sound and acoustics.[19] As a nod to the innovative magic lantern scenes conjured up by Étienne-Gaspard Robertson, projection technologies are at the forefront of the latest range of animatronics. Instead of complex mechanical movements, animations of a figure's vivid facial expressions are projected onto its head. Savings in time and cost

John Sunderland's original time-car concept for the JORVIK Viking Centre transports people through a show of sound, light, and image immersion.

York Archaeological Trust / The Jorvik Viking Centre

Design drawing by RMA Themed Attractions authentically recreates a Viking city in northern England using street tableaux's, animatronics, and pungent smells.

York Archaeological Trust / JORVIK Viking Centre / RMA Themed Attractions Ltd.

are realized because there is no need to take apart or remake the whole animatronic when the character needs changing.[20] Other developments include stunt-double animatronics that can perform acrobatics—Stuntronics can swing and fall from point A to point B in death-defying style.[21]

Bots and machine learning

First automata, animatronics, and now artificial intelligence have offered a new addition to the exhibition designer's box of tricks with infinite possibilities. Venues are experimenting with machine learning in a myriad of ways with websites, chatbots, and analytics tools that play a role in improving the audience experience.

Innovations in robots have increased their ability to convey, interpret, and customize exhibition content. In 2018, Pepper (not related to Pepper's ghost), a humanoid robot developed by SoftBank Robotics, was introduced at three Smithsonian museums with the purpose of answering visitors' questions and telling stories using voice, gestures, and an interactive touch screen.[22] The Smithsonian Institution says Pepper is particularly successful at attracting people to exhibit spaces that tend to be less visited and introducing them to content that is otherwise overlooked. People love to interact with Pepper, and the bots even pose for selfies.[23]

The eye movements so cleverly incorporated in the Android Clarinetist hundreds of years ago have evolved into animatronics that can track people's eye movements and where they look. Stare at your favorite character long enough and they will talk to you, and the next generation of bots will also address you by name.[24] Machine learning has the potential to deliver an experience that responds to audience preferences and is not beholden to a singular curator-led narrative. Elaine Heumann Gurian describes audiences who will wander through a multiplicity of sources that are visual, tactile, and verbal, and will personalize their interests through surfing, combining, and recombining.[25] This scenario presents new and exciting challenges for exhibition designers to accommodate this open-endedness, and no doubt the illusionist, performer, and magician in them will rise to the occasion.

Tips and Tricks

When using illusion and deception, keep the following design techniques in mind:

1. Minimize breakdown; have a backup plan.
2. Make it believable—hide the inner workings or infrastructure; do not spill the beans.
3. Be ethical—make deception fun, not discriminatory, elitist, or cruel.
4. Model accessibility—make exhibits easy to participate in for all.
5. Keep it simple—tried-and-tested methods are always best.
6. Bang for your buck—mirrored surfaces are inexpensive and readily available; they can augment object viewing and create a sense of spaciousness.
7. Practice safety—inset glass/mirrored panels so that their edges cannot be touched.
8. Think big—projection systems are a powerful storytelling tool that mask reality, add drama and theatrics, and are doable on a big scale.
9. Do no harm—Pepper's ghost can superimpose still or animated images on top of an object or background without leaving a mark; it is reversible and sustainable.
10. Use humor and empathy—animatronics and bots connect people with objects and ideas.

Notes

1. Uwe R. Brückner and Eberhard Schlag, *Scenography: Staging the Space* (Basel: Atelier Brückner/ Birkhauser, 2019), 158–59.
2. Virtual webinar interview and discussion, "Disney Legend Imagineer Bob Gurr." Walt Disney Family Museum, April 15, 2020.
3. Barbara Maria Stafford and Frances Terpak, *Devices of Wonder: From the World in a Box to Images on a Screen* (Los Angeles: Getty Publications, 2001).
4. "About teamLab," accessed August 5, 2020, https://www.teamlab.art/e/amosrex/.
5. "E.G. Robertson and the Phantasmagoria," accessed June 12, 2020. https://www.glassarmonica.com/ armonica/phantasmagoria.php.
6. "SEGD Awards," accessed July 2, 2020, https://segd.org/london-mithraeum-bloomberg-space.
7. "IBM Pavilion NY World's Fair," accessed August 21, 2020, https://www.eamesoffice.com/the-work/ ibm-pavilion-ny-worlds-fair/.
8. Jason Surrell, Marty Sklar, and Tom Fitzgerald, *The Haunted Mansion: Imagineering a Disney Classic*, 3rd ed. (Los Angeles: Disney Editions, 2015), 18.
9. *The Haunted Mansion: Imagineering a Disney Classic*, 35.
10. "D23," accessed February 22, 2021, https://d23.com/a-to-z/haunted-mansion/.
11. "David Wilson," accessed August 18, 2020, https://www.macfound.org/fellows/678/.
12. Albert R. Rice, "The Android Clarinetist by Cornelis Jacobus Van Oeckelen (1838)," *Journal of the American Musical Instrument Society* 40, (2014), 163–89.
13. "The Android Clarinetist by Cornelis Jacobus Van Oeckelen (1838)," 188.
14. "D23," accessed September 15, 2020, https://d23.com/a-to-z/audio-animatronics/.
15. "Great Moments with Mr. Lincoln animatronic segment at Disneyland Park," accessed July 5, 2020, https://www.youtube.com/watch?v=WeMRxOTzOOQ.
16. "Viking language returns to York," University of York, accessed July 6, 2020, https://www.youtube. com/watch?v=_OKxzSKzJe0.
17. John Sunderland, *On My Way to Jorvik: A Memoir* (UK: CreateSpace Independent Publishing; 1st edition, 2013), 12.
18. Sarah Maltby. Interview with Timothy McNeil about the JORVIK Viking Centre, November 14, 2019.
19. "Animatronics," accessed August 12, 2020, http://www.theatrecrafts.com/pages/home/topics/ animatronics/.
20. "Taking a Look Back at the History of Animatronics in the Disney Parks," accessed August 27, 2020, https://allears.net/2020/03/30/taking-a-look-back-at-the-history-of-animatronics-in-the-disney -parks/.
21. "Stuntronics—Disney Research," accessed June 22, 2022, https://la.disneyresearch.com/stuntronics/.
22. Lauren Styx, "How are museums using artificial intelligence, and is AI the future of museums?" accessed July 2, 2021, https://www.museumnext.com/article/artificial-intelligence-and-the-future -of-museums/.
23. "Smithsonian Launches Pilot Program of 'Pepper' Robots," accessed August 28, 2020, https://www .si.edu/newsdesk/releases/smithsonian-launches-pilot-program-pepper-robots.
24. "How Disney plans to track guests' eyes to improve the theme park experience," accessed August 28, 2020, https://www.bizjournals.com/orlando/news/2016/12/08/how-disney-plans-to-track-guests-eyes -to-improve.html.
25. Elaine Heumann Gurian, "On the Importance of 'And': Museums and Complexity," in MacLeod et al., *The Future of Museum and Gallery Design: Purpose, Process, Perception* (London; New York: Routledge, 2018), 39.

Designer's Toolbox: **Communication**

Advanced production processes have increased the availability and durability of experience-based print, environmental, and digital graphic applications, while promotional communications and social media outside the exhibition space are growing exponentially. Commune with the designer's toolbox and be amazed at the typology, anatomy, and array of exhibition graphics and their applications.

Visualization: Leidy Karina Gómez Montoya. Composition of exhibition graphics designed by the team at Parque Explora, Medellín, Colombia

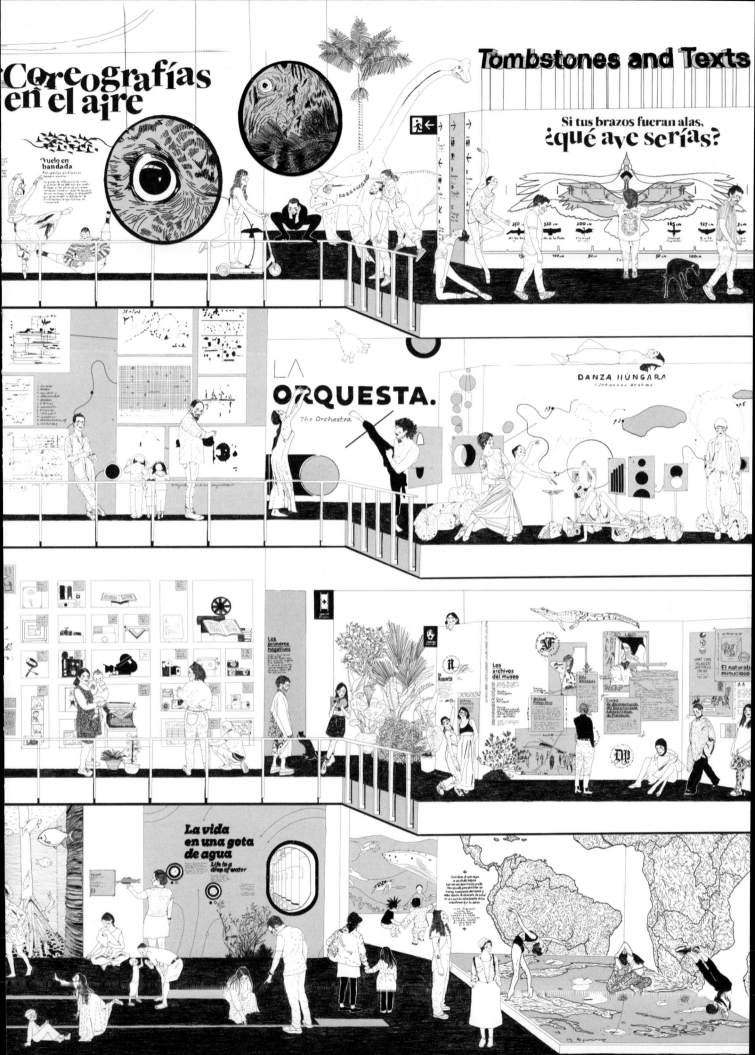

CHAPTER 11

Tombstones and Texts

Designed words and images are essential vehicles for communication in the exhibition environment.

Key message: Design makes exhibition messages clear, communication direct, and visuals pop.

Key word: communication

Object labels are one of the most contested exhibition design elements. They represent a microcosm where knowledge, learning, and clear communication compete and often clash. Experts debate about telling the whole story, educators want the content to reach the broadest possible audience, and designers insist on a consistent visual style and clarity.

When objects first went on public display—be it at markets, fairs, or museums—people needed to know an item's worth, maker, or provenance. These basic messages still endure, but technological production advances have moved information graphics from static, to dynamic, to interactive, using a plethora of seductive imagery, typography, and visually striking messages.

At their most basic level, tombstone labels provide key object information. This chapter uses this common communicator as an entry point to understand the legacy, design, and making of exhibition graphics. Often invisible to the average eye, design facilitates the interpretation of text- and image-based content to engage and orient exhibition audiences, creates a cohesive visual voice that holds an experience together, and forms a consistent graphic identity that reassures audiences. Designing exhibitions and experiences is not about architectural form; it is about communication.[1]

Ubiquitous Object Label: A Microcosm for Developing Exhibition Content

A series of cylindrical clay drums baffled archaeologists excavating the ancient Ur palace and temple complex of Babylonian King Nabonidus, who ruled in the sixth century BCE. Positioned next to dozens of Mesopotamian artifacts with origins spanning 1,500 years, these cylinders were, in fact, the earliest designed object labels resplendent with descriptive tombstone information.[2] The king's daughter, Princess Ennigaldi-Nanna, curated and arranged the objects for what could be the first educational museum of antiquity. Little did she know that these drums would chart the evolutionary course for the ubiquitous object label and the explanatory graphics we have come to expect in contemporary exhibition making.[3]

First tombstone

Object labels communicate an artifact's historical context, function, appearance, value, maker, and provenance to elevate its importance.[4] They also convey a story about graphics production. Ennigaldi-Nanna's cylinders were intended to spin and reveal their information—like a Buddhist prayer wheel, they predate interactive flip-and-turn versions. Casting graphics in clay, the method of production in 540 BCE, made way for handwritten and letter-press examples in the first formal museums of the eighteenth century. Exhibition graphics in the twentieth century used typewritten, photo-composite, silkscreen, transfer lettering, and cut vinyl. Today's large-format inkjet printing and digital projection/screens reflect rapid technological advances in graphics production, turnaround, and durability.

Babylonian clay cylinders intended to spin and reveal their object information are the earliest form of exhibition graphics at the Palace of Bel-Shalti-Nanna, about 530 BCE.

Library of Congress, Prints & Photographs Division, LC-DIG-matpc-09949.

Clay drums to e-ink

Ennigaldi-Nanna's clay drums were cast in three different languages—even today, exhibition makers find multilingual graphics challenging because of the physical display space they require. E-paper displays placed next to objects at the Estonian National Museum (2016) cleverly circumvent this

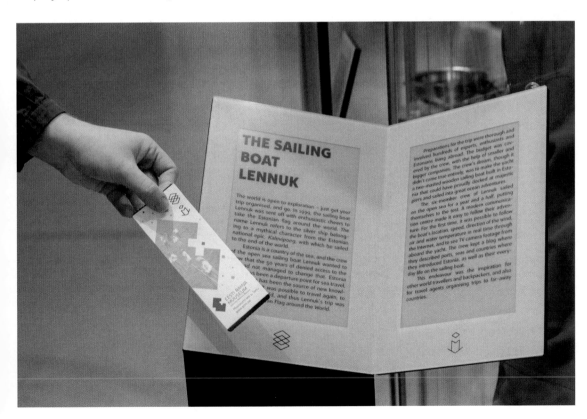

RFID activated labels next to objects at the Estonian National Museum activate and display information in a visitor's chosen language.

Photo: Estonian National Museum

issue. Guests use Radio Frequency Identification (RFID)–coded tickets to activate electronic object labels (in the shape of an open book) and display information in their chosen language (Estonian, English, or Russian). E-readers are thin and light, using power only when changing the
content on the screen. Connecting wirelessly, they allow the artifacts to remain the main focal
point, take up less room, and are infinitely expandable.[5]

Didactic Graphics Enter the Stage

There is an informative photograph of designer Barbara Fahs Charles spacing 9-inch dimensional
letter-forms on rolls of brown paper and carefully tracing around them to make stencils for their final composition at the exhibition site.[6] Pictured in the Eames design studio, designers are creating
exhibition elements for *A Computer Perspective* (1971), which opened at the IBM Corporate Exhibit Center in New York and presented inventions that eventually evolved into desktop computing
and design software.[7] This ironic moment represents a figurative and metaphoric transformation
from analog to digital graphics production.

Information delivery
Large-scale experiential graphics were solidified by the political and ideological movements in
early-twentieth-century Europe. Notably, the work of Russian Constructivist El Lissitzky, whose
supersized sculptural forms, adorned with layered, overlapping montages of striking imagery and
bold sans-serif typography, ascended from the floor, covered the walls, and plastered the ceiling
in an unorthodox and experimental manner. His expanded photographic reproductions, contact
paper, cut lettering, and sign-painting for the Soviet Pavilion at the International Press Exhibition
(*Pressa)* in Cologne (1928) foreshadowed Photoshop filters and image manipulation and provided
an opportunity for modernist and traditional designers to work alongside each other and employ
current technologies in mass media.[8]

Herbert Bayer's exhibition explorations were influenced by El Lissitzky and indebted to
the work of Otto Neurath, whose large information graphics were installed at the Gesellschafts-
und Wirtschaftsmuseum (Museum for Society and Economy) in Vienna (1924). Neurath collaborated with graphic designer Gerd Arntz to humanize knowledge and pictorialize complex data for

El Lissitzky's super-sized environmental graphics for the 1928 International Press Exhibition (*Pressa*) in Cologne foreshadowed digital image manipulation.

El Lissitzky: © 2022 Artists Rights Society (ARS), New York. Image courtesy of The Collection of Fostin Cotchen.

Otto Neurath's large statistical supergraphics for the Museum for Society and Economy in Vienna were the focus, not the exhibit structures that displayed them.

Image courtesy of the Otto and Marie Neurath Isotype Collection, University of Reading.

a general audience. Where Bayer and El Lissitzky worked downward from the spatial environment to the message, Neurath's statistical supergraphics worked from the message upward.[9] They exploited the exhibition medium to communicate to the masses until their tools became coopted as propaganda machines and they fled an increasingly repressive 1930s Europe.

Supergraphics

As interpretive graphics rather than exclusively discreet object labels became a critical method of exhibition information delivery, professional designers embraced a grander visual spectacle.

These supergraphics, at the intersection of communication and the built environment, eventually evolved into digital billboards and dynamic building façades. Designer Deborah Sussman described supergraphics as bigger than the architecture.[10] Exhibitions enabled Charles and Ray Eames to indulge their inner polymath. Never ones to stay in their own lane, they considered design as all categories of architectural and graphic design.[11]

Primary case study

Words (and numbers) become graphic display and play

Mathematica: A World of Numbers... and Beyond, **California Science Center, March 1961–January 1998**
Designer: Office of Charles and Ray Eames

Design challenge: Intense design process

Mathematica: A World of Numbers... and Beyond demonstrated how didactic exhibitions could make complex knowledge meaningful and fun.[12] Charles Eames thrived on having an intellectual sparring partner. In this case, his content collaborator was University of California, Los Angeles mathematics professor Raymond Redheffer. Their infectious excitement and competitiveness rippled through the office as everyone became unwittingly committed to delivering an interactive learning environment about mathematical phenomena. In the center of the 3,000-square-foot IBM-sponsored exhibition space were live demonstrations, nine push-button interactive displays (ranging from the topics of probability to celestial mechanics), and five "peep-show" films about more mathematical concepts.[13] A fifty-foot *History Wall* (chronology of mathematical discovery), and *Image Wall* (diagrammatic representations of mathematical concepts) flanked the hands-on exhibits, and quotations by mathematicians were suspended on panels hung from the ceiling. As Barbara Fahs Charles notes, "*Mathematica* is a brilliant visualization of mathematical theories and a classic manifestation of the intense Eames design process."[14]

Design solution: A sum of its parts

The interactive exhibits in *Mathematica* influenced future hands-on science museums.[15] The graphics on the other hand are often overlooked despite representing an evolutionary moment in exhibit communication, the transmission of information, and the pleasurable but serious business of learning.[16] Words are typographically playful, overlapping images convey stories and use mnemonic devices, diagrams organize data, and color accents important messages. This tantalizing tapestry of headings, descriptions, quotes, timelines, and imagery jump off the walls onto posts, hanging signs, gameboards, and floating panels. Instead of an afterthought assigned to a convenient location near the exhibits, the information is liberated and embedded into the exhibition surfaces. The integrated design works as a unified whole rather than a sum (literally) of its parts.

Typography for the *History Wall* and *Image Wall* was set using metal type, larger elements used wood block type, and the emerging Linotype (phototypesetting) for the smaller characters (up to 14 point). Large letter-forms and dimensional letters festooned the Eames Office walls as scale reference, images were cut out and mounted with glue to paper substrates, and black-and-white photographs were printed in the studio darkroom or pilfered from pages in books. It was common to grab a book from the office library and find it peppered with gaping holes.[17]

Design impact: Limited by production

While "Mathematica" was ahead of its time, the density of content, awkward Bodoni, Helvetica, and Times letter spacing, and pieced-together photographic elements pale in comparison to the typographic control made possible by a few clicks of the Adobe Suite. Today's sophisticated audiences are accustomed to seamless graphic displays where printed or digital words and images are wallpapered onto surfaces.

The Eames Office employed many designers to create *Mathematica*. Deborah Sussman quietly steered the graphic compositions and production. Glen Fleck magically said a lot with a few well-chosen words and succinct graphics.[18] Commercial exhibit fabrication companies did not exist, so studio designers painstakingly marked up copy to be typeset, tediously trimmed and pasted up images, and sourced catalogue display letters in suitable fonts and sizes. No doubt contemporary cut vinyl lettering, large inkjet printing, and CNC milling would have been fully embraced and elevated the pioneering design work of *Mathematica* to even greater heights.

The Eames's *Mathematica: A World of Numbers... and Beyond* included interactive displays and didactic graphics including a 50-foot History and Image Wall.

Charles and Ray Eames assembling their informative, statistical, and playful graphics for *Mathematica: A World of Numbers... and Beyond.*

Robert Staples installing cut-out images and phototype-set graphics on the *History Wall* for *Mathematica: A World of Numbers... and Beyond.*

Didactic to Dynamic Graphics

Mathematica was part of a growing interpretive movement that paralleled the emerging professionalization of exhibition making with a goal to educate and explain. Exhibition graphics responded with clarity, hierarchy, and accessibility. The communication of science was fertile ground for a generation of designers who carefully integrated visual communication into the overall exhibition experience and used multimodal methods of interpretation to engage and seduce audiences.

Graphics that were once static and plastered on flat surfaces adopted dynamic forms. Color photography, backlit transparencies, explanatory diagrams, and commissioned illustrations and murals visualized complex content. Manipulative (flip) object labels challenged audiences to discover information. Pushbuttons illuminated dimensional maps, models, and activated understanding. Advances in signage production opened the door to consistency, color, clarity, and an intentional typographic hierarchy.

Science popup book

Dynamic graphics responded to the prevailing visitor studies and educational theory that advocated for accessible content using less words, bigger messages, and fewer objects to cater to informal learners (school group visits). *Story of the Earth* (1972) at the Geological Museum in London embraced this populist, graphics-driven integration. Designed by James Gardner, it represented a significant breakthrough in science museum design (including an active volcano model and earthquake machine) and was critically acclaimed and imitated worldwide.[19] The exhibition's hierarchical presentation of image-driven information and hands-on elements mirrored an illustrated popup book about science on a large scale.

The success of *Story of the Earth* germinated an in-house design team led by Giles Velarde (head of exhibition design at the Geological Museum 1974–1988) that collaborated with scientists and technicians to develop a series of groundbreaking temporary and permanent exhibitions. *Treasures of the Earth* (1985) succeeded Gardner's initial exhibition and is credited as the first installation to integrate image and text information adjacent to artifacts using computer terminals.[20]

Audience tested

Mathematica elevated the role and integration of interpretative graphics. *Story of the Earth* made complex information easy to follow, hierarchical, and diagrammatic. Despite these advances, the expert's voice prevailed. Audiences could be excused for finding the onslaught of technical information overwhelming and the resulting graphic elements difficult to read. To the rescue came an enlightened, people-focused cadre of educators, editors, experts (and designers) who "developed" and audience-tested exhibition content, expedited by the next iteration of graphics fabrication. Nimbler, computer-driven production processes like large-format inkjet replaced photographic and silkscreen printing, and when embedded behind protective laminates fused to a wider range of substrates, increased a graphics shelf life.

James Gardner's design for *Story of the Earth* featured hierarchical, image-driven information that resembled an oversize popup book about science.

Photo: © The Trustees of the Natural History Museum, London

Graphics that respond to learning theory and visitor evaluation

Monterey Bay Aquarium, Monterey, CA, Exhibit halls, 1984–present
Principal Designers: Judy Rand; Jim Peterson; Don Hughes

Design challenge: Message-driven

The Monterey Bay Aquarium's (MBA) circular emblem is a swirl of giant kelp. The interwoven fronds represent an unexpected approach to design, the amazing art to be found in nature, and that kelp and other seemingly obscure aspects of the ocean are as fascinating as its animals.[21] Like the Japanese Enso mark, the circle is never complete because the aquarium continuously refines an exhibit philosophy that is "mission-driven, message-driven, and visitor-driven."[22]

Perched on the edge of the bay and lapped by crashing waves, the Aquarium's state-of-the-art building opened in 1984 with a unique focus on the diversity and beauty of marine life found specifically in the Monterey Bay and California's Central Coastal waters. Judy Rand established the Exhibit Research and Development department initially with design lead Jim Peterson, and two years later, Don Hughes took over the Exhibition Design division.[23] With their teams, they set new standards for exhibit development, interpretation, writing, and the design of the visitor experience. This distinctive style, tone, and voice launched groundbreaking special exhibitions.

Changing exhibitions with ocean conservation themes are now common in the aquarium world.[24] *Fishing for Solutions: What's the Catch* (1997–2021), inspired the sustainable seafood movement by highlighting overfishing and habitat destruction.[25] *Hot Pink Flamingos: Stories of Hope in a Changing Sea* (March 2010–September 2011) connected the public's love for marine life with the impacts of climate change on ocean ecosystems. Formative and summative audience evaluations at the MBA inform multiplatform (exhibit and social media) conservation messages that are graphically styled to be concise, engaging, and humorous.[26]

Design solution: Interpretive framework

The industrial-looking aquarium (designed to resemble the original Cannery Row sardine factories) features light-filled, open interiors, where exhibits take advantage of the spectacular ocean views. The Pacific Ocean feeds enormous kelp tanks that house a stunning diversity of marine life—sea otters, sharks, and sunfish. Lacing these exhibits together is a series of graphic design elements that follow a legible, consistent, and interactive house style, fabricated to withstand the rigors of a hands-on family environment and the temperate ocean air.

Interactive flip labels and touchscreens nest into exhibit surfaces adorned with cut letter-forms, dimensional images, and layered graphics. Typography, image, and color selections are synchronized throughout. Elements are scaled according to their reading distance and sequenced in order of hierarchical importance: Headings are installed above height (primary), section and focus texts mid-height (secondary), object and descriptive captions below (tertiary).

Exhibit text is written to carefully chunk and organize relevant information. Messages begin with direct, declarative sentences emphasizing what people know and play to their interests.[27] This tried-and-tested interpretive graphics framework is used to hook people and reel them into the content.

Design impact: People-driven

Founder Julie Packard wanted the Aquarium to be "elegant but fun." Today's design team continues this philosophy through a clever interplay of words and images. In contrast to an art museum, the MBA relinquishes sophisticated, serifed, and small tombstone texts. An informal whiff (and salty ocean air) permeates the exhibit graphics as versatile Optima and playful sans-like fonts like Tekton happily rub shoulders.

The look, feel, and intent of the Aquarium's graphics are intentionally friendly, accessible, and shaped by audience feedback. Since its inception, the in-house team has served as an incubator for audience-driven exhibit development and design excellence. There is a calming consistency to the graphic interpretation. Audiences quickly learn the systematic visual language at the beginning of their exhibition journey. Graphics at the MBA feel familiar, approachable, and conversational. Easy to comprehend, they require minimal effort and allow people to focus on the real stars of the show: the living plants and animals.

Fishing for Solutions: What's the Catch used audience evaluations to inform conservation messages that were consistent, concise, and graphically engaging.

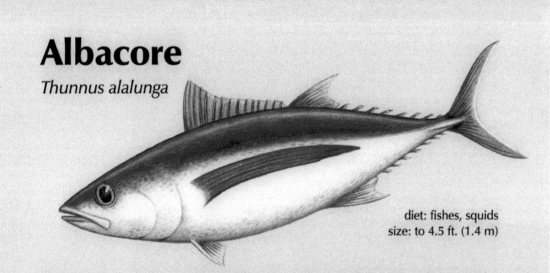

Albacore
Thunnus alalunga

diet: fishes, squids
size: to 4.5 ft. (1.4 m)

Born to run, schools of streamlined albacore swim from here to Japan, circling the Pacific. When they need to speed, they'll fold those fins and go faster than 40 miles an hour.

Opening a major new wing in 1996, designers follow Monterey Bay Aquarium standards—clean layout; consistent fonts; short, readable text—as they increase label legibility, contrast, and size to meet visitors' needs.

Image courtesy of Judy Rand

Bilingual interpretive graphics at the Monterey Bay Aquarium continue to use bold headlines to draw the reader into short sentences that are active and conversational.

Photo: Jamie Pham / Alamy Stock Photo

Local Projects designed Scalable interpretative graphics to shift from gesture activated screens to handheld tablets at The Cleveland Museum of Art's *Gallery One*.

Courtesy of The Cleveland Museum of Art

Dynamic to Digital Graphics

Integrated into exhibits or conveyed via handheld devices, digital graphics are ubiquitous in contemporary exhibition experiences. The immediate styling of words and images makes these seductive visuals easy to update compared with their static cousins. Whereas digitized graphics were once as clunky as the computer terminals that displayed them (Knoxville World's Fair, 1982), or discreetly housed in adjacent galleries (Micro Gallery, National Gallery London, 1991), they were eventually released to roam exhibition spaces in direct competition with the objects (Art Access, J. Paul Getty Museum, 1997).[28]

Gallery One's space at the Cleveland Museum of Art (2012) proved that interpretative graphics could be digitally deployed from large gesture activated surfaces (Collection Wall) to handheld tablets (ArtLens app). A tablet's augmented reality portal can liberate nested overlays about the artworks in the galleries using supplemental graphics, videos, and a variety of voices. *Gallery One* meets the real (visceral) versus the virtual halfway—where art objects in a dedicated room are a teaser to the gallery adventure that awaits.[29]

Nested graphics

Where *Gallery One* confines graphic overlays within rectangular screens, other experiences released digitally generated graphics into the physical space. *Sparking Reactions* at the British Nuclear Fuels' Visitor's Centre in Sellafield, Cumbria (2002), created a public forum for debate about the future of energy production and supply. Dynamic typographic messages (the audiences' own opinions) were displayed in an immersive audiovisual installation of six giant screens with wall and floor projections in a darkened environment called the Core. The energy debate at the Centre, therefore, was evolving during its three-year life span.[30]

Casson Mann and designer Nick Bell were also responsible for the nested information graphics on the meters-long interactive touch table at the Churchill Museum in London (2005). This installation was one of the first to use gestural, sensor-based interaction, in this case, to display thousands of documents, images, and film clips relating to Churchill's eventful life. Digital graphics had reached a turning point where they combined seamlessly with physical graphics in one heady multimodal mix.

Sparking Reactions at the British Nuclear Fuels' Visitor Centre released large digitally generated motion graphics into the physical space.

Courtesy of Science Museum Group, Casson Mann, photo by Andreas Schmidt

1899
1898
18
1895
1894
1893
1892
1891
1890

1889
Jan '89: continues at Harrow School
Mar '89: Army career for Winston
Sep '89: joins Army class at Harrow
Nov '89: 15th birthday

1888
Jan '88: last term at school in Hove
Apr '88: starts Harrow School
Nov '88: 14th birthday

1886-87
Jan '86: continues at school in Hove
Mar '86: seriously ill with pneumonia
Jul '86: Lord Randolph Chancellor
Nov '86: 12th birthday
Dec '86: Lord Randolph resigns
Jan '87: continues at school in Hove

1884-85
Apr '84: leaves St George's School
Sep '84: starts new school in Hove
Nov '84: 10th birthday
Jan '85: continues at school in Hove
Jun '85: Lord Randolph India Secretary
Nov '85: 11th birthday

Designers Casson Mann with Nick Bell and David Small created one of the first gestural, sensor-based interactive touch tables at London's Churchill Museum.

Courtesy of Casson Mann

Primary case study

Multimodal graphic experiences

Impact of the Bible in the World,
**Museum of the Bible, Washington, D.C.,
2019–present
Principal Designer: C&G Partners**

Design challenge: Designer multiples

The Museum of the Bible positions the Bible as a powerful artifact for making sense of the world rather than, as some would see it, proselytize, and promote the history of Christianity. The exhibition design is anticipatory, fusing entertainment and education into a one-stop-shopping cultural experience.[31]

Amassed above the arrival and gift shop level are three floors that engage audiences in a spiritual exhibition journey created by multiple design firms. PRD Group designed the fourth-floor exhibits, BRC Imagination Arts and Jonathan Martin Creative (JMC) the third-floor experiences, and C&G Partners crafted the second-floor, 30,000-square-foot exhibition *Impact of the Bible in the World*. With so many design hands involved in one singular museum, it is a smorgasbord of exhibition methods and techniques. Their brands of interpretive design oscillate from literal recreation to immaculate abstraction, and everything in between. These various approaches play an instrumental role in choreographing the sensory experience of visitors.[32]

C&G Partners were commissioned to convey the contemporary portion of the museum story: "Bible in America," "Bible in the World," and "Bible Now." Their creative team had a degree of autonomy to exert control over the research, development, and design to successfully unify the content, graphics, and digital media solutions.

Design solution: Graphic multiples

Impact of the Bible in the World illustrates today's multimodal graphic design philosophy where traditional and progressive communication mediums collide. C&G's design director Alin Tocmacov uses *phy-gital* to describe this integration of physical and digital content.[33] A plethora of absorbing graphic and interactive elements guides the exhibition narrative using the "streaker, stroller, studier" method of information delivery; the experience is rewarding even for people who read little. Headings applied to illuminated lanterns called "candles"—spiritual and symbolic of the light that first illuminated the study of the Bible—guide people to the specific exhibit themes. They hang above strata of primary, secondary, and tertiary graphic elements: headings and quotes, introductory section texts, focus texts, floor graphics (section markers), object labels, and images. Each forms the interpretive backbone for an array of digitally driven dimensional maps, touch tables, gestural screens, and audio testimonies. The exhibition's typographic language infiltrates every medium and is surprisingly restrained. Avenir flexes its range of weights, sizes, and upper-/lowercase combinations to assert hierarchy as the exhibition's singular typeface.

Design impact: Multiple mediums

Anchoring the linear exhibition space is a two-hundred-foot-long allegorical tapestry. The tapestry weaves together an illustrated story of the Bible's impact throughout American history to connect the galleries. The woodblock illustration style evokes an oversize graphic novel with broad audience appeal. Digitally projected quotes and facts activate the tapestry surface as people walk by.[34] This digitally woven masterpiece is the perfect metaphor for the modern age and being *phy-gital*. "Impact of the Bible" does not come across as extravagant despite its multimodality of graphic methods. The strong visual language and competent communication remains copasetic to the content—a hallmark of C&G Partners' work that goes back to their founding DNA (see chapter 5).

Graphics to learning

Contemporary exhibitions merge multimodal experiences to engage audiences on every level using many graphic mediums. While this chapter touched on interpretation, interaction, participation, and exhibition development, what follows will expound on this further and how multimodality extends to a range of other design methods to foster learning in the exhibition space.

Impact of the Bible in the World unfurls a 200-foot-long allegorical tapestry, an interpretive backbone for an array of static and dynamic graphic applications.

Photo: Museum of the Bible

The designers unified text content, illustrative graphics, and digital media solutions at the *Impact of the Bible in the World*.

Photo: Francis Joseph Dean / Deanpictures / Alamy Stock Photo

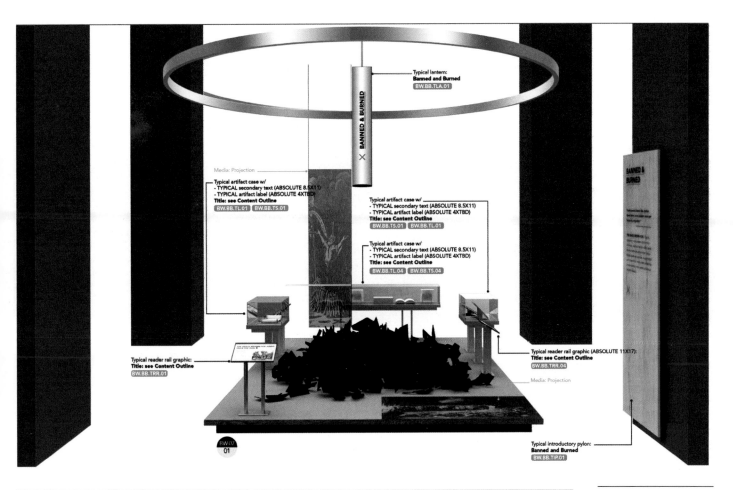

Labels in diagram (top to bottom, left to right):

Typical lantern:
Banned and Burned
BW.BB.TLA.01

Media: Projection

Typical artifact case w/
- TYPICAL secondary text (ABSOLUTE 8.5X11)
- TYPICAL artifact label (ABSOLUTE 4XTBD)
Title: see Content Outline
BW.BB.TL.01 BW.BB.TS.01

Typical artifact case w/
- TYPICAL secondary text (ABSOLUTE 8.5X11)
- TYPICAL artifact label (ABSOLUTE 4XTBD)
Title: see Content Outline
BW.BB.TS.01 BW.BB.TL.01

Typical artifact case w/
- TYPICAL secondary text (ABSOLUTE 8.5X11)
- TYPICAL artifact label (ABSOLUTE 4XTBD)
Title: see Content Outline
BW.BB.TL.04 BW.BB.TS.04

Typical reader rail graphic:
Title: see Content Outline
BW.BB.TRR.01

Typical reader rail graphic (ABSOLUTE 11X17):
Title: see Content Outline
BW.BB.TRR.04

Media: Projection

Typical introductory pylon:
Banned and Burned
BW.BB.TIP.01

BANNED & BURNED

BW.07
01

Title and sub-title	(1–10 words) - identifying what the exhibit is about; large, attention grabbing, design over content, mood setting
Section headings and quotes	(10–20 words) - large and easy to read from a distance, more informational than titles, topic oriented
Introductory text or statement	(50–200 words) - words divided into succinct, concise paragraphs; near entry; explanatory; relates exhibition rationale, introduces major concepts
Section or focus text	(75–150 words) - associated with groupings of objects or a section; unifies the grouping conceptually; informative, interpretive
Object label	(25 words) - wall, display case, group, singular; contain basic facts, give objects a name
Extended object labels	(75 words) - interpretive, specific to object or small group
Brochure	unlimited text length, optional, portable, target to interested visitor, information intensive
Explanatory graphic	interactive; timeline; map; photographs/images; illustrations/diagrams; pictograms/symbols; mural or super-graphic; floor graphic; banner, scrim, or fabric; video kiosk, flat screen; projected; film/image; gobo; handheld device (AR); headset (VR)

Detailed design specifications for a vocabulary of multimodal graphics applications at the Museum of the Bible's *Impact of the Bible in the World*.

Image courtesy of C&G Partners

Exhibitions use a typology and hierarchy of graphic elements with specific communication criteria.

Diagram: Timothy J. McNeil

Tips and Tricks

The anatomy of an exhibit graphic consists of five basic design factors:

1. **Message (content):** Consider the voice, comprehension level, word count, and language. Use bold lead-in phrases, active verbs, and the present tense. Break the content into paragraphs and easy-to-read logical chunks. Apply information hierarchy (primary, secondary, tertiary levels) to place emphasis on what people need to know first. Graphic styling should be dictated by content type: identification (heading); explanatory (text); instructional (caption).

2. **Placement (perception):** Consider the graphics location, height, visibility, and lighting. Orient to a person's plane of vision and scale graphics relative to the viewing distance. Place graphics off the walls to create spatial divisions and unexpected encounters.

3. **Graphics (style):** Consider fonts (typography) that have enough variety to interpret and style the range of content. Create a grid that accommodates short, easy-to-read line lengths, symbols/pictograms, arrows/lines, maps, diagrams, and images. Use color and contrast effectively. Adhere to a size/layout system and consistent visual language.

4. **Form (physical):** Consider the graphics shape, size, and depth, as well as the materials it is made from and how will it be mounted or secured using adhesives, fasteners, or hardware. Explore printed, projected, or screen-based (power required) graphic applications.

5. **Accessibility (people-centered):** Consider legibility and scale and use 70 percent minimum contrast between the figure and ground. Can the graphic be tactile, use audio (listening device), and be understood by everyone? Follow any accessibility standards (ADA, universal design, Smithsonian, etc.).

Notes

1. For a deeper analysis of graphics in the physical environment, see Jona Piehl, *Graphic Design in Museum Exhibitions: Display, Identity and Narrative*, 1st ed. (Abingdon, Oxon; New York: Routledge, 2020).

2. "The Case for Museums Today (Video)," Khan Academy, 1:34 minutes, accessed September 6, 2021, https://www.khanacademy.org/humanities/approaches-to-art-history/tools-for-understanding-museums/
museums-today/v/the-case-for-museums.

3. Louise Pryke, "Hidden Women of History: Ennigaldi-Nanna, Curator of the World's First Museum," The Conversation, accessed September 6, 2021, http://theconversation.com/hidden-women-of-history-ennigaldi-nanna-curator-of-the-worlds-first-museum-116431.

4. See Beverly Serrell, *Exhibit Labels: An Interpretive Approach*, 2nd ed. (Lanham, MD: Rowman & Littlefield, 2015).

5. Ursa Primozic, "Estonian History Now on Electronic Paper," *Visionect* (blog), November 21, 2016, https://www.visionect.com/blog/estonian-museum-on-eink/.

6. Barbara Fahs Charles. Interview by Timothy McNeil about designing the "Mathematica" exhibition and working in the Eames Office, October 29, 2021.

7. Barbara Fahs Charles, "Peaks of Perception and Excitement: Exhibition Making at the Eames Office," in Catherine Ince et al., *The World of Charles and Ray Eames* (London: Thames & Hudson Ltd in association with Barbican Art Gallery, 2015), 290–301.

8. Jeremy Anysley, "Pressa Cologne, 1928: Exhibitions and Publication Design in the Weimar Period," *Design Issues* 10, no. 3 (1994): 53, https://doi.org/10.2307/1511692.

9. Roger S. Miles et al., *The Design of Educational Exhibits* (London: Routledge, 2002), 8.

10. "Interview with Deborah Sussman" from the exhibition "California's Designing Women," at the Autry National Center, 2012, https://www.youtube.com/watch?v=0_Qx9eC3DvE.

11. Charles Eames, Ray Eames, and Daniel Ostroff, *An Eames Anthology: Articles, Film Scripts, Interviews, Letters, Notes, Speeches* (New Haven; London: Yale University Press, 2015), 32.

12. Eames Demetrios, *An Eames Primer: Revised Edition* (New York: Universe Publishing, 2013), 179–91.

13. John Neuhart et al., *Eames Design: The Work of the Office of Charles and Ray Eames* (New York: H.N. Abrams, 1989), 255.

14. Barbara Fahs Charles, "Peaks of Perception and Excitement," 291.

15. Neuhart et al., *Eames Design*, 257.

16. Pat Kirkham, *Charles and Ray Eames: Designers of the Twentieth Century* (Cambridge, MA: MIT Press, 1995), 264.

17. Barbara Fahs Charles. Interview. October 29, 2021.

18. Catherine Ince, Lotte Johnson, and Barbican Art Gallery, eds., *The World of Charles and Ray Eames* (London: Thames & Hudson Ltd in association with Barbican Art Gallery, 2015), 277.

19. Frederick W. Dunning, "The Story of the Earth," *Museum International* 26, no. 2 (June 1, 1974): 99–109, https://doi.org/10.1111/j.1468-0033.1974.tb01823.x.

20. "Geological Museum," in *Wikipedia*, August 2, 2021, https://en.wikipedia.org/w/index.php?title=Geological_Museum&oldid=1036829954.

21. "Giant Kelp | Wallpapers | Monterey Bay Aquarium," accessed September 14, 2022, https://www.montereybayaquarium.org/animals/wallpapers/giant-kelp.

22. Jenny-Sayre Ramberg, Judy Rand, and Jaci Tomulonis, "Mission, Message, and Visitors: How Exhibit Philosophy Has Evolved at the Monterey Bay Aquarium," *Curator: The Museum Journal* 45 (January 15, 2010): 302–20, https://doi.org/10.1111/j.2151-6952.2002.tb00067.x.

23. Judy Rand. Interview by Timothy McNeil about the early design philosophy at the Monterey Bay Aquarium. September 12, 2022.

24. "Introduction and History | Monterey Bay Aquarium Media Kit | Newsroom," accessed September 29, 2021, https://www.montereybayaquarium.org/newsroom/media-kits/introduction.

25. Geoff Drake, "Seafood Watch: Celebrating 20 Years of Sustainable Seafood—a Look Back at Our History," Wriding, November 13, 2019, http://www.wriding.com/seafood-watch-celebrating-20-years-of-sustainable-seafood-a-look-back-at-our-history/.

26. Julie Packard, "Effective (and Ineffective) Engagement: Lessons Learned from Exhibitions & Programs with a Conservation Message," *Exhibition* 39, no. 01 (Spring 2020): 25.

27. Ramberg, Rand, and Tomulonis, "Mission, Message, and Visitors," 305.

28. Alex Morrison, "The Micro Gallery: Observations from Three Projects: London; San Diego; Washington D.C.," International Conference *Hands on Hypermedia and Interactivity in Museums,* San Diego, CA, 1995, https://www.archimuse.com/publishing/ichim95_vol2/morrison.pdf.

29. "Transforming the Art Museum Experience: Gallery One | MW2013: Museums and the Web 2013," accessed October 11, 2021, https://mw2013.museumsandtheweb.com/paper/transforming-the-art-museum-experience-gallery-one-2/.

30. "Nick Bell Design," accessed October 11, 2021, https://nickbelldesign.co.uk/#projects-exhibition-design.

31. Philip Kennicott, "Perspective | The New Bible Museum Tells a Clear, Powerful Story. And It Could Change the Museum Business," *Washington Post*, November 15, 2017, https://www.washingtonpost.com/entertainment/museums/the-new-bible-museum-tells-a-clear-powerful-story-and-it-could-change-the-museum-business/2017/11/15/6fc76f40-c98e-11e7-8321-481fd63f174d_story.html.

32. James S. Bielo, "Experiential Design and Religious Publicity at D.C.'s Museum of the Bible," *The Senses and Society* 15, no. 1 (January 2, 2020): 98–113, https://doi.org/10.1080/17458927.2019.1709303.

33. Alin Tocmacov. Interview by Timothy McNeil about *Impact of the Bible* exhibition. October 25, 2021.

34. "Museum of The Bible: Impact of the Bible—100% Final Design Document" (C&G Partners, October 28, 2015), 25.

Designer's Toolbox: **Learning**

Designers instinctively respond to visual, visceral, and environmental factors. Equally important is understanding the cognitive and behavioral attributes affecting how people learn, and to design for a range of experiential preferences. Activate the designer's toolbox to specify the appropriate type of learning modality.

Visualization: Magnús Elvar Jónsson is an interaction and exhibition designer at Gagarín in Reykjavik, Iceland

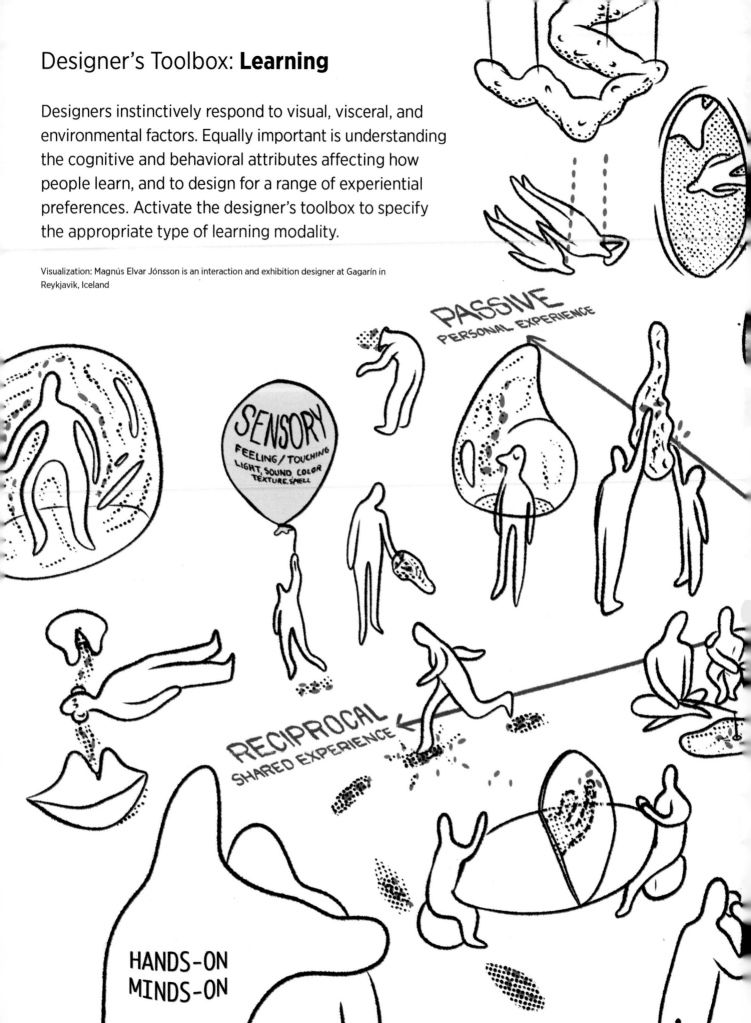

PASSIVE
PERSONAL EXPERIENCE

SENSORY
FEELING / TOUCHING
LIGHT, SOUND, COLOR
TEXTURE, SMELL

RECIPROCAL
SHARED EXPERIENCE

HANDS-ON
MINDS-ON

CHAPTER 12

Hands-on, Minds-on

Never lose sight of the fact that 90 percent of people learn through doing and discovering.

Key message: Design encourages learning using engaging and interactive exhibit techniques.

Key word: learning

Metamorphosis is one of the earliest interactive phenomena. Optical devices such as thaumatropes (which, when spun quickly, appear to place one image on top of another) demonstrate the science behind visual perception, and such trickery continues to be incorporated into hands-on learning activities; indeed, these uncanny illusionary toys anticipated minds-on flip, turn, and reveal didactic labels.

This chapter derives its "hands-on, minds-on" trope from the American educational reformer John Dewey (1859–1952), who advocated for educative experiences that positioned "learning through doing" as the most effective method of acquiring knowledge.[1] Dewey's educational philosophy inspired the design of "please touch" exhibits and experiences that use buttons, handles, levers, spinners, pulleys, and human gesture to activate content, reveal information, solve problems, or simply enthrall audiences. From modest pushbuttons to highly integrated digital interfaces the range of minds-on modalities that designers use to inform, engage, and educate a range of people are reflective of a diverse and global community.

Learning and interpretive theory advocates
Visitor studies, backed up by respected educational and interpretive theory, informs learning goals for audiences in the museum/cultural sector. While visitor studies increased the opportunities for achieving learning, resistance came from content experts who preferred less-didactic interpretations of their research, and designers who felt they lost creative bite when their solutions became so pedantically educational.[2]

The list of contributors to these studies and critiques is historically authored by people who confidently, willingly, and regularly visit exhibitions and attractions. Today, not everyone is as enthused, and a diversity of new voices is addressing this imbalance, advocating for greater inclusion, intersectionality, and dictating a different intellectual tempo.[3]

Lifting flaps and pushing buttons as a meritorious method of hands-on learning is mixed and hotly debated. Learning advocates will quickly point out that understanding how to apply a concept (use it) needs to be directly connected to the concept being taught. Simply asking audiences to do something besides just stand there is worthy, but those actions often have little

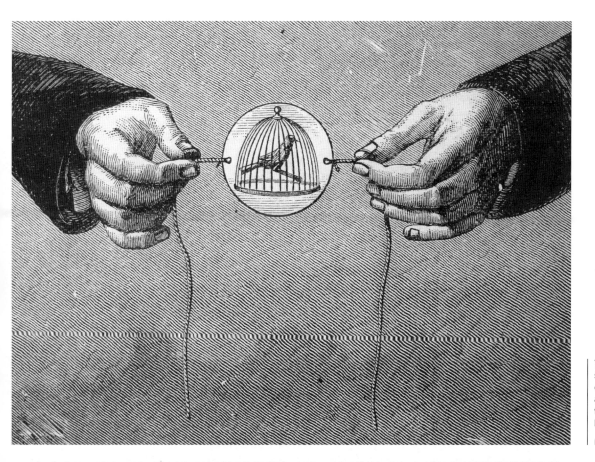

Thaumatropes, which when spun quickly appear to place one image on top of another, anticipated minds-on flip, turn, and reveal didactic labels.

Public domain

Learning through doing at Gateway Science Museum.

Gateway Science Museum

to do with "minds-on" understanding. Finding ways to get people to comprehend complex ideas through doing them—a core piece of the learning cycle—is hard. The more abstract an idea, the more difficult it is to get people to be able to "try it" in some way.[4] The question is can "real learning" occur within the confines of a public exhibition space and not in the classroom.

Multimodal, multisided, multiuser, and multi-outcome experiences

Consensus exists within exhibition development teams (in the cultural, commercial, and entertainment sectors) that a "something for everyone" approach reaches the broadest possible audience, and that multiple entry points make accessing various kinds of learning easier.[5] Adults may prefer a contemplative reading and looking experience. Children a discovery-based experience that involves touching and doing. It is unusual to find an exhibition environment today that is not responding to its audience, participation-friendly, and centered on learning.

Hands-on, minds-on experiences (both analog and digital) employ multiple design modalities ranging from passive (personal) to interactive (social), and exclusive (individual) to the reciprocal (shared). These include:

Contemplative (looking/viewing): passive two-dimensional graphic elements such as words, images, and illustrations that go further than simply reading in the built environment.

Sensory (feeling/touching): emotive elements such as sound, smell, and light that transcend multiple languages, cultural identities, and demographic forces.

Discovery (doing/making): hands-on elements such as manipulating, assembling, simulation rides, solving puzzles, and dress-up that physically engage people to discover content.

Participatory (exchanging/modifying): reciprocal and interactive elements such as collaborative making, activities/games, facilitated discussion, and role playing that create immersive and memorable experiences.

Design for Hands-on, Minds-on: Learning Through Doing and Making

Exhibition spaces offer alternatives to the formal educational settings found in schools and classrooms and provide unique opportunities for self-directed informal learning in a social setting. From galleries to gallerias, a full range of cultural, entertainment, and commercial environments initiate experiences that enhance cognitive skills, divergent thinking, and educate by curiosity, discovery, and exploration.[6]

Education theory in exhibitions

New York's Brooklyn Museum and Metropolitan Museum of Art were some of the first institutions to employ staff instructors (educators) and incorporate educational programming during the 1920–1930s.[7] Learning through experiencing launched entire organizations in the 1960s, notably San Francisco's Exploratorium (1969), and educational theorists who observed patterns of behavior and how people learned in exhibition environments. Toward the end of the 1970s, visitor and interpretive studies challenged elitist mindsets, shifting from the mechanics of exhibition design to the complexities of the exhibition experience.[8] Researchers dove into what they now saw to be the heart of the encounter: the interests, attitudes, and values that shaped the way audiences experienced an exhibit (American Alliance of Museums standing committee on museum education founded in 1970). The resulting educational tone reflected this change, and designers became less of a solitary artist in charge of a visually driven experience and more of an embedded team player willing (often having) to compromise.

First hands-on learning

Early museum education, while "a distinctly American idea," contrasted with a European tradition that remained scholarly and elite.[9] No wonder modernist exhibition designers like Herbert Bayer flourished in a postwar America with its latest ideas about audience participation and learning. The concept of "hands-on" learning, however, got its start in Europe. Munich's Deutsches Museum

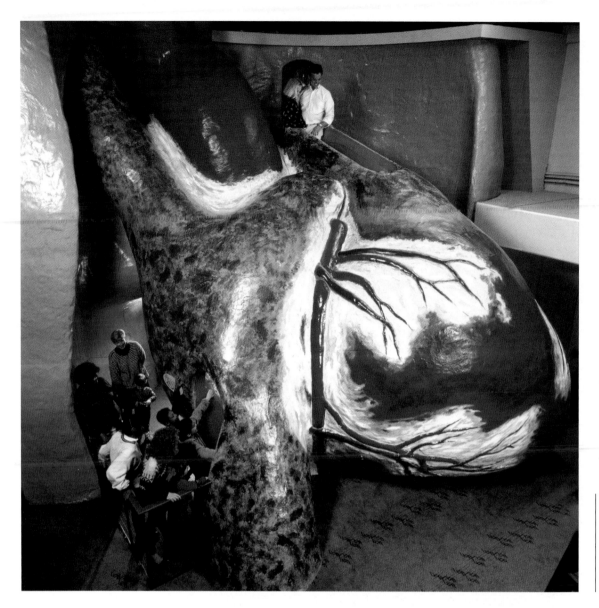

Suspension of disbelief is climbing through the *Giant Heart* (1954–present) and hearing the dynamic human heartbeat at Philadelphia's Franklin Institute.

Photo: H. Mark Weidman Photography / Alamy Stock Photo

(1906) was a place for education, entertainment, and immersion, and it developed the first exhibits where people could initiate technical demonstrations by the push of a button and work levers in the name of scientific discovery. The museum used explanatory diagrams, scale models, and dioramas. The mining exhibit (1925) staged life-sized costumed figures with electric borers whose thudding sound added realism to the space.[10] The museum informed other groundbreaking centers of science learning, including the Museum of Science and Industry in Chicago (1933) and the Children's Gallery at the Science Museum in London (1931).

First multisensory learning

Paris's Palais de la Découverte (Discovery Palace, 1937) was designed to offer an experience that was multisensory with advanced approaches to the presentation of scientific data and information that could promote new forms of education.[11] Live demonstrations and experiments by renowned scientists beguiled audiences in a purposefully designed building that housed a range of stunning exhibits. Unlike the Deutsches Museum, which highlighted the history of science, the Palais was promoted through innovation where contemporary lectures, screenings, and interactive exhibits immersed audiences in the forefront of scientific development.[12]

Paris's Palais de la Découverte offered a multisensory experience where live demonstrations (like the moon exhibit, 1937) and experiments by renowned scientists beguiled audiences.

Designer Taizo Mlyake led a team of young designers to envision the Ontario Science Centre as an interactive wonderland with a focus on participatory learning.

Explosion of interactivity

Popular science inspired by the space race and 1960s progressive ideologies placed the learning needs of the ordinary person over the exhibition specialist. Simple, attractive exhibits with interactive working models became the favored method to interpret scientific (complex) principles. This profound shift away from static displays and explanatory text panels toward engaging people in creative, hands-on learning experiences was met with some resistance by experts who had to share or relinquish control. The designers involved in these projects anticipated this transformation and led the way.

Learning by play

Around the time the Eames Office was harnessing play and discovery and using hands-on exhibits to help people understand obtuse formulas in *Mathematica: A World of Numbers . . . and Beyond* (1961), Physicist Dr. Frank Oppenheimer received a grant from the National Science Foundation to develop pedagogical models for teaching science to elementary and high school children. Oppenheimer initially flirted with hiring the Eames Office to turn these models into core exhibits at the new Exploratorium, but their exhibit design aesthetics were incompatible. Oppenheimer's emerged from the on-site Machine Shop, where engineered exhibits were democratized, constantly under scrutiny, retooled, and propagated using salvaged materials and everyday products that people have at home—a "cookbook" approach to hands-on exhibit making. The Exploratorium's "learning by experimenting" method of audience engagement directly influenced other hands-on museums, who took their exhibition design aesthetic in different directions.

Primary case study
Learning by doing

Ontario Science Centre, 1969
Principal Designers: Taizo Miyake;
Raymond Moriyama

Design challenge: Hands-on architecture

Celebrated Canadian architect Raymond Moriyama was commissioned to design a science museum that eschewed static artifacts for ideas imparted through a form of active participation, emotional experience, and intellectual satisfaction.[13] A product of the Canadian Centennial Project, the Ontario Science Centre (OSC) was conceived as a teaching machine in which the public could find answers to questions presented in an unbiased reliable fashion. The museum is still exemplary for its open and flexible architecture and exhibit halls that connect indoor exhibition spaces with the lush outdoor natural spaces that change with time and in themselves become interactive. Even the textured wall surfaces of the brutalist architecture are temptingly touchable, like the hands-on exhibits inside. Collaborating with Moriyama during the design of the building was Japanese American designer Taizo Miyake who led a team of young designers to plan the exhibitions and envision an engaging

interactive wonderland with a multisensory focus on what participatory learning really means?[14]

Design solution: I hear and I forget. I see and I remember. I do and I understand (Confucius, 551 BCE–479 BCE)

Rather than the educational theories of Dewey, Moriyama and Miyake's hands-on, minds-on approach to the building and exhibition design was founded on the Confucianist principle that people learn better by doing than by watching.[15] Contrary to the Exploratorium's concrete floors, and style of rough, adaptable exhibit prototypes fashioned by scientists, engineers, and artists, the Ontario Science Centre offered a version of exhibition design that was polished and harmonious—even spiritual. The designers created black boxes (to manage the atmosphere) with a minimum of interior finishes and a maximum of hidden services (like electricity). The architecture disappeared and nothing detracted from the exhibits.[16] Interactive displays about muscular topics (e.g., steam engines) used trendy forms (geodesic domes) and were presented using fashionable colors, curved contours, wood laminates, and wall-to-wall carpets. The exhibits were designed to make learning engaging and attractive. Contrary to the severe concrete exterior the exhibit halls used brilliant colors, lighting, and bold graphics to inject warmth and enhance the dramatic ambiance. This highly design-driven aesthetic was the product of a design team consisting of European-trained crafts-men working with scientists and industrial designers.[17] Evocative of a swanky 1960s apartment, this domesticity was intentional. It felt welcoming, familiar, and approachable for all audiences—true to the Centre's mandate, it exhibited the softer, more touchy-feely side of scientific discovery.

Design impact: **Designing hands-on is not easy**

The Ontario Science Centre's elevated level of exhibition design detailing combined with a philosophy of active audience participation is both a blessing and curse. While the designer enjoys the creative freedom the maintenance and wear and tear on the exhibits can make upkeep challenging or impossible.[18]

Taizo Miyake later went on to develop a powerful theatrical medium for holding an audience's attention. Object Theater is a decidedly hands-off exhibition strategy that brings objects to life using a combination of light projection and spoken/recorded narrative. Object Theaters were later developed at the Minnesota Historical Society, the Children's Museum in Boston, the Connecticut Historical Society, and elsewhere.[19]

The Kaleidoscope Room at the Ontario Science Centre offered a version of exhibition design that was hip, polished, and harmonious.

Ontario Science Centre

Contrasting with the Ontario Science Centre's concrete exterior, bold colors, lighting, and graphics inject warmth and enhance the drama of the exhibit halls.

Ontario Science Centre

Exhibits at the Ontario Science Centre were designed to be universally appealing through attractive and interactive experiences.

Ontario Science Centre

Design for Interaction, Gaming, and Fun: Learning Through Feeling and Touching

Celebrated for early contributions to informal interactive learning, the Boston Children's Museum threw away the "do not touch" labels when it appointed Michael Spock (son of the famous child psychologist Benjamin Spock) as director in 1962. The next year Spock hired designer Michael Sand, and together they set about transforming a traditional museum into an environment that was active and experimental rather than passive and pedantic, where children explored freely.[20] It was personified by *What's Inside?* (1964), an exhibition where children clambered into a series of spaces from a drop of water to a toaster, seeking answers to questions about their place in the world.[21]

Learning through play

Michael Sand graduated from the Rhode Island School of Design and worked briefly at the Eames Office (1962–1963), designing exhibits for the 1964/1965 New York World's Fair. His career as a designer and educator helped further the use of hands-on and technology-driven practices in museums and other learning environments.[22] Sand was attentive to people-centered design as it related to childhood development, promoted simple interpretive design tools with replaceable components, and thought hard about what is enticing to children. No surprise that his favorite substrate was cardboard.

Over time the Boston Children's Museum fostered an internal exhibition co-design/creative process that was non-hierarchical and actively encouraged team tinkering. Influential exhibit developers, such as Janet Kamien and Dan Spock, came through this design incubator, and later Margaret Middleton, whose design work considers intersectionality and LGBTQ perspectives. While Sand left his staff role in 1966 to launch a design consultancy, he continued to work with the museum for at least the next decade.[23] Notable exhibition spaces such as *Playspace* (1978) are part of his legacy.

Pictured in his design studio, Michael Sand threw away the "do not touch" labels and transformed the Boston Children's Museum into an active, experimental environment.

Image courtesy of the Michael Sand Estate (online at michaelsand .com)

Exhibit makers who have taken this learning legacy further are founder of ESI Design Edwin Schlossberg, who launched his experience design career in 1977 with the design of one of the world's first interactive museums, the Brooklyn Children's Museum, and chief design instigator Paul Oselli, whose blog and Cheapbooks are universally available to those who design exhibits for science and children's museums.

Screens-on learning

One of the most successful exhibitions at the Boston Children's Museum was the *Giant's Desktop* (1974). Children could scramble over typical office supplies up to twelve times their original size.[24] Fast-forward a few years, and the exhibition would have included a desktop computer, keyboard, and mouse in anticipation of a new form of interactivity that was to transform "hands on" into "screens-on."

If the design of hands-on exhibits revolutionized interactivity in exhibition halls during the twentieth century, computer-driven new media in the twenty-first century expanded "minds-on" exponentially, using a plethora of nested content behind seductive digital interfaces. With less need to battle the constraints of the physical space, touch-sensitive displays with an ability to retrieve thousands of images from a video disk (later laser disk and CD-ROM) disseminated information to a greater number of people with a smaller spatial footprint.

First touchscreens

Designer's Ramirez and Woods touchscreen computer kiosks debuted in the U.S. Pavilion at the 1982 Knoxville World's Fair with a little help from IBM. The goal of these state-of-the-art interactive computer/video disk systems was to impart a depth of information while still engaging visitor participation in the exhibit.[25] Responding to the theme of "energy" the design team assimilated forty-two instructional kiosks into the display space. While tame by today's standards, the interactive interface impressed audiences with its highly personal, nonlinear presentation, which allowed for specific interest selections while bypassing familiar information. The system made full use of its powers, employing text, sound, images, and video.[26] There is no question that people

Designers Carlos Ramirez & Albert H. Woods together with a team of technologists debuted touchscreen kiosks with random-access video-disks at the 1982 Knoxville World's Fair.

1984 SIGGRAPH Conference Catalogue

spent time at these kiosks, but possibly the uniqueness factor led to streaking rather than strolling through the content?

Hands-off learning

Today, countless examples exist of exhibit-based digital interfaces that facilitate contemplative, sensory, discovery, and participatory learning. Instead of announcing their presence, designers thoughtfully integrate new media into spatial environments without drastically changing how audiences behave in the exhibition, and the technology feels more natural and cohesive with the experience.[27]

Touchless personalization using RFID tags facilitate tailored experiences based on people's interests, abilities, and adopted personas—choose to traverse an exhibition as a soldier, spy, or famous sports person. This persuasive technology also doubles up to track people's dwell time and monitor hotspots and crowded areas.

With the wave of a hand, gesture-based interaction offers hands-on digital surfaces that are hygienic and hands-off. Touch tables at the Cooper Hewitt, Smithsonian Design Museum (2014) allow people to retrieve and collect content to augment their learning experience using interactive pens that can be sanitized after use. Virtual sandbox exhibits demonstrate the environmental interconnectivity of the landscape and watersheds—magically flutter your fingers and it begins to rain, dig a hole, and fill with water to create a virtual lake.

Touchless haptics simulate physical feedback from a surface or screen sent through ultrasound. The waves are felt on people's fingertips, it's like pressing a button with a physical sensation, but there is no physical touch. Gesture recognition is a form of synesthesia that evokes more than one sense and adds accessibility options to the designer's toolbox.

Gestural interaction debuted with experimental motion activated artworks (rear projection) triggered by movement in front of a video camera. The participant's movement speed and frequency generated an abstract kaleidoscopic portrait with a sonic accompaniment. First developed for hip art-science fusion conferences like SIGGRAPH and Ars Electronica in the late 1990s, the lamascope and other hands-on magical digital experiences seeded a groundbreaking exhibition at the Millennium Dome in London.[28]

With intuitive pointing, the design team at Gagarin make volcanoes erupt using hands-off gesture-based interaction at Iceland's LAVA Centre, 2017.

© studio: Gagarin / photo: Magnús Elvar Jónsson

Touch tables at the Cooper Hewitt, Smithsonian Design Museum allow people to retrieve and collect content using interactive pens.

Courtesy of Cooper Hewitt Design Museum. Photo: Local Projects.

Primary case study

Learning through gaming, fun, and interaction

PlayZone at the Millennium Dome, London, December 31, 1999–December 31, 2000
Principal Designer: Land Design Studio (Shirley Walker, Peter Higgins, and Robin Clark)

Design challenge: Welcome to the twenty-first century

The controversial Millennium Dome was modeled after the Dome of Discovery at the Festival of Britain (1951) to welcome the twenty-first century. Fourteen exhibit zones beneath one vast celebratory canopy tackled the themes "who we are," "what we do," and "where we live," An assemblage of teams assigned to each zone had their own design and budget brief and received conflicting oversight from the organizers. The ensuing audience experience was critically branded as overwhelming and incongruous, and the project did not attract the expected footfall. PlayZone was the exception for the way it prototyped equitable (all ages) state-of-the-art hands-on technology that anticipated how people will learn and play in the future.[29]

Design solution: Learning as entertainment

Land Design Studio created a responsive architectural structure inside the dome ringed by distinctive cantilevered "snouts" (or cones) to house the rear projection units that illuminated/activated the activities inside. Sequencing potentially 3,500 visitors per hour meant that people entered via an escalator and were afforded views down to the hubbub below from a long pathway before descending a ramp into the exhibit area. This "reveal" anticipated the "reward," managed visitation time, and provided experiences for the streaker, stroller, and studier depending on a person's appetite for participation.[30]

PlayZone consisted of three areas: Play to Discover, Express, and Learn. Participants were immersed in a series of multimedia activities that put them in control of the narrative—such as affecting the direction of a raft through participant's movement tracked by overhead cameras, playing musical games activated by gestural and tactile interfaces, and attempting to score a goal against a virtual goalkeeper controlled by a surrogate player.

Performance specifications were incorporated into the exhibits that defined the mode of interaction, engagement prompts, numbers of players, and dwell time (games were designed to time out). Lead designer Peter Higgins reflected on "passive interactivity" where non-participants also enjoyed watching the performance if they could understand the protocols and the output media was at a suitably

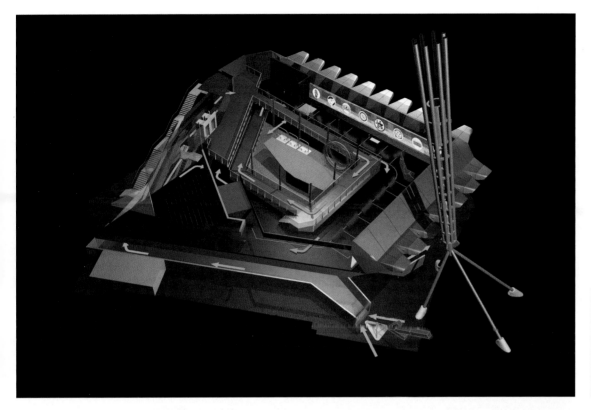

Rendering of the Millennium Dome's PlayZone showing the sequenced entry pathway and distinctive cantilevered 'snouts' that housed the games rear projection units.

Land Design Studio, Photo by Nick Wood

PlayZone participants were immersed in a series of screen-based activities activated by gestural and tactile interfaces.

Land Design Studio, Photo by Nick Wood

PlayZone's exhibits offered gamified versions of passive or active hands-on learning for a range of audiences.

Toshio Iwai / Land Design Studio, Photo by Nick Wood

large scale.[31] The educational benefits of both active and passive interaction were expounded on by the early science museums discussed previously.[32]

Design impact: Future of play

Because the impetus for PlayZone was a gallery of computer-driven artists experiments, the design team initially struggled to convince their client that the technology would appeal to a younger audience and "museum play" wouldn't override "real play." The exhibits offered a gamified yet cerebral version of hands on learning.[33] Many of the activities bordered on awesome new-age arcade games,

but the seamless digital veneer made learning less pedantic and more subliminal.

The fact that these illusions and interactive games were possible in the late 1990s was itself educational. Back-end systems and screen resolutions were still in their infancy—touchscreens were cumbersome and still a rarity and the iPhone and Facebook did not appear for at least another decade.[34] The designers were challenged to create an experience in the Millennium Dome to anticipate how people will play in the future. Reflecting on the current digital world, Peter Higgins said we can genuinely claim that this is what we delivered.[35]

Design for Participation: Learning Through Exchanging and Modifying

PlayZone's innovative art and technology projects were assembled by internationally renowned artists whose work descends from *Cybernetic Serendipity* (1968) an experimental art exhibition that was well received in Europe and was shown at the opening of San Francisco's Exploratorium in 1969.[36] A few of these pioneering exhibits still grace their interactive exhibit floors today.

Oppenheimer considered artists to be science teachers whose installations not only made things look better but tendered discoveries that were different to physicists or biologists.[37] Situating the exhibits in one expansive room and publicly showing exhibit tinkering in the back-of-house Machine Shop, emphasized connectedness and cross-pollination as much as visibility. This air of transparency put exchanging and modifying at the heart of the exhibition design process.

The Exploratorium's signature open floorplan provides participants with agency to draw their own conclusions and shape their own exhibit experiences.

Gayle Laird, © Exploratorium, www.exploratorium.edu

Testing and prototyping

To advance audience engagement beyond mindless button pushing, the progressive science centers of the 1960s embraced live exhibit prototypes. The Exploratorium's open floorplan provides participants with agency to draw their own conclusions and shape their own experiences free of one prescribed by the institution. The exhibits use scientific principles learned through observation, speculation, and experimentation rather than instruction and explanation. This self-directed and open-ended exhibit architecture can inhibit learning because of overstimulation, tiredness, and mental exhaustion.[38] Over the years, strategies have been developed to not only attract people using hands-on gizmos but prolong and sustain "minds-on" engagement such as EDGE (Exhibit Design for Girl's Engagement) and APE (Active Prolonged Engagement).

Psychologist Chandler Screven's influential visitor studies work encouraged a "suck it and see" system of trial-and-error where an

iterative process of exhibition making allowed audiences to judge mock-ups to see if the exhibit design measured up to expectations.[39] Prototyping with the intended audience as well as the exhibition team allows for three-dimensional re-tooling, and alternative ways of looking at design problems and working collaboratively despite the possible increased time and cost (refer to chapter 1).

Role playing and discovery

Reciprocal role-playing experiences with costumed guides can be found at theme parks, attractions, and living history sites such as Old Sturbridge, Massachusetts (1946), Beamish, County Durham, UK (1970), and Sovereign Hill, Ballarat, Australia (1970). The Battle of Bannockburn visitor center in Scotland took this a step further and incorporated game theory into their participatory experience (see chapter 9). "Ask the expert" audience participation experiences are not new to museums but designers for *Q?rius* (2016) at the Smithsonian National Museum of Natural History in Washington, D.C., put visitors in charge as they riffle through once off-limits collections and get to ask questions of exhibition facilitators. The loving (or not) exchange of microbes during an impassioned kiss between visitors at *Micropia* (2014), the Museum of Microbes in Amsterdam causes either delight or disgust.

Contemporary exhibitions, experiences, and attractions abound with interactive hands-on, minds-on learning devices. Increasingly, co-creation and co-design during the exhibition development process is reframing the definition of hands-on to hands-off as established exhibition makers succeed content generation and design execution to their communities. This method of reciprocity requires a form of nimble design favoring flexibility to accommodate open-sourced material. Digital frameworks embedded into the exhibition infrastructure work particularly well for venues which emphasize community participation and inclusion.

Primary case study

Learning through exchanging and modifying

The Mixing Room: stories from young refugees in New Zealand, **Museum of New Zealand Te Papa Tongarewa, 2010–present**
Principal Designers: Ben Barraud (3D); Nick Clarkson (2D)

Design challenge: Shared learning

Commonly known as Te Papa (te reo Māori for "treasure box"), New Zealand's national museum opened its new building in 1998. Immediately, the museum became globally influential as an institution representing its nation's culture and indigenous people, fundamentally rewriting the ethics of being a museum.[40] Te Papa is known for its consultative methods of working with communities to develop exhibitions, sharing decision-making with iwi (tribes) and individuals with respect to managing and understanding their taonga (treasures).

In 2010, the museum opened an exhibition on the fourth floor of the museum in the Community Gallery. *The Mixing Room* experimented with novel approaches to exhibition making that went a step further than community consultation. Guided by the "community knows best" the project incorporated theories of educational and social inclusion with youth development and participatory action research.

Initial workshops developed themes for an exhibition about the settlement of refugee background youth in New Zealand, with subsequent versions for community participants to create works responding to their experiences. Expressions of poetry, performance, music, photography, film, and art were captured digitally in a form of two-dimensional storytelling. About seventy young people from at least twenty different former refugee communities took part in the co-creation process.[41]

Design solution: Making hands-on, minds-on

The Mixing Room sidesteps thematic divisions and objects to focus on capacity building for the young people and staff involved. All the content was generated by community participants and delivered in the first-person voice with minimal editorial intervention.[42]

Entering the low-lit gallery audiences are flanked by two introductory pylons that describe the exhibition in the participant's words. Glass steppingstones on the floor lead people into the space. They contextualize the work on view and chronical the history of New Zealand's refugee communities. The walls enveloping the space display an array of first-person quotes and salon-style hung backlit images featuring refugee journeys from camps and resettlement to their homes in New Zealand neighborhoods. On axis with the entrance is a large dynamic digital mosaic generated by a database containing thousands of images provided by the project's participants. This spatial sightline is compelling and the perfect "wow" moment.

Delegating the content generation meant accepting the participant's creative work in its entirety. The nested material is made available via three interactive touch tables (themed around connection, freedom, and challenge) found centrally in the space. When seated around the tables people interact with an interface of selectable icons floating in a simulation of rippling water. Touching the icons reveals the work, participatory process, and biographical statement about the artists.[43]

Design impact: Balancing excellence with access

The Mixing Room employs sophisticated interactive learning and design methods to enhance audience engagement. Community driven exhibition making may sometimes struggle to generate this "museum quality" because participants tend to gravitate to conventional forms of exhibition design that are object-based, familiar, and comfortable.[44] Te Papa is guided by the concept of mana taonga (sharing authority). *The Mixing Room* practices a co-creative process to develop a version of co-design where the participants as well as the exhibition audience are learning.

Glass steppingstones chronicle the history of New Zealand's refugee communities and lead people into *The Mixing Room* at Te Papa.

Photo by Kate Whitley, 2013. Te Papa (216803)

**Te Papa's *The Mixing Room*
is an example of community
driven exhibition making,
interactive learning, and design that enhances audience
engagement.**

Photo by Michael Hall, 2015. Te
Papa (94405)

Intersectional design

This chapter traced the design evolution of exhibition and experiential hands-on, minds-on education starting with teaching and learning to the advent of engaging and participating—the hallmarks of late-twenty-first-century museums and attractions. Reacting to a legacy of entrenched patriarchy and lack of "real" involvement, audience participation now follows models forged by social media and mobile technologies that allow people to co-create on the fly and at will. If exhibitions embrace "reciprocal" methods of shared learning where the audience dictates the aesthetic rather than the "finish-fetish" commonly associated with (ego-driven) design practice, where does the designer fit into this emerging equation? Design stems from empathy, nuance, and understanding. Creating experiences, whatever platform they happen to be designed for requires listening to multiple voices that traditionally have been marginalized, overlooked, and dismissed, and the response needs to be informed by these different realities. It is inevitable that successful experiences in the future will practice a method of "intersectional design" where learning is made inclusive, egalitarian, and socially equitable.

Tips and Tricks

Activate learning and design for interaction using the following design techniques:

1. Minimize breakdown—"temporarily out of order" signs send the wrong message.
2. Work with tinkerers and professionals who know their craft.
3. Employ a variety of kinesthetic, auditory, visual learning methods (McCarthy, 1997).
4. Balance form with functional, robust, foolproof design.
5. Model inclusivity—make exhibits and interactives easy to reach, pull, push.
6. Multimodal learning—exploit contemplative, sensory, discovery, and participatory methods.
7. Prototype—lean into the edict "less prep more presence" and be more responsive by being less perfect.
8. Design for touch—leverage people's innate predisposition for sensory confirmation.
9. Reciprocal design—incorporate moments for people to exchange and modify.
10. Intersectional design—be informed by people's different realities.

Notes

1. "John Dewey," Biography, accessed May 2, 2022, https://www.biography.com/scholar/john-dewey.
2. Frank Oudsten, "The Exhibition as Theatre," *Museum International* 47, no. 1 (March 1, 1995): 15, https://doi.org/10.1111/j.1468-0033.1995.tb01217.x.
3. "Cartography: A Black Woman's Response to Museums in the Time of Racial Uprising," The Incluseum (blog), June 10, 2020, https://incluseum.com/2020/06/10/cartography-a-black-womans-response-to-museums-in-the-time-of-racial-uprising/.
4. Susan Spero. Correspondence with Timothy McNeil about learning in exhibitions. September 14, 2022.
5. Michael Spock and Children's Museum of Boston, eds., *Boston Stories: The Children's Museum as a Model for Nonprofit Leadership: 1960s–1980s, 30 Years of Experimentation* (Boston, MA: Boston Children's Museum, 2013), 192.
6. "Museums and Informal Education—Infed.Org," accessed May 3, 2022, https://infed.org/mobi/museums-and-informal-education/.
7. Lisa C. Roberts, *From Knowledge to Narrative: Educators and the Changing Museum* (Washington, D.C.: Smithsonian Institution Press, 1997), 4.
8. Roberts, *From Knowledge to Narrative*, 4–5.
9. Roberts, *From Knowledge to Narrative*, 4.
10. H.S. Williams, "Germany's Greatest Museum: The Deutsches Museum in Munich," *Century Magazine*, Vol. LXXXIV, New Series LXII, No. 6, October 1912, 933–94.
11. James Housefield, *Playing with Earth and Sky: Astronomy, Geography, and the Art of Marcel Duchamp* (Hanover, NH: Dartmouth College Press, 2016), 180.
12. Andrée Bergeron and Charlotte Bigg, "Built in Thoughts Rather than Stone. The Palais de La Découverte and the 1937 Paris International Exposition," 2019, 111.
13. Douglas N. Omand, "The Ontario Science Centre, Toronto," *Museum International* 26, no. 2 (June 1, 1974): 76–85, https://doi.org/10.1111/j.1468-0033.1974.tb01821.x.

14. Mary Jane Conboy and Elgin Cleckley, "Thinking Big: Raymond Moriyama's Ontario Science Centre," *ACORN Architectural Conservancy Ontario* 41 (2), 2016, 18–20, https://acontario.ca/files/pub/32/ ACORN_2016_Fall.pdf.

15. "I Was Starting to Bleed from Top to Bottom: The Agony and the Ecstasy of Raymond Moriyama | TVO. Org," accessed May 5, 2022, https://www.tvo.org/article/i-was-starting-to-bleed-from-top-to-bottom -the-agony-and-the-ecstasy-of-raymond-moriyama.

16. Omand, "The Ontario Science Centre, Toronto," 79.

17. Tom Kasanda, "Improving the Future of Learning Through Enhanced Collaboration Methods and Plat- forms," 2017, 5.

18. Omand, "The Ontario Science Centre, Toronto."

19. Leslie Bedford, "Storytelling: The Real Work of Museums," *Curator: The Museum Journal* 44, no. 1 (Jan- uary 1, 2001): 27–34, https://doi.org/10.1111/j.2151-6952.2001.tb00027.x.

20. Suzanne MacLeod, *Museums and Design for Creative Lives* (London; New York: Routledge, Taylor & Francis Group, 2021), 40–41.

21. Marjorie Schwarzer, *Riches, Rivals & Radicals: 100 Years of Museums in America* (Washington, D.C.: American Association of Museums, 2006), 148.

22. "About Michael Sand," *Michael Sand Archives* (blog), accessed May 2, 2022, https://michaelsand.com/ about-michael-sand/.

23. Jessica Sand. Interview by Timothy McNeil about Michael Sand. August 24, 2022.

24. "100 Years: The Boston Children's Museum," accessed May 6, 2022, https://bostonchildrensmuseum .org/history-timeline/index.html.

25. Allen E. Beach and Anita Grinvalds et al., "United States Pavilion at the Knoxville International Energy Exposition. Final Report, Department of Commerce," 1982, 17–18, https://www.state.gov/wp-content/ uploads/2019/04/Knoxville-Expo-1982.pdf.

26. Ramirez and Woods Inc., Knoxville World's Fair Exhibition featured in 1984 SIGGRAPH Conference Catalog, 34. ACM SIGGRAPH Art Show Archives, accessed May 7, 2022, https://digitalartarchive .siggraph.org/artwork/ramirez-and-woods-inc-knoxville-worlds-fair-exhibition/.

27. "ARTLENS @ Gallery One: A Look at the Future of Museum Engagement," AMT Lab @ CMU, accessed October 11, 2021, https://amt-lab.org/reviews/2014/10/artslens-gallery-one-a-view-to-the-future.

28. Ernest Edmonds, Greg Turner, and Linda Candy, *Approaches to Interactive Art Systems*, 2004, https:// doi.org/10.1145/988834.988854.

29. *A History of the Future*, Land Design Studio, 2020, https://vimeo.com/402910682.

30. Peter Higgins, "Land Design Studio Portfolio of Completed Projects," 58, http://www.landdesignstudio .co.uk/files/LDS_Pack_1702.pdf.

31. *A History of the Future*.

32. Steve Bitgood, "Suggested Guidelines for Designing Interactive Exhibits," *Visitor Behavior*, January 1, 1991, 9, https://www.academia.edu/1093650/Suggested_guidelines_for_designing_interactive_exhibits.

33. David Taylor, "Learning from the Dome," *Architects' Journal* (blog), February 10, 2000, http://www .architectsjournal.co.uk/archive/learning-from-the-dome.

34. *A History of the Future*.

35. *A History of the Future*.

36. "Cybernetic Serendipity," accessed May 9, 2022, https://cyberneticserendipity.net/?og=1.

37. "Exploratorium Founder Frank Oppenheimer," Exploratorium, April 4, 2013, 4, https://www.exploratorium .edu/press-office/press-releases/exploratorium-founder-frank-oppenheimer.

38. Gareth Davey, "What Is Museum Fatigue?" *Visitor Studies Today* 8 (January 1, 2005): 17–21.

39. Roger S Miles et al., *The Design of Educational Exhibits* (London; Boston: Allen & Unwin, 2002), 15.

40. Conal McCarthy, *Te Papa: Reinventing New Zealand's National Museum, 1998–2018* (Wellington, New Zealand: Te Papa Press, 2018), 10.

41. Sara Kindon and Stephanie Gibson, "The Mixing Room Project at Te Papa: Co-Creating the Museum with Refugee Background Youth in Aotearoa/New Zealand," *Tuhinga* 24, 2013, 76.

42. Kindon and Gibson, 70.

43. "The Mixing Room: Stories from Young Refugees in New Zealand," 2012, https://www.youtube.com/ watch?v=Bh2sWjXWpfg.

44. Conal McCarthy. Interview by Timothy McNeil about Te Papa history and exhibition design. May 19, 2022.

Afterword

Call to Action—SCORECARD

Key message: A methodology for measuring the experiential impact of an exhibition.

Key words: evaluate/measure/share

The next generation of exhibition and experience designers are defined by their ability to adapt, their ethics and advocacy for social justice and the environment, and their questioning of content, purpose, audiences, outcomes, and the impact of their work. All these facets mean taking risks and embracing failure as much as success. There is much at stake, and we will not accomplish this journey without feeling comfortable with testing, and the associated trial and error.

One of the most rewarding aspects of being an exhibition designer is witnessing firsthand the reactions of people to your work. Taking the time to observe and talk with audiences, evaluate what works and what does not, and then reflect on the teams' accomplishments is a vital component of the design ideation process.

Formal and informal feedback mechanisms (front-end; formative; remedial; summative evaluation) are commonplace, but few contemporary frameworks exist for critically evaluating the effectiveness of exhibition design and the corresponding quality of an audience's experience. Afterall, good design engages visitors, making them ready and willing to experience more.[1]

The series of recurring tropes (principles, or conventions) covered in this book constitute a methodology for evaluating exhibitions and experiential design. Employ all twelve as tools to measure the multimodality of the design response and the engagement level of experience, whether it is a museum, trade show, attraction, retail space, or festival. While the associated SCORECARD was developed as a response to environments and exhibitions, it also performs well on digital and interaction applications. Keep it nearby next time you participate in the expanding array of experiential encounters.

Exhibition/Experience Design Scorecard

Rate each question from 0-10

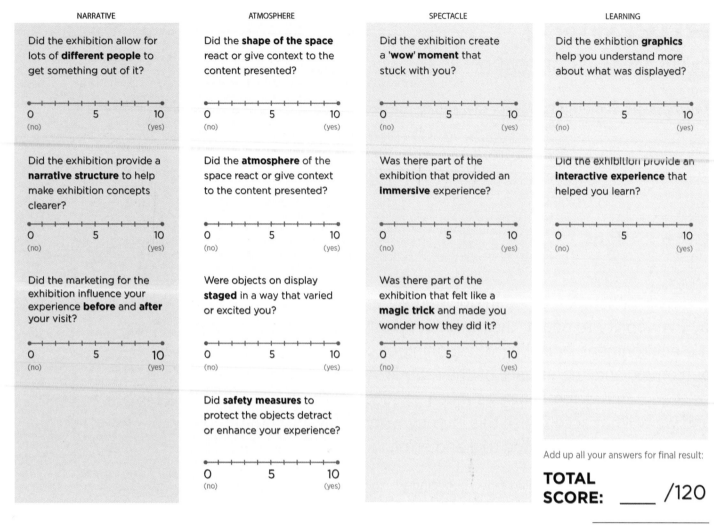

NARRATIVE

Did the exhibition allow for lots of **different people** to get something out of it?

0   5   10
(no)   (yes)

Did the exhibition provide a **narrative structure** to help make exhibition concepts clearer?

0   5   10
(no)   (yes)

Did the marketing for the exhibition influence your experience **before** and **after** your visit?

0   5   10
(no)   (yes)

ATMOSPHERE

Did the **shape of the space** react or give context to the content presented?

0   5   10
(no)   (yes)

Did the **atmosphere** of the space react or give context to the content presented?

0   5   10
(no)   (yes)

Were objects on display **staged** in a way that varied or excited you?

0   5   10
(no)   (yes)

Did **safety measures** to protect the objects detract or enhance your experience?

0   5   10
(no)   (yes)

SPECTACLE

Did the exhibition create a **'wow' moment** that stuck with you?

0   5   10
(no)   (yes)

Was there part of the exhibition that provided an **immersive** experience?

0   5   10
(no)   (yes)

Was there part of the exhibition that felt like a **magic trick** and made you wonder how they did it?

0   5   10
(no)   (yes)

LEARNING

Did the exhibtion **graphics** help you understand more about what was displayed?

0   5   10
(no)   (yes)

Did the exhibition provide an **interactive experience** that helped you learn?

0   5   10
(no)   (yes)

Add up all your answers for final result:

TOTAL SCORE: _____ **/120**

A new methodology for understanding exhibition and experience design.

© Timothy J. McNeil and Edward Whelan, 2022

Note

1. Beverly Serrell, *Judging Exhibitions: A Framework for Assessing Excellence* (Walnut Creek, CA: Left Coast, 2006), 30–33.

Bibliography/Appendix

Twenty years of teaching exhibition and experience design has allowed me to compile an extensive bibliography and key references that have proven helpful for students and scholars. The following snapshot focuses on resources that put "design" front and center—and it serves as an historical compendium that is perhaps more useful for the field given this publication's design emphasis. Writing this book involved extensive bibliographic references, and I refer the reader to the chapter notes for a comprehensive listing.

Organizations

Experiential Designers and Producers Association (EDPA)
National Association for Museum Exhibition (NAME)
Society for Experiential Graphic Design (SEGD)
Themed Entertainment Association (TEA)

Resources

A Guide to Exhibit Development. Smithsonian Exhibits, http://exhibits.si.edu/wp-content/uploads/ 2018/04/Guide-to-Exhibit-Development.pdf.
A Guide to the EDGE (Exhibit Design for Girl's Engagement). Exploratorium, https://www .exploratorium.edu/sites/default/files/pdfs/EDGE_GuideToDesignAttributes_v16.pdf.
Design Thinking. Stanford d.school, https://dschool.stanford.edu/resources/getting-started -with-design-thinking.
Exhibition. A journal of exhibition theory and practices for museum professionals, https://www .name-aam.org/past-issues-online.
Exhibit Planning, Design, and Fabrication Specifications. National Park Service—Harpers Ferry, https://www.nps.gov/subjects/hfc/upload/NPS-Exhibit-Planning-Design-and-Fabrication -Specifications-2019.pdf.
Green Exhibit Checklist. OMSI, https://omsi.edu/sites/default/files/ExhibitSEED_Green% 20Exhibit%20Checklist.pdf.
How to Make a Pop Up Museum: An Organizer's Kit. Santa Cruz Museum of Art and History, http://popupmuseum.org/wp-content/uploads/2013/09/Pop-Up-Museum-Edited.pdf.
Smithsonian Guidelines for Accessible Exhibition Design, https://www.sifacilities.si.edu/sites/ default/files/Files/Accessibility/accessible-exhibition-design1.pdf.
The Designer's Critical Alphabet by Dr. Lesley-Ann Noel, https://criticalalphabet.com/about/.
Tools and Approaches for Transforming Museum Experience. Cooper Hewitt Interaction Lab, https://www.cooperhewitt.org/interaction-lab/tools-and-approaches-for-transforming -museum-experience/.
Writing Gallery Text at the V&A: A Ten Point Guide, https://www.vam.ac.uk/blog/wp-content/ uploads/VA_Gallery-Text-Writing-Guidelines_online_Web.pdf.

Selected Bibliography

Atelier Brückner, Uwe Brückner, and Beverley Locke, eds. *Scenography. 2: Staging the Space = Szenografie 2: Der Inszenierte Raum*. Basel, Switzerland: Birkhäuser Verlag GmbH, part of Walter de Gruyter GmbH, 2019.

Austin, Tricia. *Narrative Environments and Experience Design: Space as a Medium of Communication*. Routledge Research in Design Studies. New York: Routledge, Taylor & Francis Group, 2020.

Bayer, Herbert. *Fundamentals of Exhibition Design*. New York: The Composing Room/P.M. Publishing Co, 1940.

Bedford, Leslie. *The Art of Museum Exhibitions: How Story and Imagination Create Aesthetic Experiences*. Walnut Creek, CA: Left Coast Press, 2014.

Black (Ed), Misha. *Exhibition Design*. London: The Architectural Press, 1950.

Carboni, Erberto, and Herbert Bayer. *Exhibitions and Displays*. Milan: Silvana, 1957.

Carmel, James H. *Exhibition Techniques: Traveling and Temporary*. New York: Reinhold Publishing Corporation, 1962.

Casson, Dinah. *Closed on Mondays: Behind the Scenes at the Museum*. London: Lund Humphries, 2020.

Cooks, Bridget R. *Exhibiting Blackness: African Americans and the American Art Museum*. Amherst: University of Massachusetts Press, 2011.

Dernie, David. *Exhibition Design*. 1st American ed. New York: W.W. Norton, 2006.

Escobar, Arturo. *Designs for the Pluriverse: Radical Interdependence, Autonomy, and the Making of Worlds*. New Ecologies for the Twenty-First Century. Durham: Duke University Press, 2018.

Falk, John H., and Lynn D. Dierking. *The Museum Experience Revisited*. Walnut Creek, CA: Left Coast Press, Inc, 2013.

Franck, Klaus. *Exhibitions: A Survey of International Designs*. New York: Frederick A. Praeger Publisher, 1961.

Gardner, James, and Caroline Heller. *Exhibition and Display*. London: B.T. Batsford Ltd., 1960.

Gibson, David. *The Wayfinding Handbook: Information Design for Public Places*, Design Briefs. New York: Princeton Architectural Press, 2009.

Hall, Margaret. *On Display: A Design Grammar for Museum Exhibitions*. 1st ed. London: Lund Humphries, 1987.

Hughes, Philip. *Exhibition Design*. Second edition. London: Laurence King Publishing, 2015.

Hughes, Philip. *Storytelling Exhibitions*. London; New York: Bloomsbury Visual Arts, 2021.

Klein, Larry. *Exhibits: Planning and Design*. New York: Madison Square Press: Distributors in North America, Robert Silver Associates, 1986.

Kossmann, Herman, and Mark W. de Jong. *Engaging Spaces: Exhibition Design Explored*. Amsterdam: Frame, 2010.

Kossmann, Herman, Suzanne Mulder, and Frank den Oudsten, eds. *Narrative Spaces: On the Art of Exhibiting*. Rotterdam: 010 Publ, 2012.

Locker, Pam. *Exhibition Design*. Basics Interior Design 02. Lausanne: AVA Publishing SA, 2011.

Lohse, Richard P. *New Design in Exhibitions*. New York: Praeger, 1954.

Lorenc, Jan, Lee Skolnick, and Craig Berger. *What Is Exhibition Design?* Essential Design Handbooks. Mies: RotoVision, 2007.

Lukas, Scott A. *Theme Park*. London: Reaktion Books, 2008.

Lukas, Scott A. *The Immersive Worlds Handbook: Designing Theme Parks and Consumer Spaces*. New York: Focal Press, 2013.

Lupton, Ellen. *Design Is Storytelling*. New York: Cooper Hewitt, Smithsonian Design Museum, 2017.

MacLeod, Suzanne. *Museums and Design for Creative Lives*. London; New York: Routledge, Taylor & Francis Group, 2021.

MacLeod, Suzanne, Tricia Austin, Jonathan Hale, and Oscar Ho Hing Kay, eds. *The Future of Museum and Gallery Design: Purpose, Process, Perception*. Museum Meanings. London; New York: Routledge, Taylor & Francis Group, 2018.

Mayfield, Signe, and Ted Cohen. *The Object in Its Place: Ted Cohen & the Art of Exhibition Design*. San Diego : [Oakland] : San Francisco: Mingei International Museum; in association with the Oakland Museum of California and the Museum of Craft and Design, 2020.

McKenna-Cress, Polly, and Janet Kamien. *Creating Exhibitions: Collaboration in the Planning, Development and Design of Innovative Experiences*. Hoboken, NJ: John Wiley & Sons, 2013.

McLean, Kathleen. *Planning for People in Museum Exhibitions*. 5. repr. Washington, D.C.: Association of Science-Technology Centers, 2009.

McLean, Kathleen. "Manifesto for the (r)Evolution of Museum Exhibitions." *Exhibition* 29, no. 1 (2010): 40–50.

Papanek, Victor J. *Design for the Real World: Human Ecology and Social Change*, 2nd ed., completely rev. Chicago, IL: Academy Chicago, 1985.

Piehl, Jona. *Graphic Design in Museum Exhibitions: Display, Identity and Narrative*. 1st edition. Abingdon, Oxon; New York: Routledge, 2020.

Pine, B. Joseph, and James H. Gilmore. *The Experience Economy*. Updated ed. Boston, MA: Harvard Business Review Press, 2011.

Pressman, Heather, and Danielle Schulz. *The Art of Access: A Practical Guide for Museum Accessibility*. Lanham, MD: Rowman & Littlefield, 2021.

Rand, Judy. "The 227-Mile Museum, or Why We Need a Visitor's Bill of Rights," *Visitor Studies: Theory, Research and Practice* 9 (1997).

Serrell, Beverly. *Judging Exhibitions: A Framework for Assessing Excellence*. Walnut Creek, CA: Left Coast, 2006.

Serrell, Beverly. *Exhibit Labels: An Interpretive Approach*. Second edition. Lanham, MD: Rowman & Littlefield, 2015.

Staniszewski, Mary Anne. *The Power of Display: A History of Exhibition Installations at the Museum of Modern Art*. 1st edition. Cambridge, MA: The MIT Press, 1998.

Tunstall, Elizabeth. *Decolonizing Design: A Cultural Justice Guidebook*. Cambridge, MA: MIT Press, 2023.

Velarde, Giles. *Designing Exhibitions: Museums, Heritage, Trade and World Fairs*. 2nd ed. Aldershot, [England]; Burlington, VT: Ashgate, 2001.

Walhimer, Mark. *Designing Museum Experiences*. Lanham, MD: Rowman & Littlefield, 2021.

Index

NOTE: Page references in *italics* refer to figures and photos.

About the Author

Timothy J. McNeil is a professor of design at the University of California, Davis. He has spent over thirty years as a practicing exhibition designer working for major museums, researching exhibition design history and methods, and teaching the next generations of exhibition design thinkers and practitioners.

McNeil's research defines exhibition and experiential design practice and its impact on communities and audience engagement. He has designed hundreds of exhibition environments and contributed to building three major museums: the J. Paul Getty Museum at the Getty Center and Getty Villa, and the Jan Shrem and Maria Manetti Shrem Museum of Art.

As co-founder of *Re-envisioning Exhibition* Design, McNeil curated a series of international summits called *Chaos at the Museum* to advance academic understanding and elevate professional practice in the exhibition and experiential design field. He is the primary instructor for undergraduate exhibition and environmental graphic design courses in the UC Davis Department of Design, and he is the thesis advisor for graduate students researching exhibition related design theory, criticism, and practice. He also serves as director of the UC Davis Design Museum, which exhibits national and international design-related materials and serves as a laboratory for experimental exhibition design and interpretation.

An authority on environmental sustainability, McNeil co-founded the California Association of Museums Green Museums Accord and is an inductee into the National Environmental Hall of Fame. He has been recognized for design excellence by the Society for Experiential Graphic Design, the University and College Designers Association, the American Alliance of Museums, and the International Museum Design and Communication Association. McNeil is a frequent speaker and writer on museum and design issues. His award-winning design work is archived at the Getty Research Institute, and he has been featured in multiple publications.